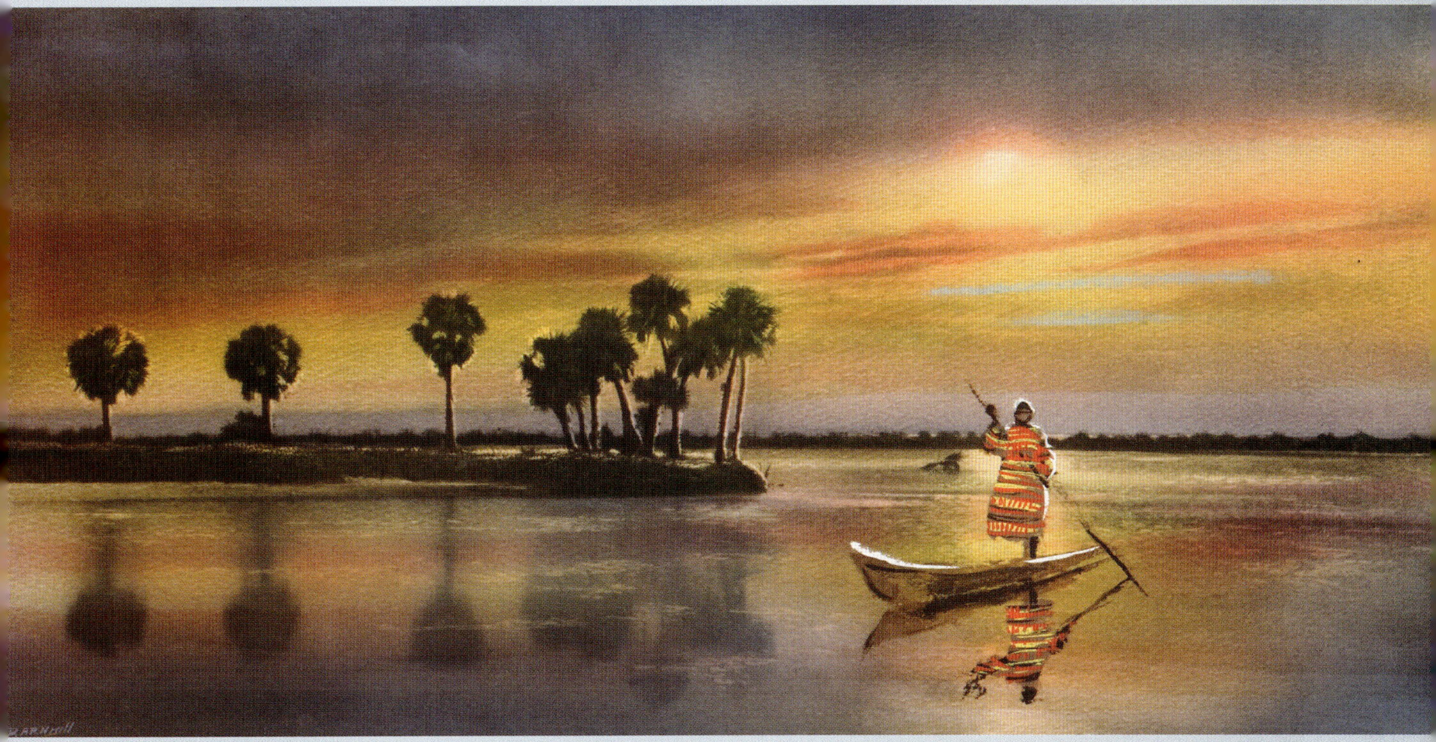

≈ **E. G. Barnhill** ≈

UNIVERSITY PRESS OF FLORIDA

Florida A&M University, Tallahassee
Florida Atlantic University, Boca Raton
Florida Gulf Coast University, Ft. Myers
Florida International University, Miami
Florida State University, Tallahassee
New College of Florida, Sarasota
University of Central Florida, Orlando
University of Florida, Gainesville
University of North Florida, Jacksonville
University of South Florida, Tampa
University of West Florida, Pensacola

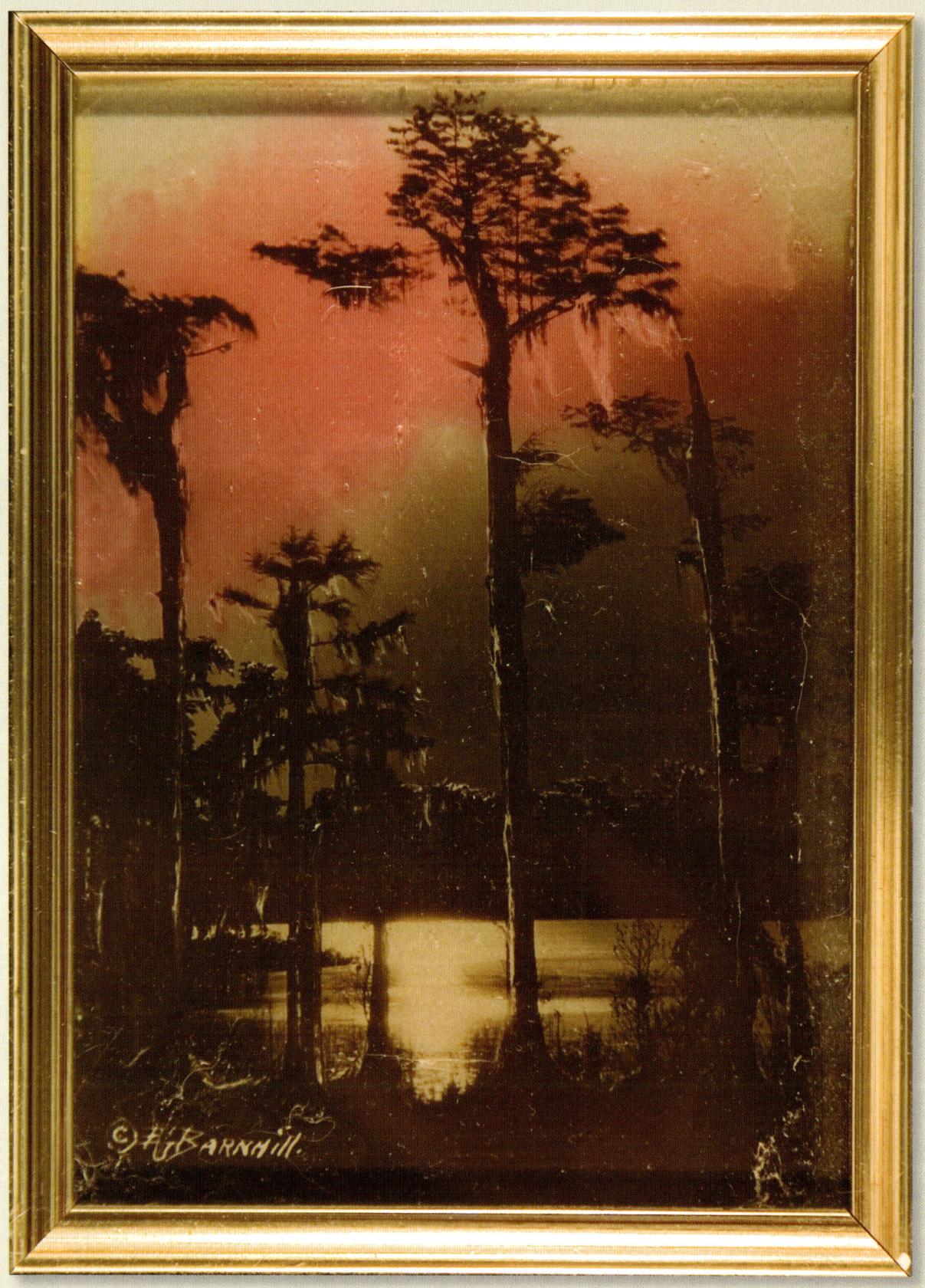

E. G. Barnhill

Florida Photographer, Adventurer, Entrepreneur

Gary Monroe

University Press of Florida

Gainesville · Tallahassee · Tampa · Boca Raton · Pensacola · Orlando · Miami · Jacksonville · Ft. Myers · Sarasota

21 20 19 18 17 16   6 5 4 3 2 1

Library of Congress Control Number: 2015953454
ISBN 978-0-8130-6277-8

The University Press of Florida is the scholarly publishing agency for the State
University System of Florida, comprising Florida A&M University, Florida Atlantic
University, Florida Gulf Coast University, Florida International University, Florida
State University, New College of Florida, University of Central Florida, University of
Florida, University of North Florida, University of South Florida, and University of
West Florida.

University Press of Florida
15 Northwest 15th Street
Gainesville, FL 32611-2079
http://www.upf.com

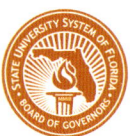

framed with a grant from
Figure Foundation
to seed a goal spectrum

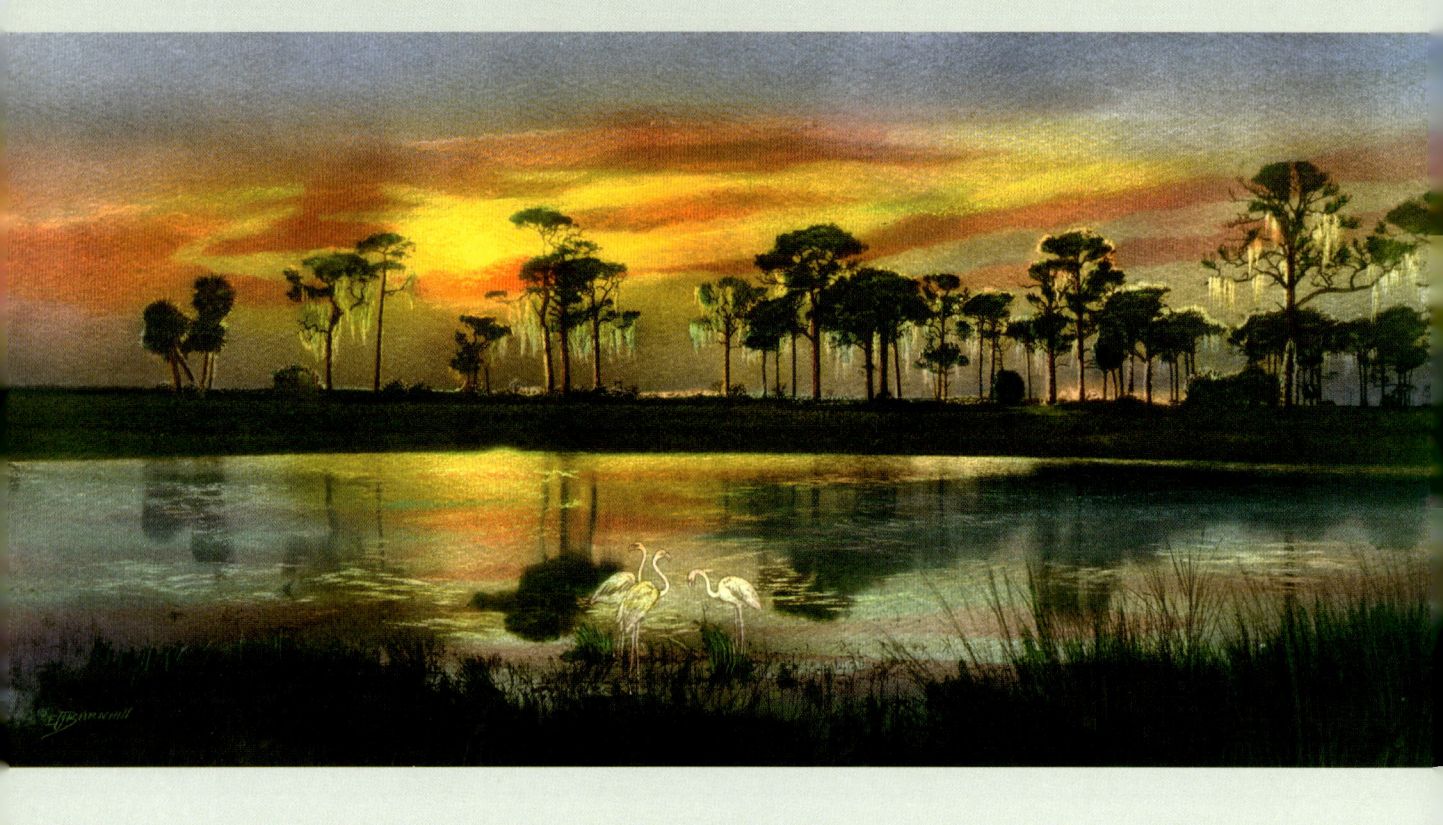

The imaginative artist willy-nilly influences his time. If he understands his responsibility and acts on it—taking the art seriously, himself never quite—he can make a contribution equal to, if different from, that of the scientist, the politician, and the jurist.

Herman Wouk

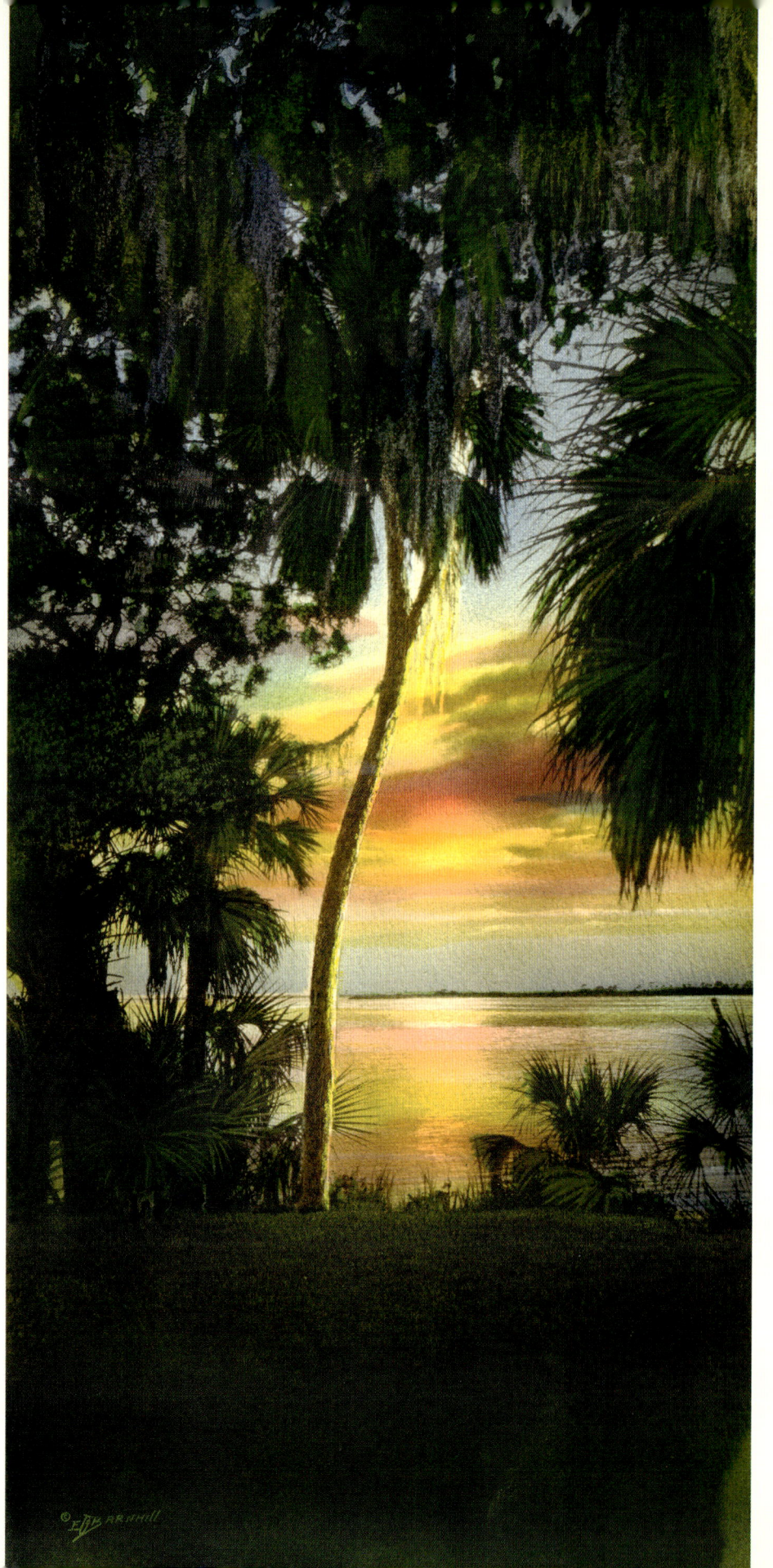

Preface

FOR WHATEVER REASON, I have always been drawn to obscure artists who work on the fringes of the art world and who often live on the edges of society. After completing graduate school in 1977 as a new-minted photographer, I had returned to my home in South Beach to document the endings of the Old World culture there that had been established by Eastern European Jewish refugees who had escaped czarist pogroms and, later, the Nazi Holocaust. Almost immediately I was torn away from my chosen field when I came upon the beautiful photographs of Gleason Waite Romer, who had captured Miami on film from 1924 to 1964. His life's work was buried in the Miami–Dade Public Library, unknown and unacknowledged by the general populace. Because I believed that his work needed to be shared, to be aired to the world, I published my first book, *Romer's Miami*, in the mid-1980s. This ultimately led to establishing the Romer Collection as central to Miami's visual history.

After that initial wandering into the world of writing, I devoted all my time to photography. Then, about twenty years ago, I took a turn off I-95 at Ft. Pierce to have lunch with three of the artists known as the Highwaymen. Their story and their artwork had not yet come to public awareness. I was quickly compelled to learn about them and understand their artistic creations. This came at a good time for me and for these painters. Their story needed to be told, and no one had yet presented their unearthed tale. Then in my mid-forties, I thought it wise to take a year or two away from photography to regroup; after all, most of my photographer-friends and mentors seemed to have either burned out or given up before their fiftieth birthdays. Twenty years later I am still, unexpectedly, writing. My books about the Highwaymen and other vernacular Florida artists and photographers have fed my spirit. Indeed, I believe that my writings have kept me vital and true in my photography.

Like those whose lives and works I have explored, my photography has become questlike, and increasingly private.

I am a native and lifelong resident of Florida; I know it as well as anyone. I have traveled around, written about, and photographed Florida during its old and new days. Ours is a rich, diverse, and often wild-and-crazy, if not a misunderstood, state. As E. G. Barnhill's photographs are finally finding their rightful place in our culture, Florida adds yet another colorful layer to its photographed records. Seemingly, like many of the subjects of my books, Barnhill had been relegated to near obscurity. Few people paid attention to him or his photographs. In Florida, W. J. Harris had captured the spotlight in the field of early-twentieth-century hand-colored photography. Once again I was attracted to a marginalized artist. Barnhill worked outside the established conventions, giving us something fresh and meaningful. I am privileged to have the opportunity to present his work to the world.

E. G. Barnhill and the Art of Tourism

JUST AFTER THE turn of the twentieth century, when Henry Flagler's railroad pushed Florida's frontier below his St. Augustine home base and when Henry Plant's railroads and steamships expanded Florida from his Tampa headquarters, two photographers found their own individual ways to this burgeoning state. These men eventually would impact the settlement of Florida from the early to middle 1900s through the art they each embraced—photo coloring. The two would settle in and work from geographically different parts of the state. As time passed, one of them enjoyed a greater renown than the other, but both contributed to the history of Florida's settlement in those years of rapid growth.

William James Harris's contribution to the advertisement of Florida through the popular arts has been well established. Harris (1868–1940), from his St. Augustine shop, portrayed the uniqueness of the beauty found in natural Florida in his dreamy creations. It was in the treatment of the subject matter of this art, however, that the less famous photo colorist, Esmond Grenard Barnhill, established his own place in Florida history while working in his photography business in St. Petersburg.

Esmond was born in Saluda, South Carolina, on March 4, 1894, to Luther Hulen Barnhill and Bonna Estella "Stella" (nee Gilbreath) Barnhill. Thereafter the Barnhills took up residence in Tallulah Gorge, Georgia, a primary tourist destination because of a local waterfall that gave the town its nickname, "Niagara of the South." Here the seeds of Esmond's later business acumen were planted as he learned firsthand, at an early age, that tourism often was built upon an elusive dream, a search for the unique place, and, perhaps, a quest for peaceful surroundings.

Some time later Luther and Stella, together with their five children, Arthur, Maude, Esmond, Delma, and James, moved to Waycross, Georgia. Their family life was unpretentious, but filled with various activities that delighted Esmond and his siblings. In the days before a radio was in every home, the family would often sit on the porch to be entertained by Luther's mandolin or banjo playing as others sang along. Summers were spent on St. Simons Island, off the coast of Georgia, where Luther tended his pecan orchard while the youngsters gathered crabs along the shore. The children developed a sense of adventure and curiosity, stimulated by the interests of their parents. Luther passed along his skills in photography to his offspring, while Stella, who was part Cherokee Indian, motivated them to study Native American culture.

Luther supported his family, in part, by working as a tinker, traveling the back roads of Georgia and Tennessee, grinding knives, selling gunpowder, tuning pianos, repairing watches, and offering notions from the back of a horse-drawn wagon, his store on wheels. Although he always had a pistol stuck in his belt, Luther often sent Esmond "down the road ahead of the wagon because no one would shoot a boy," says Esmond's son Jack. Esmond, in fact, was generally welcomed, opening the doors for Luther to offer his wares and services. Similarly, when Luther wanted to purchase pottery and other Native American crafts, Esmond was sent into a village alone; since Luther was a white man, the inhabitants "wouldn't speak to him." Esmond very likely began to hone his own business instincts at this time.

Esmond's carefree youth was cut short by the untimely death of his mother when he was ten years old. Stella was murdered by a jilted former beau, a man whom Luther tracked down and killed five years later. Probably in an effort to protect his children from the harsh reality of his mission, Luther sent Esmond, Delma, and James to an Episcopal school in Millbrook, New York, where Stella's brother, the Reverend George Valerie Gilbreath, taught. His mother's death having been avenged, Esmond was back in Georgia by his midteen years, living near Savannah. Esmond now had been introduced to the excitement of an unpredictable and nomadic lifestyle, one that he would often pursue in the years ahead.

Always seeking adventure, Esmond and his brother Arthur became treasure hunters when they built their own versions of metal detectors. In their early attempts to find buried booty they "used a magnetic needle that would find metal," recalls Jack. Later, but as early as 1921, they constructed a contraption with two wooden bicycle wheels and copper wire, which was moved around by a wooden handle. Esmond's son Clayton, a youngster at the time, remembers that it was an awkward gadget to control; furthermore, it detected only objects that were close to the surface. It was still in Esmond's garage in St. Petersburg when he died, along with stacks of his prints, souvenirs, and memorabilia.

Once again Esmond and Arthur went to St. Simons Island, where they unearthed silver coffee pots, cups, and utensils at a vacated Spanish fort. Esmond sold his share of the valuables to finance their exploration of the West Indies on a yawl, a two-masted sailboat. They went to Santo Domingo in the Dominican Republic and Porto Bello in Panama, in search of adventure and riches. The Barnhills did not strike big finds, but Esmond discovered a small one while in Panama. There he unearthed dozens of pieces-of-eight which, from beneath less than a quarter of an inch of dirt, glistened as they caught the light of a cooking fire.

Arriving in the Tampa Bay area after this experience, circa 1913, Esmond took up residence in St. Petersburg. Although eventually this was to become his permanent base, Esmond continued to indulge and nurture his wandering ways during the next few years. He traveled around Florida and, in all likelihood, went to Seabreeze, later named Daytona Beach, where he would have the opportunity to admire and even get to know the painter James Ralph Wilcox (1866–1915). Seabreeze, a promising resort town, attracted some notable photographers, who all operated studios along the same block on Beach Street.

It was a special time in this nascent city's development as "the birthplace of speed." From 1903 to 1910 tournaments were held on the beach for the entertainment of the wealthy. But as these became increasingly popular during the teens, there developed a need to alert the locals. In the twenties, a siren sounded to announce imminent speed runs. This was necessary because bad weather often forced delays in scheduled start times. But when the air-raid-like sound announced that races were about to begin, businesses closed and children were dismissed from school.

Sometime during those formative years of auto racing in Seabreeze, Esmond would have become aware of the works of photographer Richard LeSesne (1880–1946), who produced glass-plate positives with a refined gold-tone process, and William H. Gardiner (1861–1935), who expertly hand-painted photographs of the wilds. Barnhill was likely familiar, if not acquainted, with both of these men, because they utilized techniques that he admired and would soon employ.

Esmond drifted farther south to Palm Beach, where he apprenticed with a local photographer. Itinerancy was part of being a photographer back then, when the tourist seasons were especially pronounced; most of the Seabreeze photographers, for example, relocated to northern resorts in the summertime.

Esmond did not limit his wanderings solely to Florida. While in New Jersey, he met Helen Clayton and married her on March 23, 1916. That same year he ventured westward, all the way to Alaska. It is unclear whether this jaunt was the couple's honeymoon or an adventure in which Esmond, traveling solo, would further satisfy his wanderlust. Sometime during his frequent trips to the American West he might have met Edward Curtis (1868–1952), the noted photographer of Native Americans. Indeed, it is entirely possible that Barnhill first became familiar with Curtis's artistic practices during this 1916 trip when Curtis was at his creative peak. The work of the driven and innovative Curtis would greatly influence Esmond's later productions.

Having settled in St. Petersburg, Esmond and Helen had four children: Betty, William (Billy), Clayton, and Jack. Esmond Barnhill went into business here with the opening of his first independent venture, Florida Photo Studio, in November of 1917. He was no doubt increasingly aware of W. J. Harris's photography; his own practice was clearly modeled after the established photographer's enterprise. As reported in the *St. Petersburg Independent* on November 12, 1917, Harris was to launch a line of hand-colored photographs of that region in fine watercolors. Harris Pictures were already advertised in St. Petersburg's 1916 *City Directory by Advanced Art Printery*, which was near Barnhill's place of business. Two years later, Harris's photographs were also available at Smith Paint and Wall Paper and Baur's Souvenirs and Gifts.

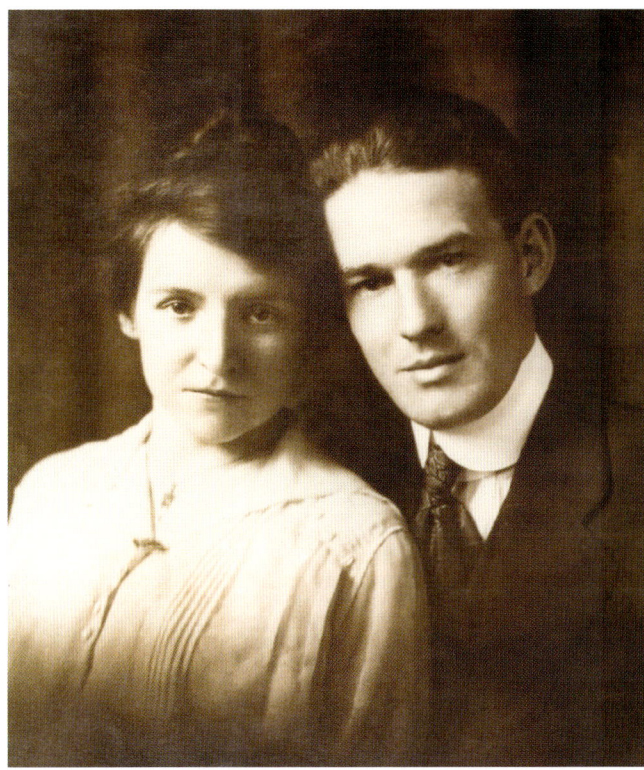

Esmond (E.G.) and Helen Barnhill, 1916

St. Petersburg was now a fertile ground for tourism. In fact, six other photography studios were listed in *Polk's St. Petersburg City Directory* in 1918.

Incorporated in 1903, St. Petersburg competed with the older, more established Florida cities along the Atlantic coast for the growing tourist trade. The Chamber of Commerce, in an effort to glean some of this trade, sponsored 10,000 promotional booklets and postcards enticing visitors to come for "good fishing and bright sunshine."[1] And come they did, on the newly paved roads, in their automobiles, which had become the dominant means of travel to Florida by the early 1920s. St. Petersburg had now established itself as a desirable spot in which to vacation. Esmond was ready to take his share of profit from its new economy.

Although Esmond had spent time in St. Petersburg circa 1913, the earliest record of his having a permanent presence there is found in the 1918 edition of *Polk's St. Petersburg City Directory*, which confirmed his residency in 1917. Esmond's shop, Florida Photo Studio, originally located at 17 Third Street North, sold the usual cameras and film, processed and printed tourists' snapshots, and vended postcards, a relatively new type of inexpensive souvenir. For the next two decades, the Barnhill name continued to be listed in this publication, usually in the "Photographic Developing and Printing" section. Dick and Yvonne Punnett, eminent researchers who concentrate on early Florida photographers, suspect that the fact that Barnhill's establishments appeared "under a different heading than just 'Photographers' hints that his principal activity was photographing views for his postcards and other paper items and marketing them as gifts rather than [merely] maintaining the usual portrait studio."

In 1924, because increased business demanded more suitable space from which to cater to the tourist trade, Barnhill moved his shop to 12 Third Street North and renamed his establishment Barnhill Studio. In 1929 he was back at the 17 Third Street North location; indeed, he may have retained a presence there all the while, as Barnhill's Camera Shop is listed at this address in the 1931 directory. In 1930, however, he appears to have relocated or branched out to yet another place, this time 24 Sixth Street North, conducting business as Alhambra Studio. Because of the Depression, no *Polk's St. Petersburg City Directory* was published in 1932, but Barnhill once again appeared in the 1933 edition under the old heading. A newspaper ad published on December 13, 1933, cites Barnhill's Camera Shop and Indian Store. Although his name does not appear at all in the 1934 directory, his business once again is listed in the 1935 edition under "Photographic Apparatus and Supplies."

As time passed, Barnhill would diversify while exercising his entrepreneurial skills. Once, as a promotion, he offered a free Brownie camera with the purchase of two rolls of film. He told his children that he had invented a part for a camera that prevented accidental double exposures by forcing the user to hand-advance the film, but explained that someone else patented the device before he got around to staking his claim.

Barnhill eventually began supplementing his income from the shop by taking publicity photographs for St. Petersburg's Festival of States

Parade. Young Jack became a participant in this endeavor when he was charged with preparing the sheet film holders for the press camera that his father used. Barnhill would photograph each of the forty-eight floats representing the states, as well as the other floats and bands constituting the procession. "People came by the thousands for prints the day after the parade," reports Jack, who, together with his brothers and their father, was up all night processing and printing 8" × 10" glossies.

National Geographic purchased some of Barnhill's photographs but never used them, although other magazines did. In a correspondence dated January 9, 1923, the chief of the magazine's illustrations division, J. L. Fisher, advised Barnhill to include a human figure in his photographs "to make them more desirable as magazine illustrations." Fisher went on to explain, "The figure should not be stiffly posed but should preferably be doing something. A pretty girl always helps such a picture and a smile provides the necessary action."

Even though he enjoyed commercial success, Barnhill was always looking for something new, something creative, something more to add to his bag of tricks. He was familiar with the practice of enhancing black-and-white photographs with applied pigments. In fact, Harris was using this technique very successfully on the other side of the state. Wallace Nutting, whose audience was primarily in New England, had demonstrated the marketability of hand-colored photographs even before Harris. Recognizing a business opportunity when he saw one, Barnhill lost no time acquiring the necessary skills to become a vendor of tinted photographs.

Before Barnhill began offering his own line of this new type of tourist art, he tinted the snapshots of his customers. Both Esmond and Helen were brushing colors onto vacation pictures, eventually instructing their children to "streak red across the horizon for the sunset," says Jack. These creations became very popular with travelers, and Barnhill, who was the first to offer this service in the St. Petersburg area, became increasingly busy. His son Jack believes that his father was the first in Florida to offer hand-coloring of snapshots taken by sojourners.

Tweaking the technique further, Esmond switched from the customary glossy paper used in photographic print development to a matte paper, because its surface better absorbed the water-based colors with which the photos were painted, and because it dried faster. A sign on the camera store offered hand-coloring for "five cents and up" for the prints from a roll of film, which amounted to less than a penny per picture. Jack remembers that soon Esmond and Helen, their four children, and a staff of as many as five women were painting all the time.

As Harris had done, Barnhill wanted to mass-produce certain images as postcards. He searched all the way to Europe for a quality printing house, and in Germany he found a company skilled in lithography which produced his subjects in sepia as postcards. Next he dealt with the Albertype Company in New York, which printed his Florida Art Series, the name Barnhill gave to his array of postcards picturing St. Petersburg's finest hotels, streets scenes, and landscapes.

At that time, during the early 1900s, photographs were relegated to black-and-white reproduction because printing presses were not yet sophisticated enough to register layers of color. Barnhill and his workers then applied color to these black-and-white postcards through a series of stencils placed over the large sheets upon which iterations of the picture had been run. Once the laborious process of tinting each card by hand was completed, the finished product retailed for five cents. Although his postcards were similar to the ones produced by the other colorists who portrayed Florida as the Garden of Eden, the hues of Barnhill's cards were especially subtle because of the Albertype printing process, which created a refinement not possible with the more pedestrian methods of the time.

Eventually Barnhill turned away from the tinting of tourists' snapshots and postcards to the hand-painting of his own pictures. His photographs were printed using the photogravure process, one in which the image was transferred from the negative onto a copper plate. This plate was then used to mechanically print richly toned multiple images on large sheets. Each print was painted by hand; Barnhill began using the descriptive Tropical Pictorial Photography tag to identify this work. Later the prints were run from the presses in color on paper stock of lesser quality.

Barnhill had entered the ranks of a legion of commercial photographers who courted the tourist trade in Florida during its formative days in the early 1900s. He could not have planned his advent any better because, oddly enough, the ever-popular state had inspired relatively few professional photographers to specialize in the hand-coloring of their photographs. Auctioneers Michael and Susan Ivankovich have documented 311 photographers who utilized the overpainting technique at that time, but only thirteen of them were in the Sunshine State.[2] Of those in Florida, W. J. Harris dominated the field. Larry Roberts, an aficionado of Florida vintage material culture, has seen "perhaps 125 different Harris pictures and approximately 40–50 Barnhills."[3] Between 1926 and 1930, Barnhill registered 59 photographs with the Library of Congress—an action he may have taken to protect his copyright of key images. However, these pictures did not represent his body of work. Actually, none of his glass-plate images, the most distinctive of his renditions, were registered.

Harris used small airbrushes to color his pictures, giving the subjects a dreamy, even ethereal, presence. Although Barnhill at times achieved bolder images through his use of the watercolors that he applied by brush, the most distinguishing feature of his work—besides the intense unearthly colors that uranium dyes yielded—is the smooth and seamless quality of his colors that his airbrushed works yielded. His sense of light and palette, the refined nature of the prints, with their inherent tonal graduation, reduced the effect of the artist's hand.

The subtle richness of Barnhill's airbrushed-tinted photographs captured Florida's distinctly clear, brisk colors. At times his dashes of brushed on highlights approached the neon colors that might be seen at sunset. Unlike Harris and the others who followed the pictorial conventions of the time, Barnhill created pictures that functioned more as windows through which to see the real Florida.

His photographs were laconic and unadorned, comparable to the future images by Walker Evans which would become the measure of the American tradition of documentary photography. They reflected an insistence on actuality, but were tempered by what photography curator

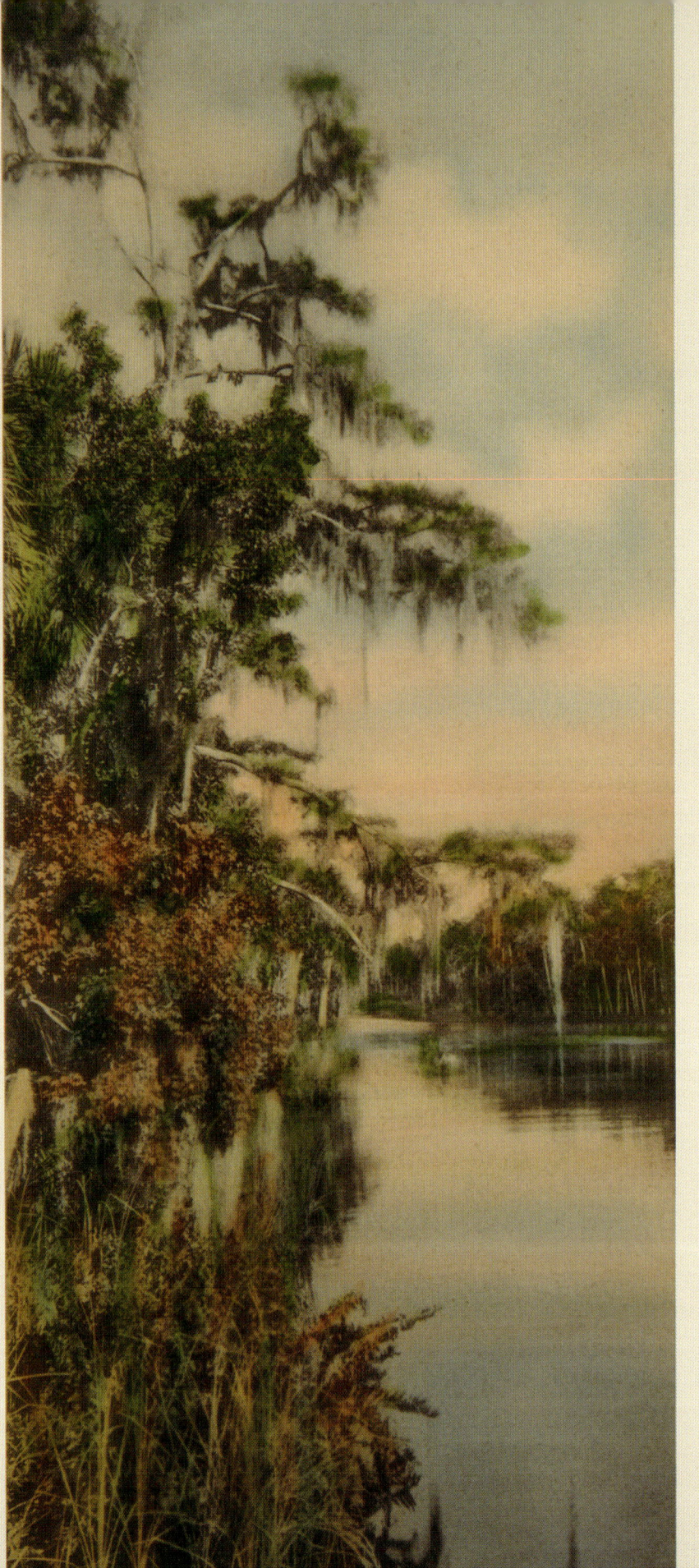

Hand-colored print
W. J. Harris

John Szarkowski referred to as the "poetic uses of bare-faced facts."[4] Barnhill did not distort reality beyond the artifice of the technique, but at the same time he was not bound by an aesthetic practice that stressed purity. Convention allowed for liberties to be taken, as far as he was concerned.

Photography has long straddled the line between high and vernacular art. The hand-painted photograph skewed this line even further toward the vernacular; it was not designed for gallery walls but rather for decoration in middle-class homes. Each one, in spite of its photographic-print basis, was an original work of art fashioned according to a photographer's own vision and interpretation of consumer demand. In the words of Elizabeth Walker Mechling and Jay Mechling, authorities on the practice, "Unique, individual handwork transformed each mass-produced photograph into a one-of-a-kind painting."[5]

Although photographers had experimented with color since the introduction of photography in 1839, it was not until 1907 that the Autochrome process offered a hope of practicality in recording this colorful world. Functional color photography became widespread with the introduction of Kodachrome transparency film in 1935. Still, even as color processes were becoming increasingly available, serious art photographers of the day did not utilize color, but preferred black-and-white prints. Photography imitating painting through a myriad of pictorialist techniques that included soft focus and hand coloring was quickly surpassed in popularity by fidelity to fact. A black-and-white image, graphically rich and suggestive, was always the norm.

At this time, the camera's descriptive prowess was revered because it captured verity rather than fantasy. The photographers who hand-colored their landscape pictures, seeking the divine and sublime, were more consistent in orientation with the painters of the Hudson River School. The nineteenth-century landscapist could instill a sense of personal affirmation and moral order without the virtuous storytelling explicit in this realm of genre painting. Barnhill's images fell somewhere in the middle of these two fields of art, the real and the ideal. Although his pictures were not more beautiful, or even as traditionally exquisite as the ones generated by others practicing in this field, Barnhill's creations stood apart. His pictures, simply put, were generally more purely photographic, if the term "pure" can be used in the realm of painted photographs.

Unlike the others who were experimenting with hand coloring, Barnhill at his best offered images that were more topographic than sentimental, seemingly more true-to-life than imaginary. While he, like other commercial photographers, would take artistic liberties with this art form, he tended to create a natural-looking picture. Sometimes his coloration was extreme, a response more to the feel of reality than reality itself; his creations reflected the sensations resulting from experiencing Florida. Barnhill's heavily painted images were without the aura of the supernatural or even the pristine motifs often found in images rendered by traditional landscape painters. Rather his works conveyed to viewers the sense of actually being present in the depicted scenes.

In order to satisfy public taste and to augment their compositions, photographers at that time were not beyond exercising some artistic license. Wallace Nutting, although valuing the straightforward approach, would retouch negatives and prints. He advised aspiring photographers to "always carry an ax," encouraging them to avoid compositional intrusions and clutter. W. J. Harris, perhaps following Nutting's basic precept that anything was permissible in the service of composition, would use a stuffed alligator or egret to enhance the foregrounds of his photographs. At times he would use both in the same picture.

Because Barnhill was an adventurer who tried many things, he was able to avoid the dogmas that often result from convention, both in his artistry and in his commerce. He would simply discard items from an original photograph to enhance his pictures. In one of his most successful images, he etched away the construction scaffolding that surrounded the Singing Tower at Bok Gardens in Lake Wales before its opening in 1929 and replaced it with clouds. This practice was in keeping with postcard production techniques. He also would recycle some images. Sailboats in an original negative might disappear in subsequent renditions, only to reappear in others.

It is easy to mistake the butterflies he superimposed on some of his pictures as cheap fancy, but they represented his interest in Native American beliefs. Butterflies, according to some beliefs, were created

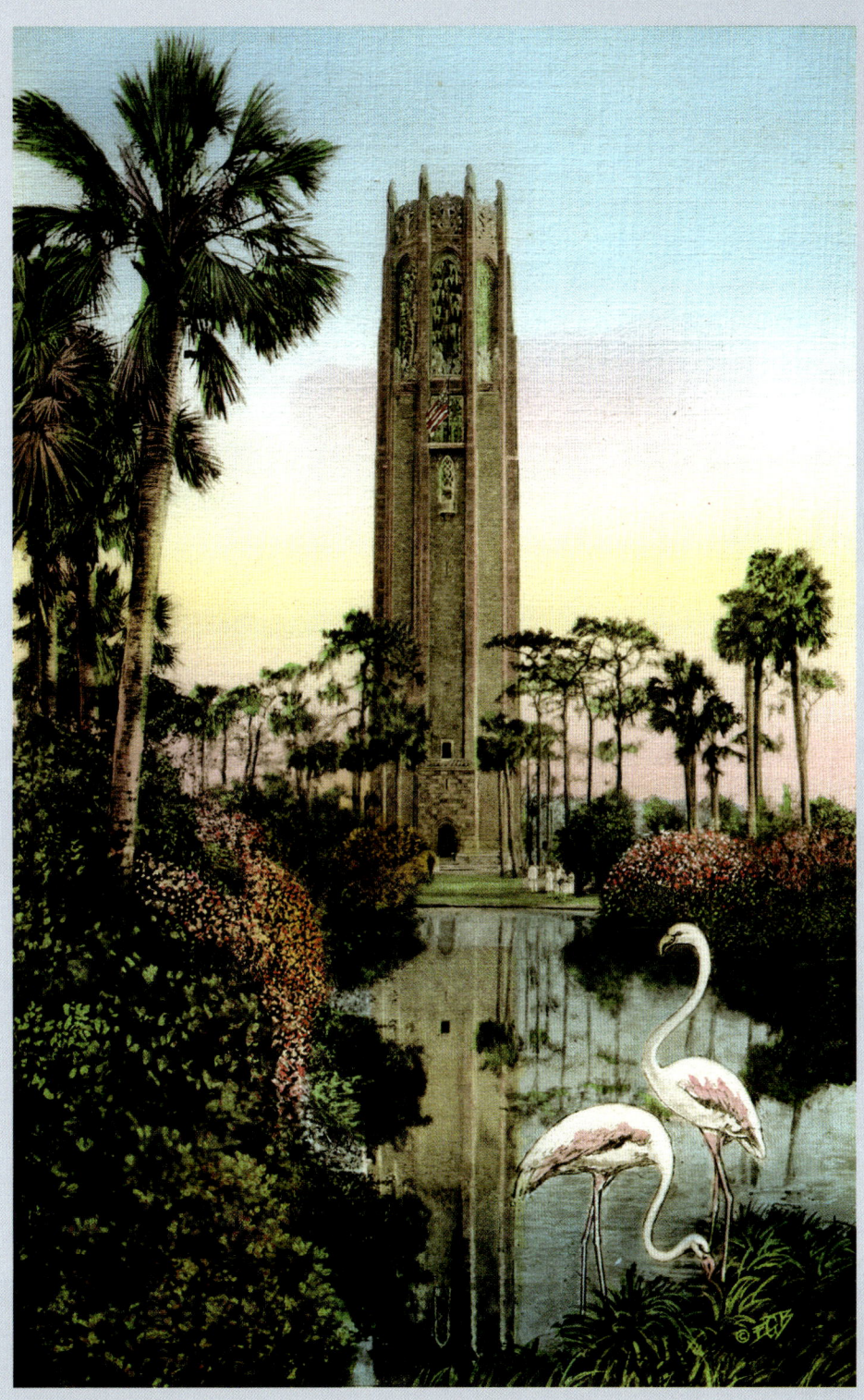

Bok Singing Tower,
Mountain Lake
[Lake Wales], Florida
E. G. Barnhill

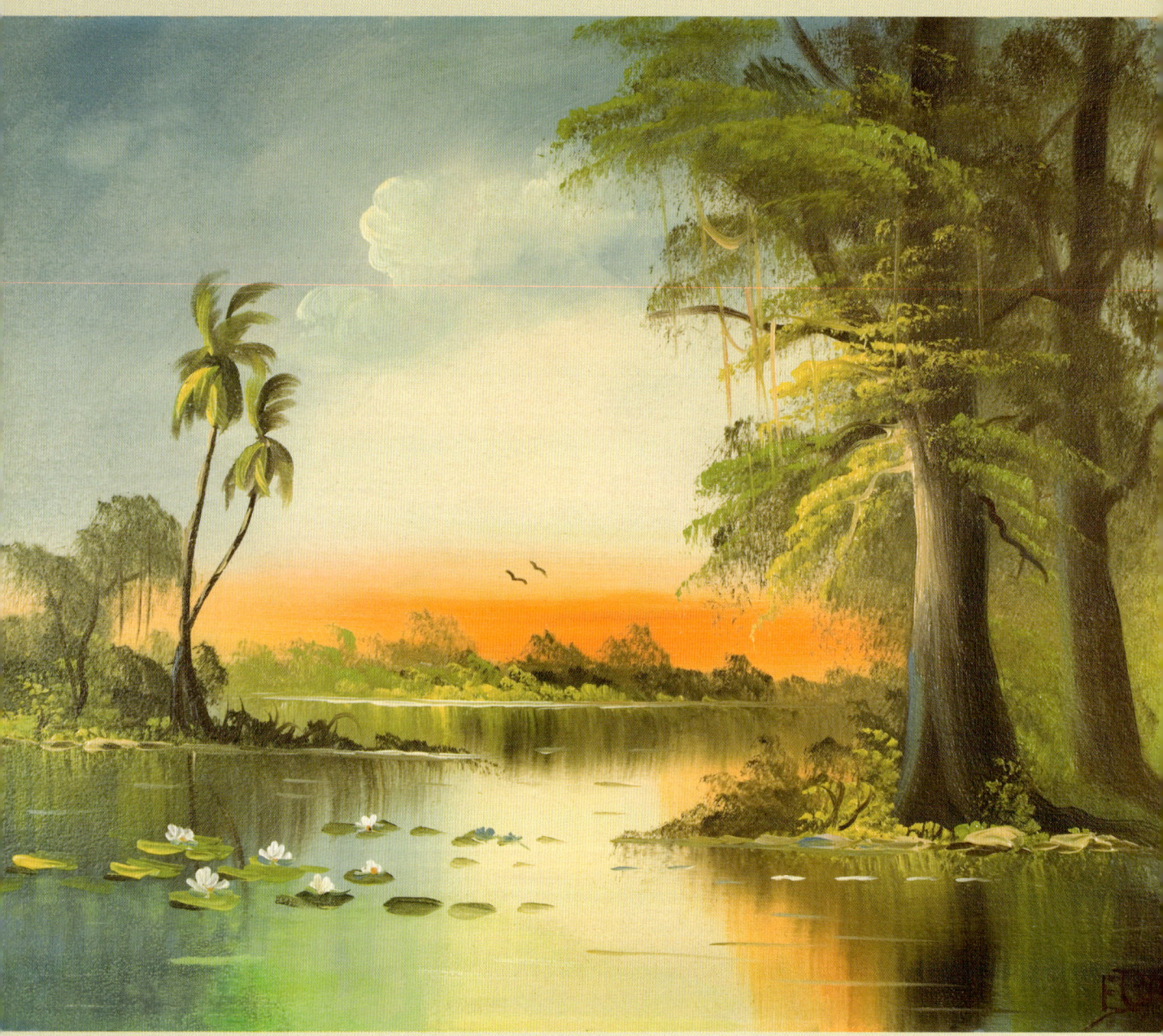

Untitled oil painting
E. G. Barnhill

from "colored stones of the mountainside and sent forth on the soft south wind to gladden the hearts of men."[6] Barnhill even added Indian princesses to his scenes, giving credence to the assertion that he had a lifelong infatuation with their culture.

But Barnhill did not adhere any further to Nutting's aesthetic feelings or failings. Heinz and Bridget Henisch, scholars of early hand-painted photography, describe the conundrum in the context of both rank commercialism and pictorial sensibility: "the banality of his [Nutting's] comments matches the blandness of his compositions: the picture 'must attract the heart, far more than attracting the eye.'"[7] Barnhill's creations maintained a high standard of veracity; he simply was truer to the photographer's central tenet of plausibility. His images had the candor of snapshots, while Harris's were increasingly formal, in keeping with established tastes and the advent of Modernism. Esmond Barnhill would not continue to use their techniques forever; he would reject the values of the new trend in favor of those borne in his romanticized, colorful past.

Eventually Barnhill had his pictures printed in color. Running them off the press this way saved time and money, though the altered process

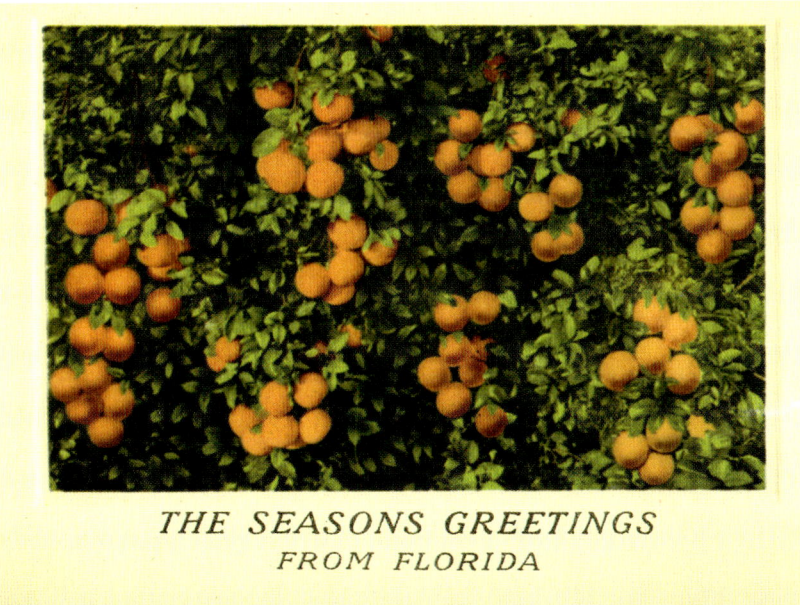

THE SEASONS GREETINGS
FROM FLORIDA

Greeting card
E. G. Barnhill

yielded less than a fine object. Now Barnhill was free to diversify. In addition to the standard fare sold to tourists, he offered greeting cards, variations of his hand-colored Florida Art Series photographs, and picture cards which often held scented blossoms or Spanish moss in tiny bottles. He sold, for one dollar each, his own unframed oil paintings of Florida landscapes to passersby who saw them in his shop's display windows. Eventually he hired two painters, Alvin Pepper and Walter Addison, to sit on the sidewalk and create pictures that could be customized to suit the tastes of a buyer who might want palm trees added, for example. These paintings, for an additional cost, could then be framed with a cypress bark edging.

Barnhill was unique in his field in another important way. He was not motivated solely by the marketability of hand-painted photographs or any other moneymaking souvenirs. His need to be mobile, his desire to explore and to create, more than anything, stimulated the wit by which he lived and by which he produced his life's work. Eventually he would make truly original contributions to photography before leaving that field and moving on to other ventures.

Among the inspirational sources for Barnhill's most notable achievements, the strongest by far was his interest in two artists of the period—the painter Ralph Wilcox and the photographer Edward Curtis.

Barnhill greatly admired Wilcox's watercolor paintings of Florida. "He thought highly of him and his art. He fell in love with his watercolors," Jack Barnhill says. However, Wilcox's prints have raised questions concerning authorship and appropriation, clouding any definitive knowledge of the works of both Wilcox and Barnhill. The Ivankoviches describe the issue: "There is some debate whether J. R. Wilcox was a photographer who sold hand-painted photographs or an artist who sold hand-painted photographic reproductions of his paintings." The latter contention is accurate. Wilcox was a painter only. But he did market hand-colored prints of his own paintings. Wilcox had the Burgman Printing Company in Seabreeze make the prints that he would tint and sell.

Jack Barnhill has long held the belief that his father and Wilcox formed a close friendship. He explains that "since [Wilcox paintings]

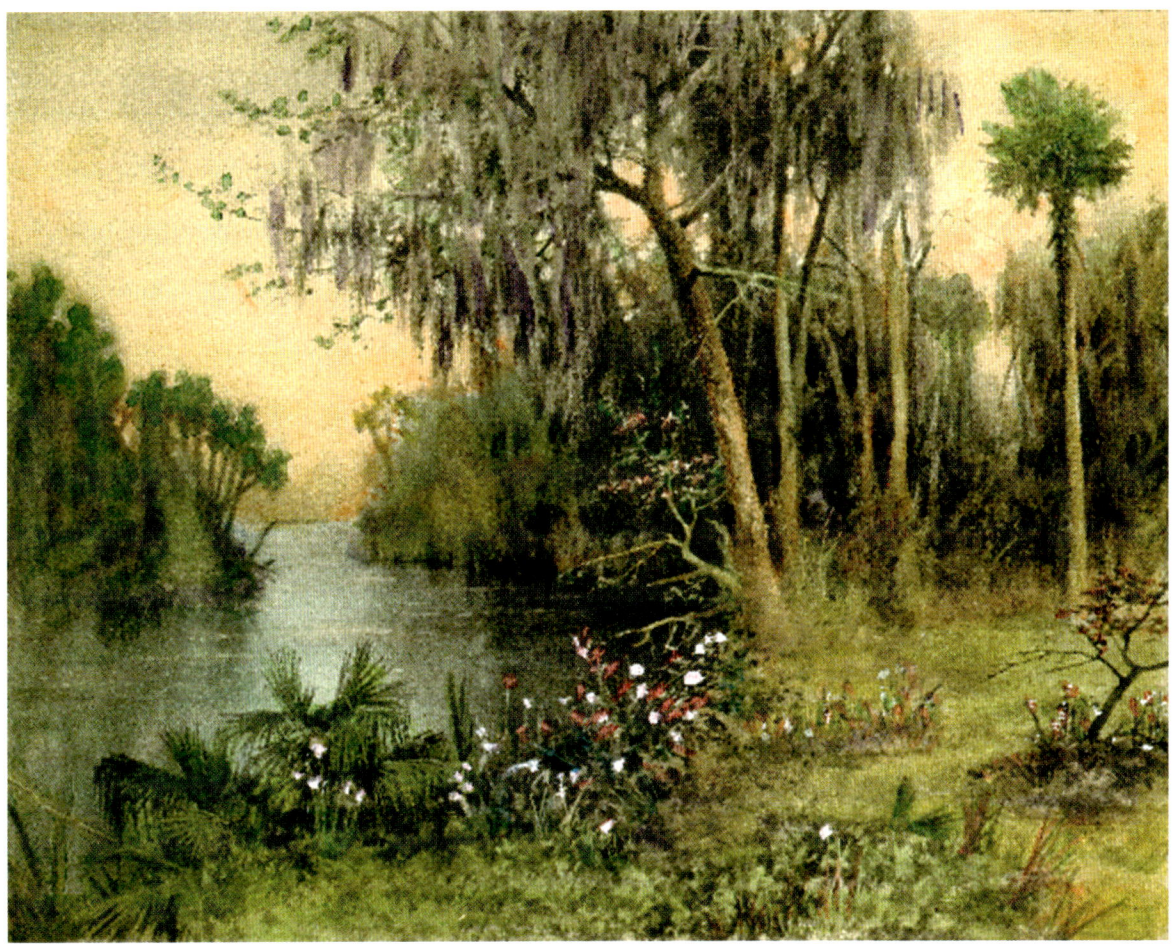

Hand-colored gravure
J. R. Wilcox

were one of a kind, Dad got the idea to photograph them, print images on bisque [matte] paper, and hand-paint them. He would do them in a variety of sizes." In this version of the relationship between Wilcox and Barnhill, Wilcox had agreed to an arrangement by which both men painted and marketed some of the prints. However, it is doubtful that a close personal relationship developed between the two men. Although each was a serious artist and businessman, Wilcox and Barnhill were nearly thirty years apart in age. Wilcox died while Barnhill was establishing himself in the field. Furthermore, there is no evidence that they socialized or colored prints together.

Because Barnhill acquired Wilcox's prints and sold them from his shop, as others were doing, it is generally accepted that the two men did meet and do business together. While there is no proof that Barnhill was ever active professionally in Seabreeze, he is believed to have been there. Historian John McSwain recently came across a signed Barnhill postcard of the often painted and photographed "Tarzan Tree" by the Tomoka River. He says, "It shows that Barnhill was at least in the area of Daytona taking photos at some point in his career." In those days, appropriating others' images was not an uncommon practice among publishers of scenic postcards. But Barnhill's view is different from the work of others who depicted the tree and its setting.

Further, Seabreeze was a center of tourism where many fine photographers could have offered him hope and inspiration, if not actual advice and trade secrets. In addition to Gardiner and LeSesne, other practicing photographers in the early part of the twentieth century were present: William Roxby, Clark Smith, Edward Harris, Seth Shear. William Coursen came in 1910, a few years after photographer-turned-industrialist Henry Kaiser (1882–1967) left town to make his fortune. Success was in the air here, attracting new and would-be artists. An ambitious and aspiring photographer, the young Barnhill could easily have stocked up on Wilcox prints while he was visiting Seabreeze.

That the two men had an amicable relationship is attested by the fact that Wilcox had traveled across Florida to St. Petersburg, a relatively easy trip by the new rail service. The *Daytona Gazette-News* reported on July 3, 1914, that "Mr. Wilcox is getting new material for his easel works this fall, and visiting the business firms he supplies with his art work in various parts of the state. Mrs. Wilcox had a letter from him, dated at St. Petersburg."

On the other hand, Wilcox's grandnephew John Leverett believes that "Barnhill purchased these unfinished prints and then finished them." This is a less than romantic version of the Wilcox-Barnhill alliance, but it is consistent with Barnhill's late-in-life conversation with Danny McKenna, a primary collector of Florida art and books. McKenna remembers Barnhill relating that when he went to see the recently widowed Mrs. Wilcox, he "saw all these prints on the floor" and that he "cleaned out the old man's garage." Surprised by this account of the relationship between his father and Wilcox, Jack Barnhill stated, "He talked about him so damn much, I can't imagine he didn't know the man."

Barnhill would say, "Wilcox was some artist," while discussing painting with Jack. Without doubt, his son adds, Barnhill "was impressed by Wilcox, appreciated his art."

Wilcox did leave behind black-and-white prints of his paintings, stacks of them. Barnhill continued to paint these, paying respect to his departed friend by signing Wilcox's name. A few times, he signed his own name on these prints, possibly taking credit for the coloring, but generally Barnhill made no attempt to usurp Wilcox's claim to these pictures. He often affixed paper labels to the mounts of these prints that read:

> Hand-Colored Gravures by J. R. Wilcox, Sea Breeze, Fla., 1890,
> who was the Best Natural scenery artist of Early Florida Scenes
> From E. G. Barnhill Collection

As time passed, collectors of these paintings found ways to authenticate the creative source of each picture, even if Barnhill had signed Wilcox's name. Wilcox's signature slanted to the left while Barnhill's slanted to the right; hence knowing who colored the print is possible. But Barnhill's tagging the date of 1890 on the paintings that he tinted and signed for Wilcox is "curious," Larry Roberts points out, "as Wilcox first visited Florida in 1901." Wilcox's obituary confirms that he did visit Florida fourteen years prior to his death, and that he relocated from Elmira, New York, buying property and setting up shop in Goodall, at the southern end of Seabreeze, in 1905.

Barnhill's date may have been chosen to further romanticize the images by placing them in the previous century, or it may have been a code indicating that he, Barnhill, had painted these prints. But Roberts offers a more mundane explanation. He "seriously doubt[s] Barnhill intended to use the 'deflated' dating of Wilcox pictures for any other purpose than to add age to the prints."

It is also possible to tell whether Barnhill or Wilcox did the painting through a study of the colors each artist chose. When Wilcox tinted one of these, he more closely maintained the soft quality of the original painting. Barnhill's brighter colors were consistent with the hand-coloring of his own photographs. He often added bright red flowers at the bases of trees in Wilcox's bucolic scenes. Harris and others always

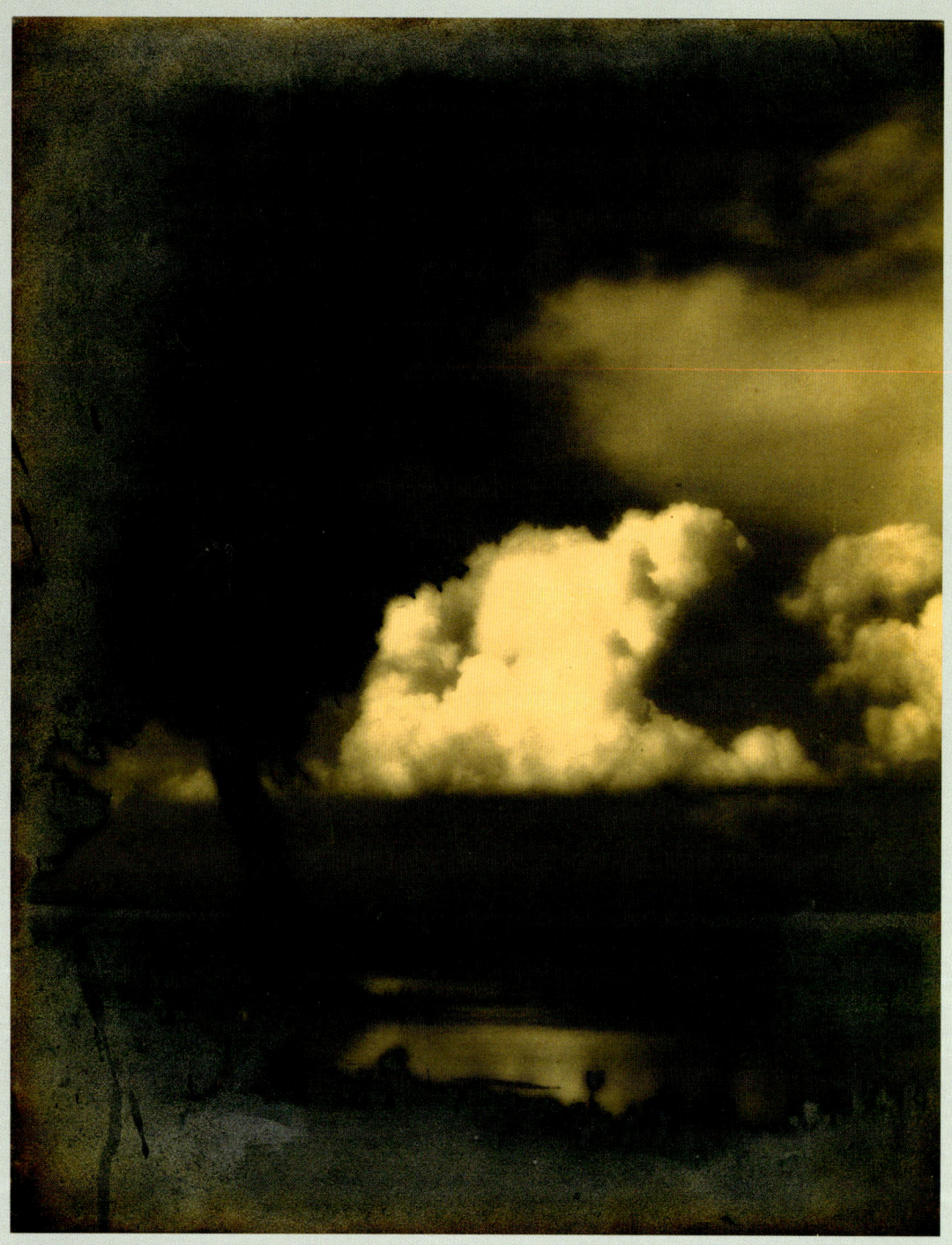

Tampa Bay Weedon Island
Silver gelatin print
E. G. Barnhill

conveyed romantic sentiment in their scenes with muted hues, but Barnhill did not try to approximate Wilcox's softer colors, or even capitalize on paradisiacal Florida. Barnhill's own hand-painted photographs were as bright as Florida's light, enriching his subject matter but making the land seem less hospitable than the seductive scenes of other artists.

A mellower Barnhill would emerge as a result of his artistic liaison with Wilcox. Perhaps Esmond had long ago buried any personal romantic longings under the trauma of his mother's death or under the harshness of his nomadic lifestyle. Seemingly, Wilcox's art fostered another eye through which Barnhill could view Florida. Now, along with his own inventory of prints, cards, and other souvenirs, Barnhill could offer reproductions of paintings to his customers.

Within a few years of starting his photographic business, Barnhill had honed his skills in a myriad of techniques in image making through which he could express himself while making a living for his family. He learned his craft as an energetic young man in the immediate prewar years. From the end of 1917 until it began to wane nearly two decades later, photographic production was his chief source of income from his shops. Indeed, it was during this period that Barnhill produced a black-and-white photograph (*facing*) that would win him recognition in Vienna, Austria. Still in good condition today, the back of the photograph reads, "Prize Winner . . . Vienna 1932 / International Photo Exhibit / Tampa Bay Weedon Island near Coluso [*sic*] Indian Ruins." The photograph was likely made during his early years, given the pictorial conventions it follows, but submitted in competition later, toward the end of his days creatively photographing.

With the souvenir photography business having peaked and with the advent of the Depression, Barnhill, like others, faced harder times. He then went west to be in on the action surrounding the construction of Boulder Dam. The *Las Vegas Age* newspaper dated December 8, 1931, reported that Barnhill "announced yesterday he will start building at once on the structure for his company's concession" at Boulder City. There he advertised himself as an Indian trader and a photographer. He sold Navajo, Zuni, Hopi, and Seminole handcrafts including silver jewelry, weavings, and pottery. Barnhill also photographed the construction of the dam, which was completed in 1935.

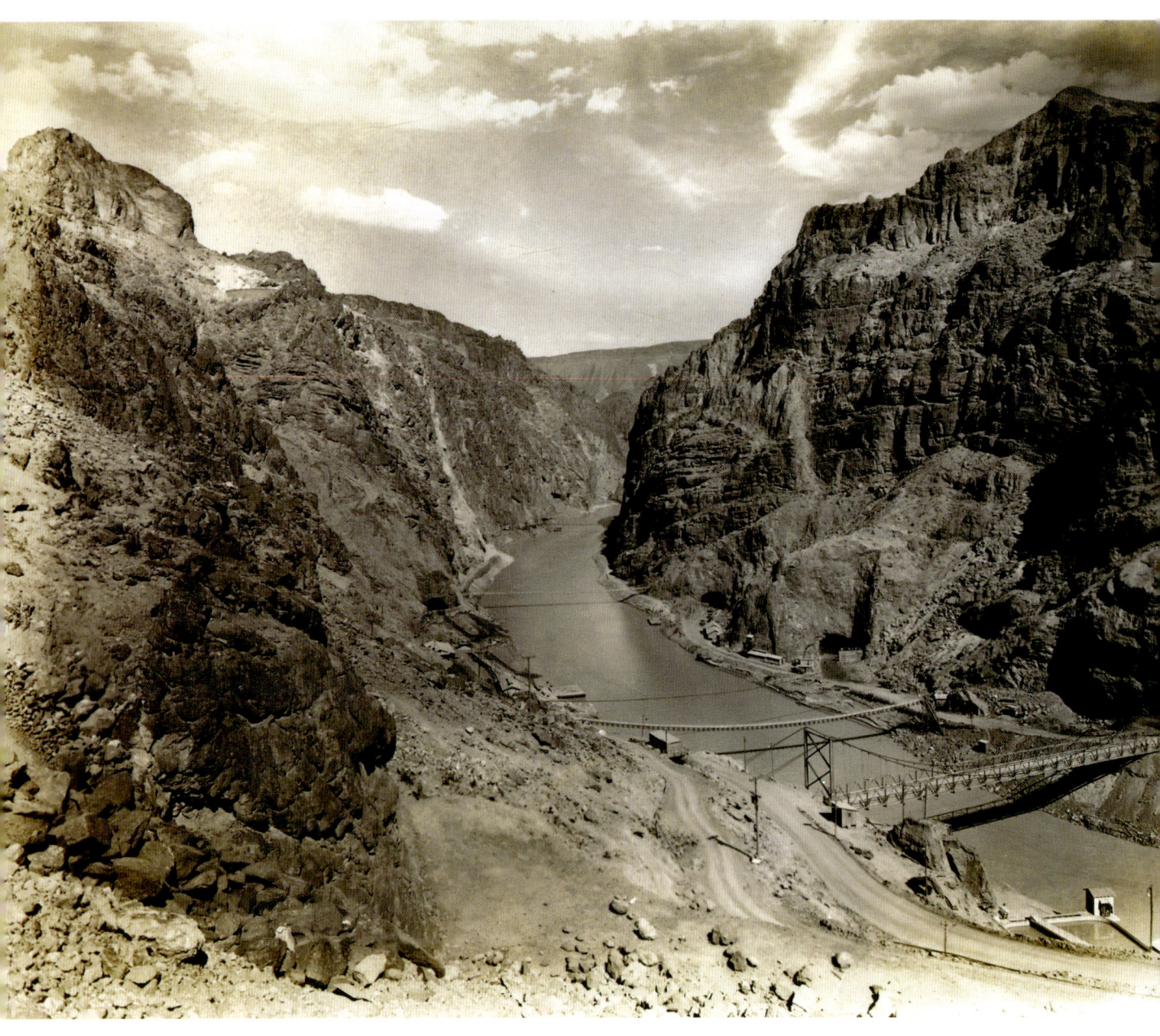

Untitled silver gelatin print
(Hoover Dam construction)
E. G. Barnhill

By the mid-1930s the St. Petersburg store had become a gift shop managed by Helen, Barnhill's wife. This was not a new venture for Helen by any means. Even during the high success of their photography business, she remained there during the summers, the off-season for tourism in Florida, while Esmond, ever the adventurer, went out west as he had done since childhood on family trips.

For many years Barnhill was the consummate photographer, demanding and accepting only the best shots. His son Clayton recalls, "He'd sit there for the longest time, till the clouds got set up. Sit for hours waiting." Working at John's Pass, near St. Petersburg, amid the junglelike vines from which children would swing, Esmond would wait with his readied view camera "till the sun set just right. He'd rush back to the shop to print it." Clayton continues, "All of a sudden, when the boom bust, he dropped photography completely." When that happened, Esmond was ready to move on to other things. His background, his personal history, and his own ingenuity would once again serve him well.

Wanting to become more involved with Native American culture, Barnhill had begun to revisit the American West in the early 1920s. Having explored Indian mounds since childhood, he became enchanted with Native American arts and crafts as he grew up. Esmond returned there in 1925 to do business. Employing native silversmiths and rug weavers, he opened trading posts in Gallup, New Mexico, and in Estes Park, Colorado, which he ran during his summers away from St. Petersburg. In Florida, at Dania, Barnhill opened his first curio shop, the Thunderbird Indian Trading Post, in the mid-1930s. There Seminole Indians were employed to make craft items that were sold to tourists. Many more trading posts and curio shops followed. In Ft. Lauderdale, at 11 Tropical Arcade, Barnhill opened Blue Wave, which sold, in addition to the Native American crafts he loved, genuine pearl shells, fish scales, pins, necklaces, earscrews, shell plaques, shell lamps, bulk shells, pearlized shells, and novelties. Still later Barnhill established other tourist shops in St. Ignace, Michigan, and in Wisconsin Dells, Wisconsin, which he ran until 1959. More of these businesses followed in Booth Bay, Maine, and in Indian Springs, Georgia.

It is the generally held belief that while working with Edward Curtis, the teenaged Barnhill learned the techniques through which he would establish his most notable contribution to photography—uranium dye–based prints on glass. Curtis's exotic images of the vanishing race, Native Americans, took many forms, the most unique of which was gold-toning. Although Curtis did not invent the process, he pioneered and perfected it, calling his finished products "Curt-Tones."

In Florida, Richard LeSesne called his gold-tones "Haberle-Tones," after his mother's maiden name, Habersham, and his own surname. A few others employed this delicate process, which yielded a translucent, three-dimensional-like image; among them were Norman Edson, James Barton, and Arthur Pillsbury. Some practitioners developed their own variations of the technique and guarded their formulas with proprietary zeal. Barnhill told his son Clayton that he "had to have good, good water" to perfect the image.

For gold-tones, which were also called orotones, a negative was first printed on a glass plate, instead of paper, as a positive image. Then a mixture of powdered gold pigment and, usually, banana oil was rolled on the back. The resulting honey-colored luminosity enriched the image, yielding a brilliance and depth not possessed by traditional photographs, or even by the silver-toned versions then being produced, which more closely approximated a traditional print. Barnhill had experimented with both silver and gold toning soon after establishing himself in Florida.

Barnhill wanted to use colors in these images on glass, so he tried various types of pigments, including paint, perfume oils, and ground minerals. Finally he discovered that uranium dyes would yield the result that he desired. In the 1870s uranium ore was mined in the American West and sent to Germany and France, where it was turned into dyes for the ceramics industry.[8] Prior to setting up in business in Florida, Barnhill had gone to Germany to study lithography; before the First World War, Germany, and Saxony especially, was a center for quality printing. Barnhill, who had a lifelong interest in mineralogy, may have become familiar with uranium ore there. With his knowledge about Native Americans, he may also have known that they used uranium to create paints for ceremonial decoration.

Ever since Marie Curie separated radium from uranium, the mining of uranium ore had boomed, making it readily available in the mid-1930s. By this time Barnhill had come into his own as an artist-photographer, had used these minerals for twenty years with a freshness reserved for pioneers, and was turning to more commercial enterprises. The uranium dyes had led him down a path as yet uncharted; not only did these colors enhance his pictures, they glowed like radiant light. To complete the process Barnhill sprayed, painted, or rolled gold pigment on the backs of the glass plates that held his images, bringing them to life. These Barnhill framed, adding labels that identified himself as the creator of the scenes portrayed therein.

The uranium-dyed images were a hybrid of the gold-tone and the hand-painted prints, but meaningfully different from each of these. The colors in the uranium-dyed images did not replicate actual colors, nor did they even come close to approximating them. The hand-colored landscape photograph had always functioned metaphorically: the viewer would eagerly suspend his disbelief of the artifice in favor of the experience of seeing and believing—believability being the crux of photographic imagery. The uranium-dyed landscapes, however, were of yet another genus. These functioned at the extremes of metaphor with their unearthly hues.

Barnhill's uranium-dyed, glass-plate photographs place him in the national dialogue of American photography. "I'm the only man in America to use the photographic process of uranium dyes on glass. I used to get uranium oxide from Germany before it was worth much," Barnhill told reporter Barbara Willy about his earlier works. She points out that this was "long before the element became known for nuclear fission."[9] Uranium oxide had been used in the photographic process in Europe then but not in its paints. Barnhill's innovative use of it yielded a new kind of glowing image.

However, it was his more-traditional and readily available hand-colored pictures on paper that established him as one of Florida's key photographers in his time. Yet Barnhill was not his work; he would not have defined himself as a photographer or as an artist. Doggedly determined in his pursuits, he was a free-spirited American original, a mercurial man who, according to his granddaughter Linda Scott, "lived his own life, and didn't go with the flow." He made a living and supported his family by being a photographer, but he gave it up for other pursuits when the fancy took him. In an odd way, he was free from being too serious, from working too predictably. He may have been influenced along the way by the likes of Harris, Wilcox, and Curtis, but he did not merely copy their techniques. Instead he massaged their methods into skills that were totally his own.

Although Barnhill had brought his love of Native American culture to Florida with businesses nearly two decades before, the most pronounced documentation of his lifelong attraction to nature and earth-centered beliefs appeared in 1953 when he opened Ancient America in Boca Raton, north of Ft. Lauderdale, where the family had located after leaving St. Petersburg. Part trading post, part zoo, and part museum, Ancient America was located between US-1 and the Intracoastal Waterway. It was built upon twenty-four acres that included an Indian burial mound, and eventually it became known as the Barnhill Mound.[10] Subsequently, with the coordination of a professional archaeologist, Barnhill and his family uncovered seventy-two Indian burials. So that tourists might be able to see the bones and artifacts from the Jeaga village that once was there, the Barnhills constructed a glassed-in tunnel to allow viewing of the inside of the mound.

Ancient America closed in 1958, when an exasperated Barnhill exclaimed, "All these tourists are interested in are dog tracks and night-clubs." He then began moving the attraction's contents to Michigan, where Jack had a 10,000-square-foot building on the lake in St. Ignace. Esmond added his collection of curiosities to his son's smaller one for display in Jack's place of business, which also had a sea aquarium, a boat line, and seaplanes. He kept his museum pieces in Michigan for about seven years and then had Jack send them back to Florida. There he started up two more museums, but neither of these was profitable.

Although the birds and animals were removed from Ancient America's zoo, the gift shop remained open for at least a few more years, and people came during subsequent winters to walk the trails and go through the tunnel to view the artifacts. "Maybe the place was officially closed in '58, but we still had visitors for several years after that," remembers Cindy Robb, Clayton's daughter. Cindy is sure of this because she used to lead tours there, something she could not have done in 1958, when she was only three years old. Her older sister, Peggy Camps, believes the doors of the stellar attraction shut for good in the late sixties.

Barnhill, however, was still not finished with his museum–trading post concept as a tourist attraction. For four years during the early seventies, farther up Florida's east coast in Palm Bay, he ran an Indian Springs Museum (he had another with the same name in Georgia), an attraction that exhibited pirate treasures as well as his then-standard fare of Native American creations, Florida souvenir items, and the remaining stacks of his own and Wilcox's prints. Eventually, noting the improved business potential stimulated by the opening of Disney World, Barnhill established the Indian Museum and Trading Post along Highway 192 in Kissimmee, a road that led to the mega-attraction's entrance. In the mid-1980s, after being beaten by robbers who took his old flintlock guns and sand-cast Navajo jewelry, a dispirited Barnhill closed his doors. He moved to Delray, on the east coast of the state, in 1986 but quickly decided to settle in Tiger, Georgia, close to where he had spent his youth.

Shortly after the move to Tiger, he sustained a head injury in a fall down some stairs. Taken to the Northeast Georgia Medical Center in Gainesville, he died there on September 16, 1987, at the age of ninety-three, and was subsequently cremated. His companion, Virginia Howard, scattered and buried some of his ashes in the memorial garden of their Four Winds Village, a spiritual retreat. The remaining ashes were laid beside his wife, Helen, who had predeceased him on November 12, 1967, under a shared headstone in Boca Raton Municipal Cemetery as the Barnhill family gathered there to memorialize his life.

The Gilded Age had come and gone before the hand-painted photograph was popular, but the visual language of the genre was more in keeping with that era than with the one it graced. In striking contrast to the idealized versions of paradise found in these photographs, social reality in Florida and its accompanying hardships were being documented by photographers working for the Farm Security Administration, a division of the federal government's Works Progress Administration. The FSA's pictures sought to shock the country, while those of the colorists attempted to soothe the populace. It was a dramatic time in our country's history, filled with much economic disparity among its citizens. Indeed, the period bracketed by the two World Wars was an extremely difficult one for our nation, and the Great Depression did much to sully the American Dream. The old ways, the old tastes, the old philosophies were, at best, waning and, at worst, dying.

It could be argued, though, that this was the perfect time for the appearance of the hand-painted photograph. Victorian genteelness was giving way to the machine age. Some Americans were doing very well, growing wealthy, living the good life. Many, however, were suffering, barely keeping food on their tables and roofs over their heads. These affordable photographs, awash with the lush colors found in Florida's tropical scenery, promised something better. They portrayed an untamed, beautiful place to which people could retreat, away from the harshness of the realities that confronted many Americans.

Florida grew, in part, because of these pictures created by Esmond Grenard Barnhill, for they gave birth to the basic building blocks of the great state of Florida—dreams.

Notes

1. A. Wynelle Deese, *St. Petersburg, Florida: A Visual History* (Charleston, S.C.: History Press, 2006).
2. Michael and Susan Ivankovich, *Early Twentieth Century Hand-Painted Photography: Identification and Values* (Paducah, Ky.: Collector Books, 2005).
3. Larry Roberts, *Florida's Golden Age of Souvenirs, 1890–1930* (Gainesville: University Press of Florida, 2001).
4. John Szarkowski, *Looking at Photographs: 100 Pictures from the Collection of the Museum of Modern Art* (New York: Museum of Modern Art, 1973).
5. Elizabeth Walker Mechling and Jay Mechling, *Embellishing Eden: Hand-Painted Photographs of Florida* (Daytona Beach: Southeast Museum of Photography, Daytona Beach Community College, 2001).
6. Mabel Altstetter, A. L. Crabb, and Lewis W. Newton, *America Yesterday and Today* (Dallas: Southern Publishing Company, 1937).
7. Heinz K. Henisch and Bridget A. Henisch, *The Painted Photograph, 1839–1914: Origins, Techniques, Aspirations* (University Park: Pennsylvania State University Press, 1996).
8. Jeffrey D. Nichols, "Southern Utah's Boom and Bust Uranium Industry," *History Blazer*, December 1996.
9. Barbara Willey, "Indian History Lives in Roadside Exhibit," *Melbourne Times*, January 12, 1977.
10. Ken Breslauer, *Roadside Paradise: The Golden Age of Florida's Tourist Attractions, 1929–1971* (St. Petersburg: RetroFlorida, 2000).

E. G. Barnhill

Barnhill's titles are not always consistent with the scenes. By using the same base image and altering the coloration, or adding elements, Barnhill would create a new marketable image. He might add a title, but it might be applied differently to another print of the same scene. Also, the same negative might be cropped differently and the same image might be printed in different sizes. Assigned dates are elusive, too; the glass plates are usually marked 1914, which is doubtful.

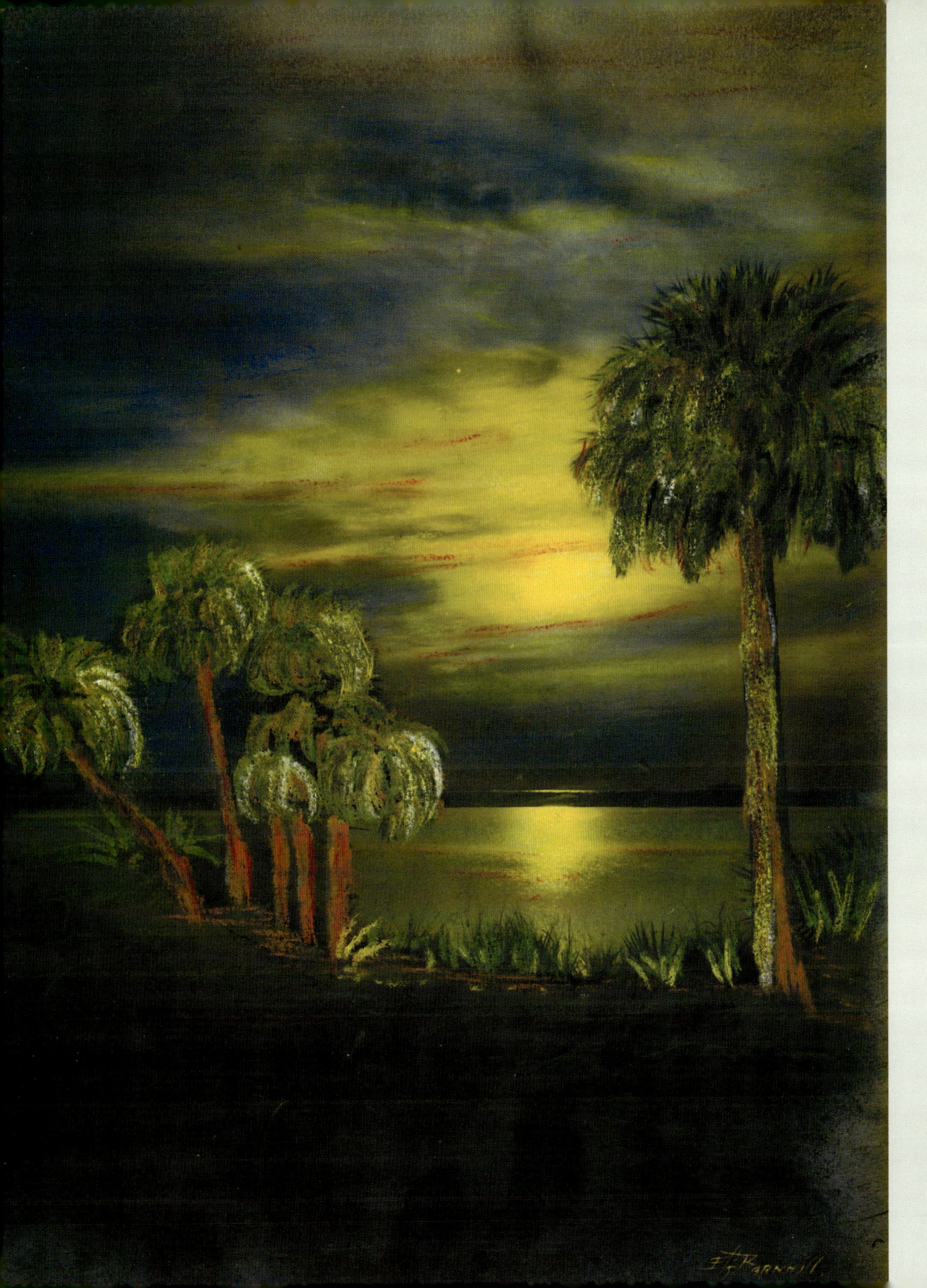

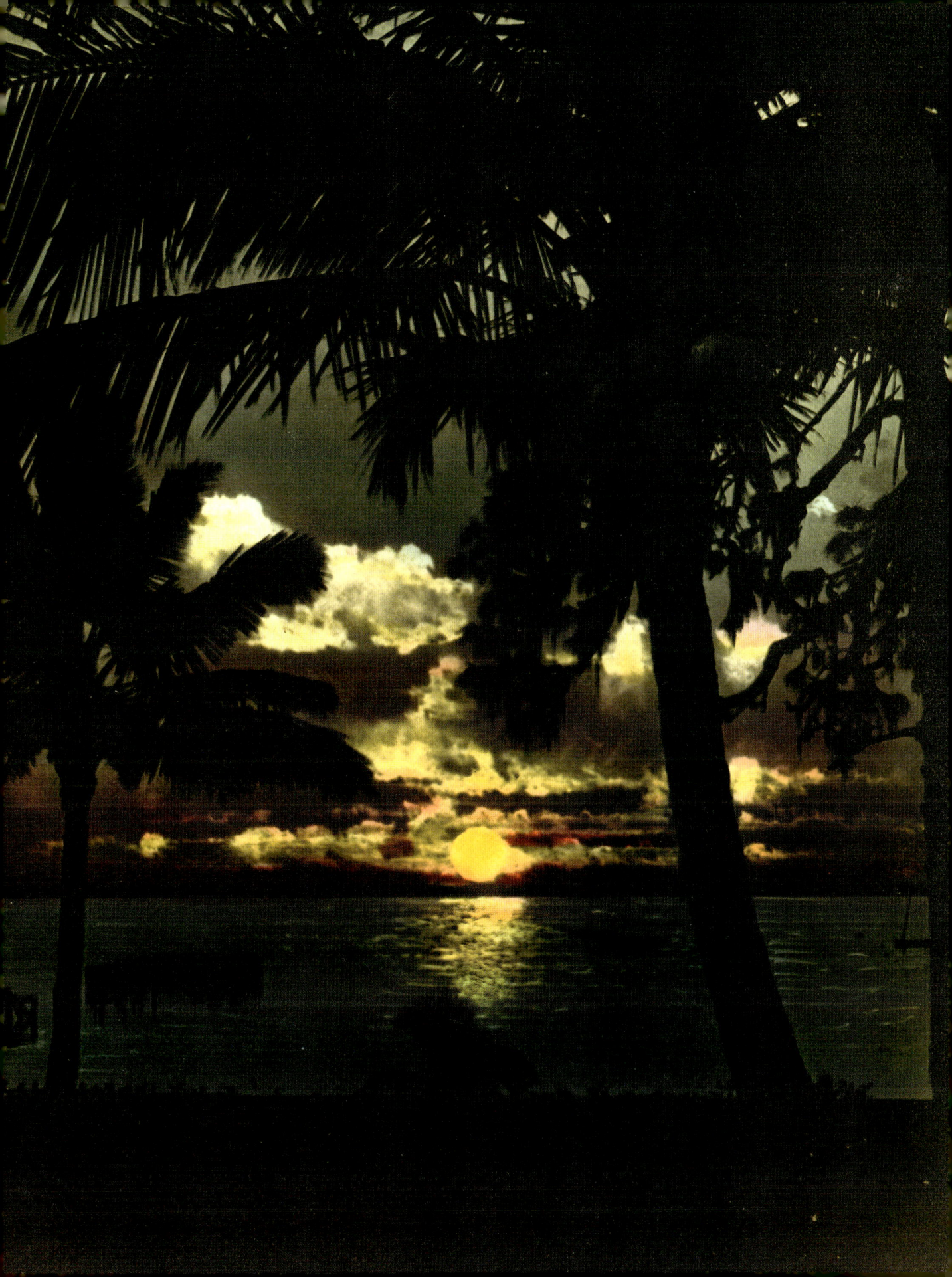

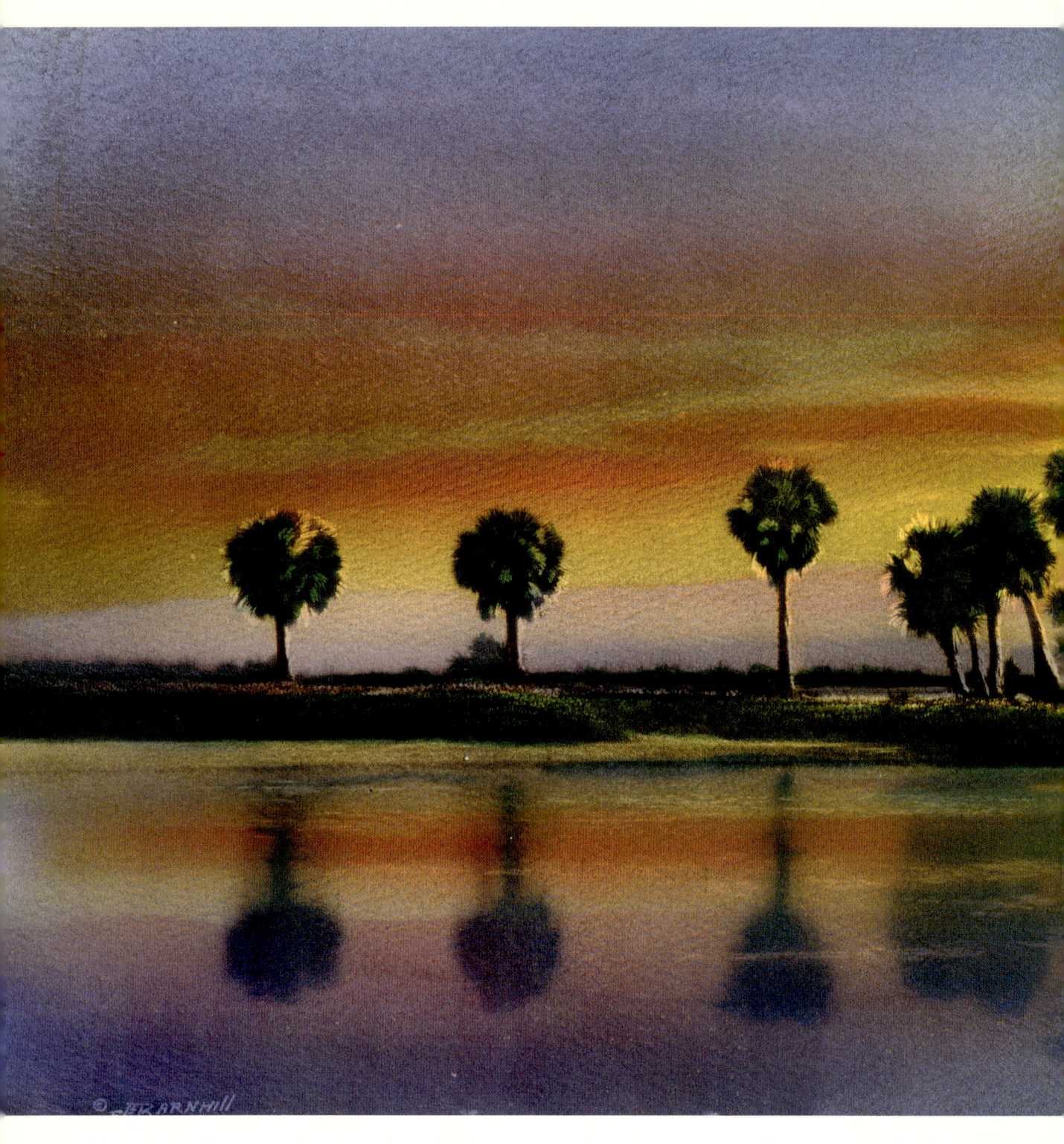

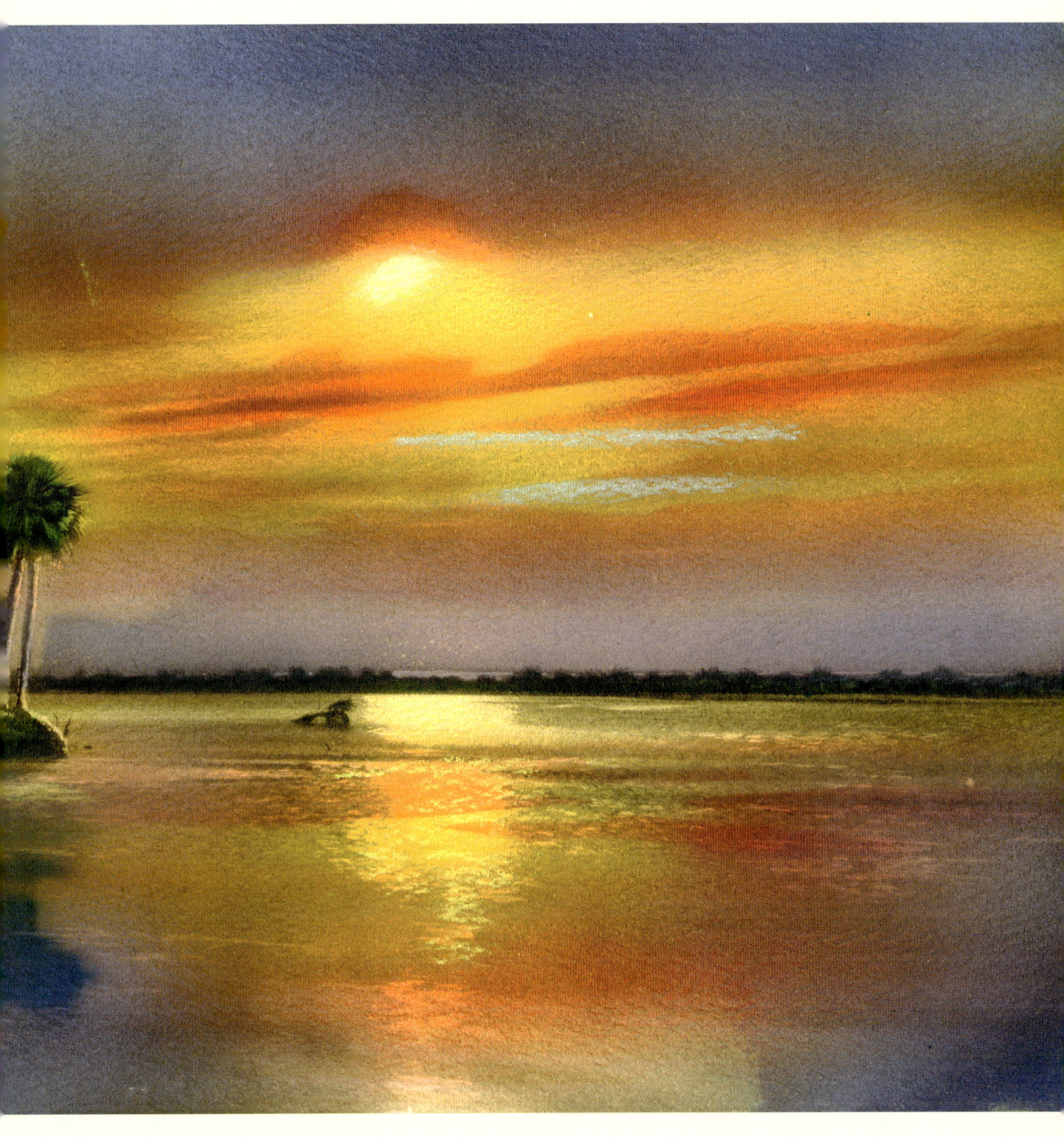

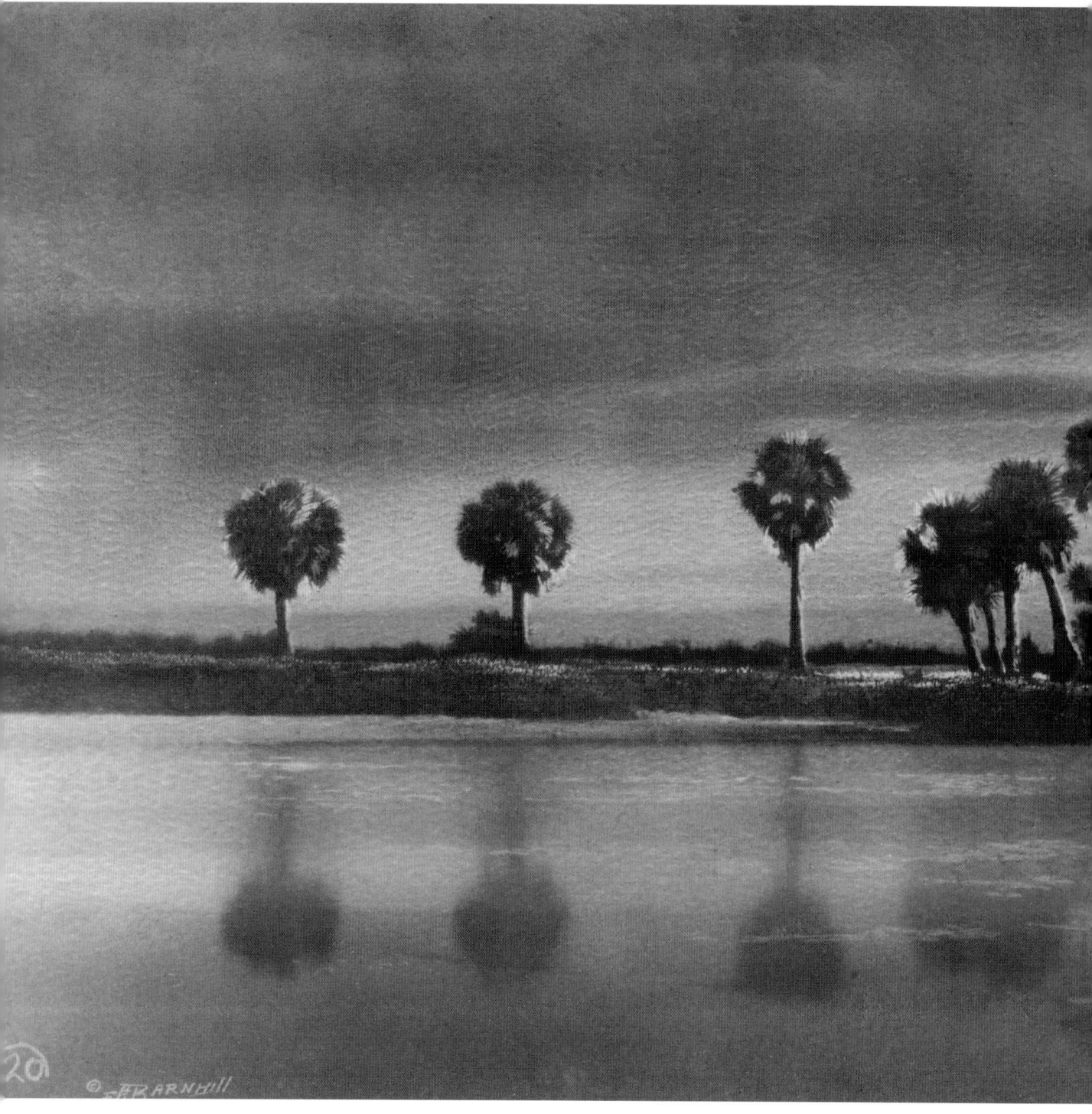

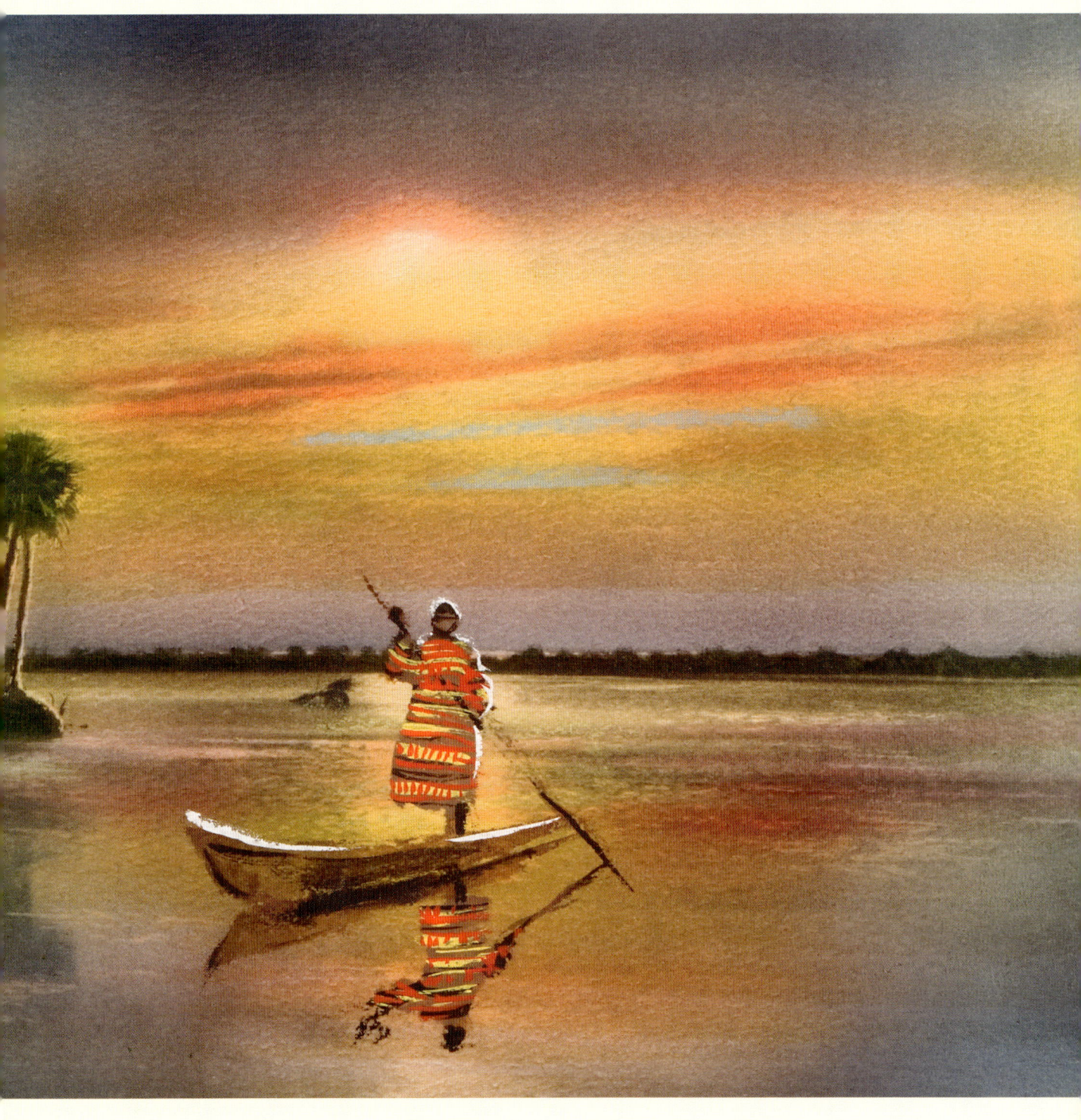

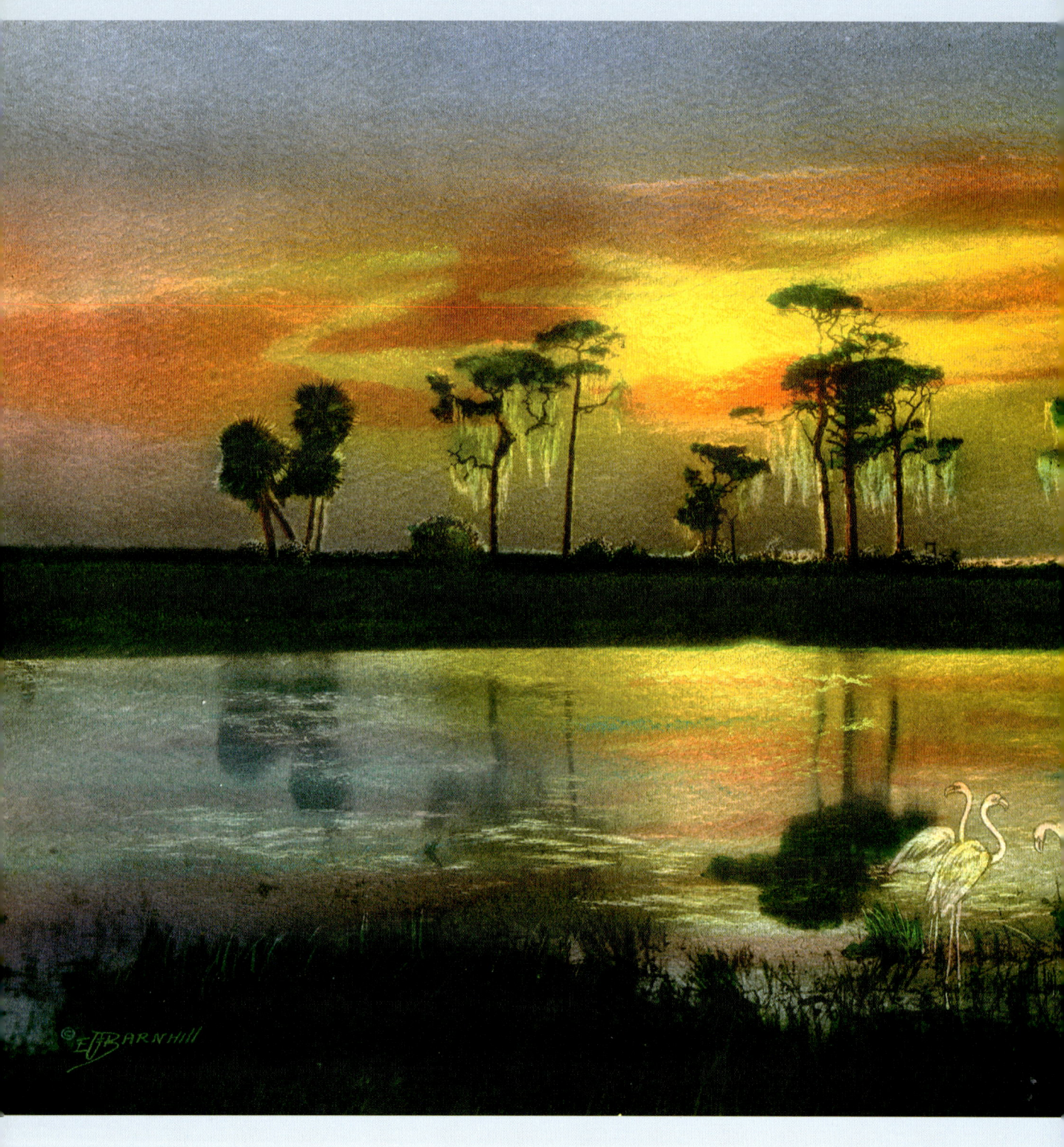

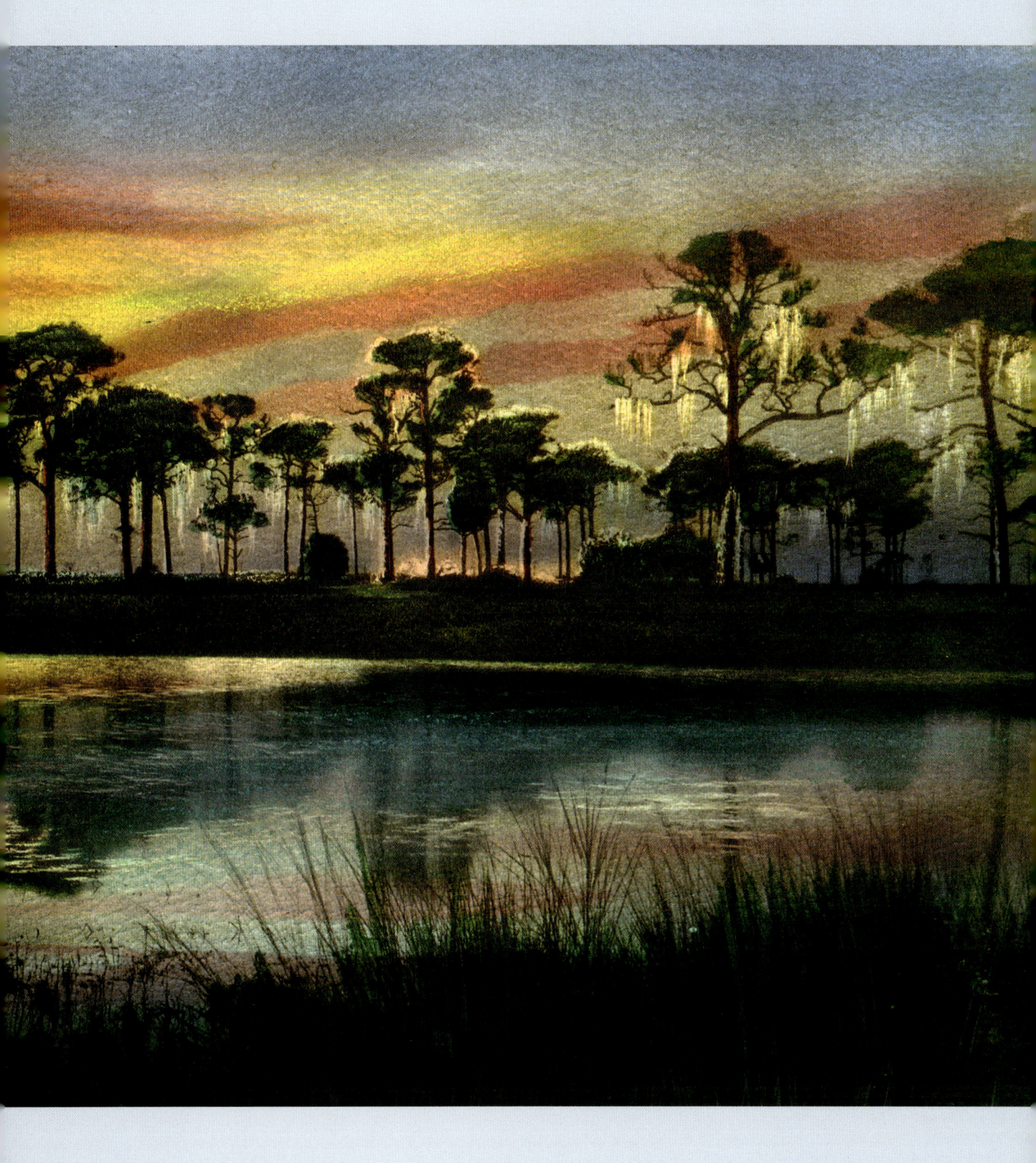

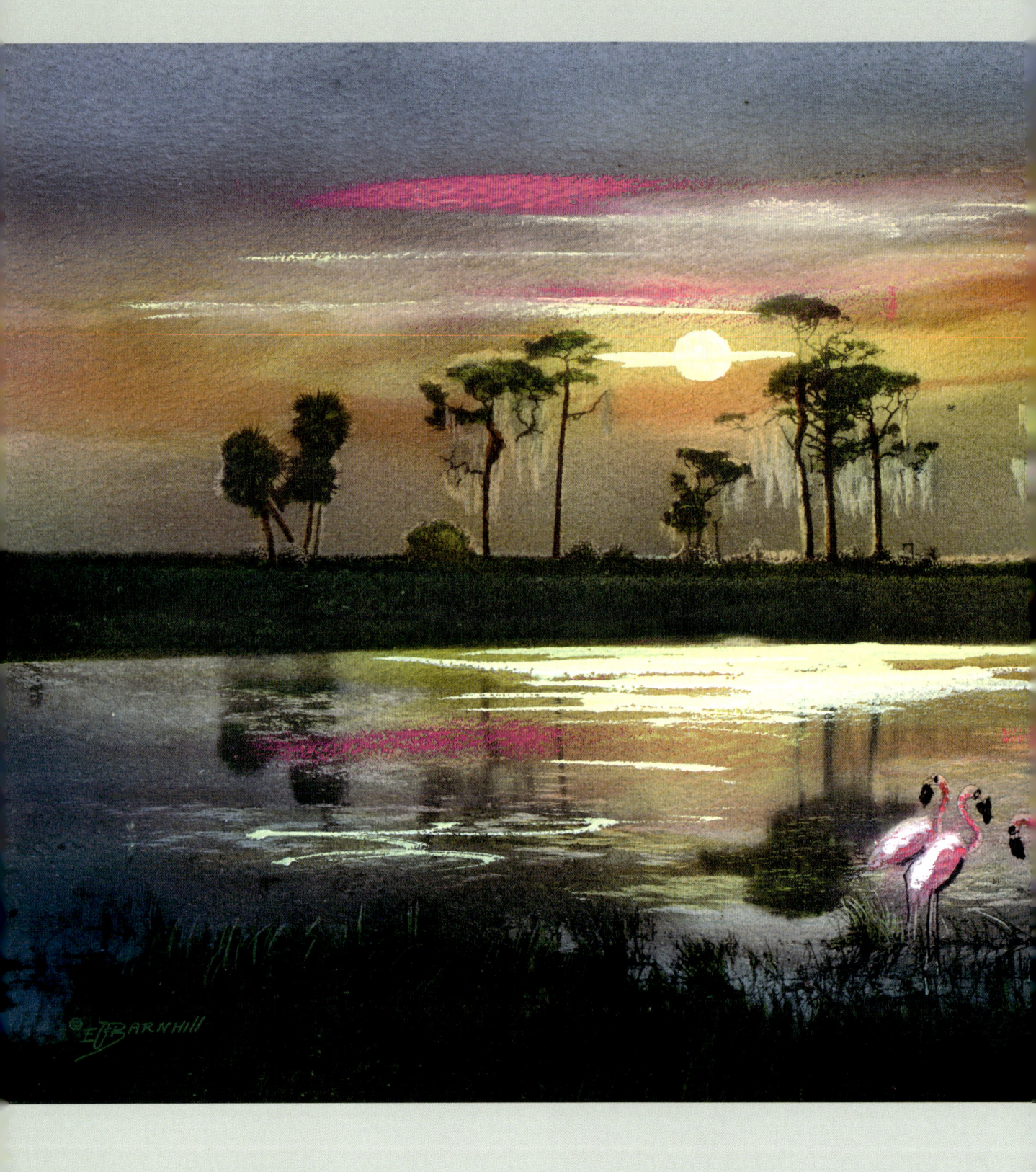

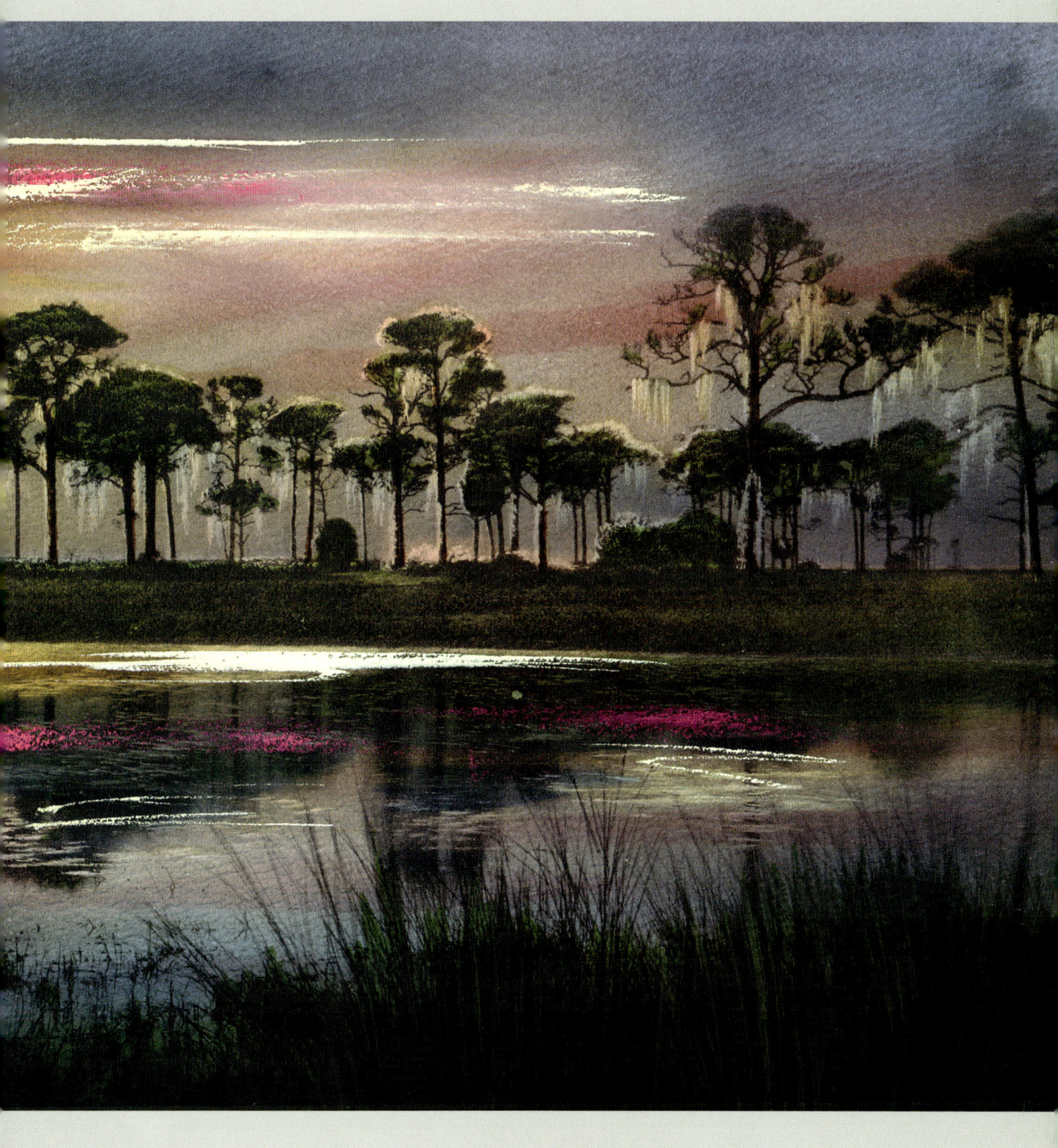

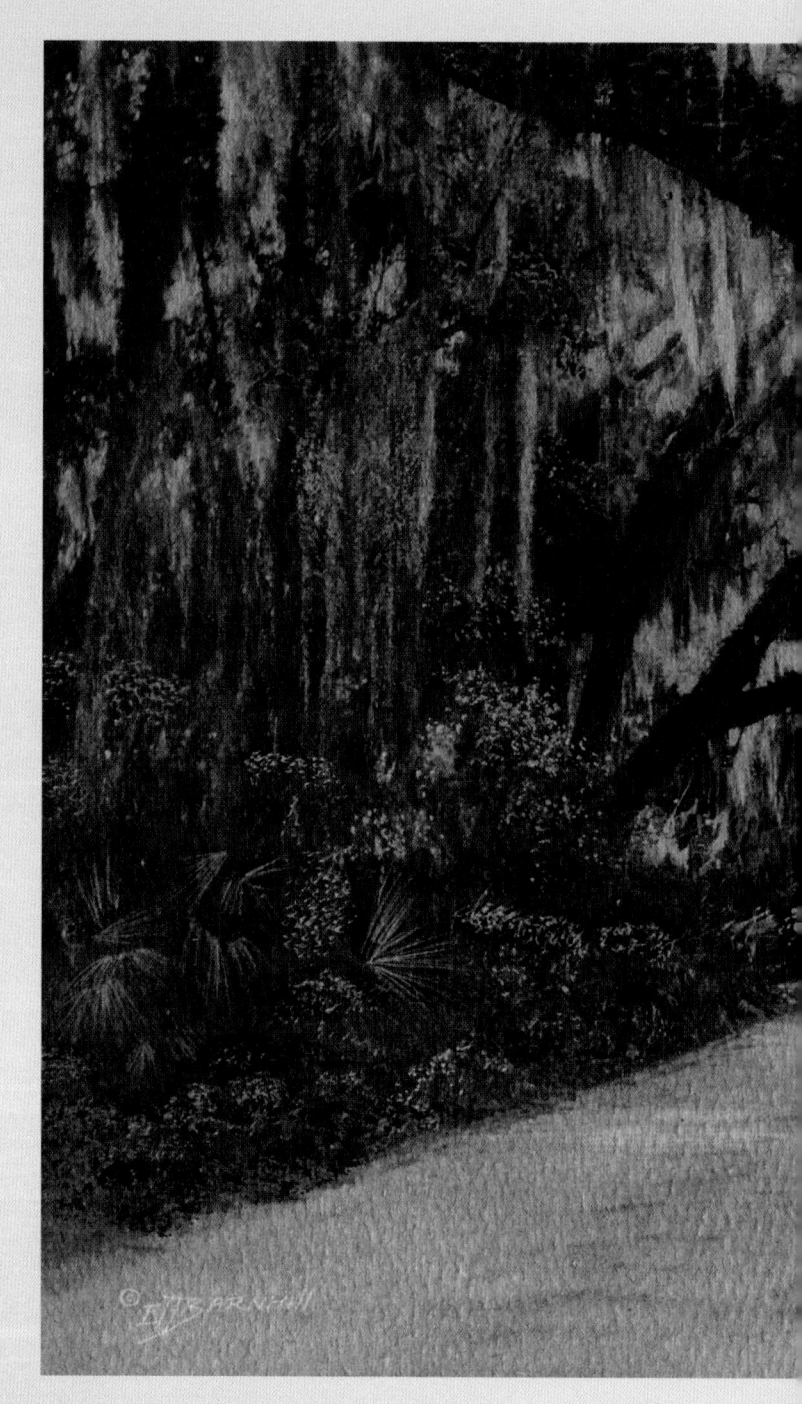

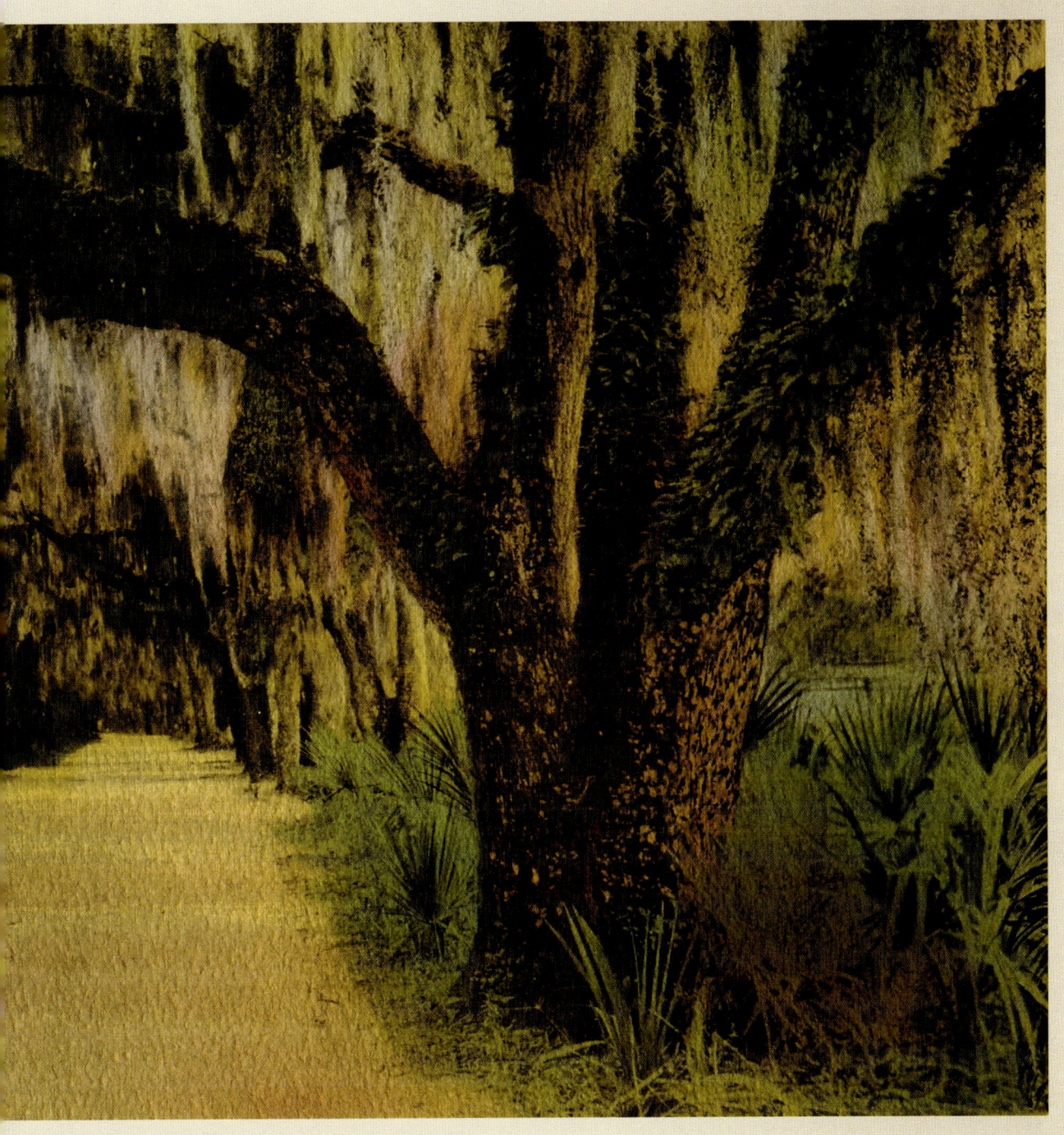

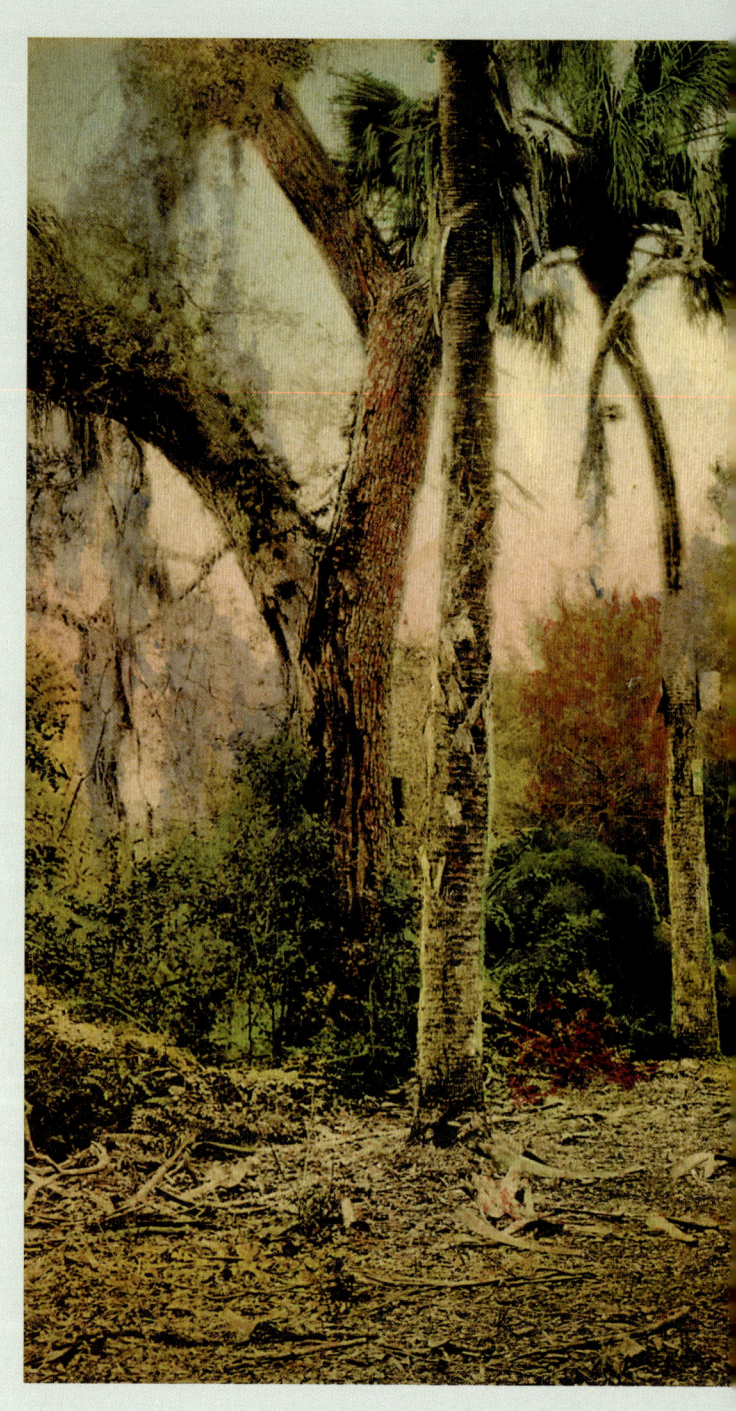

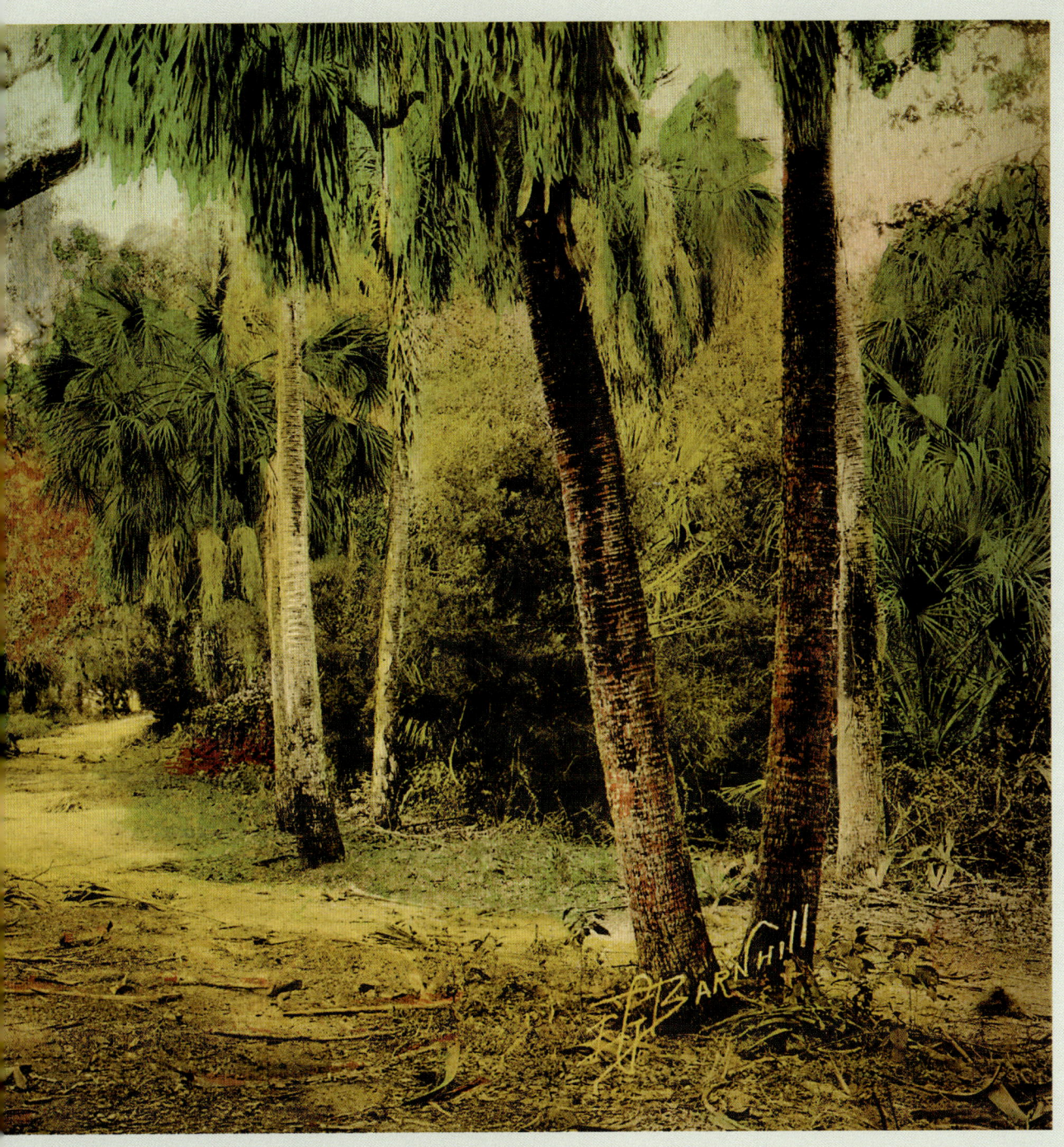

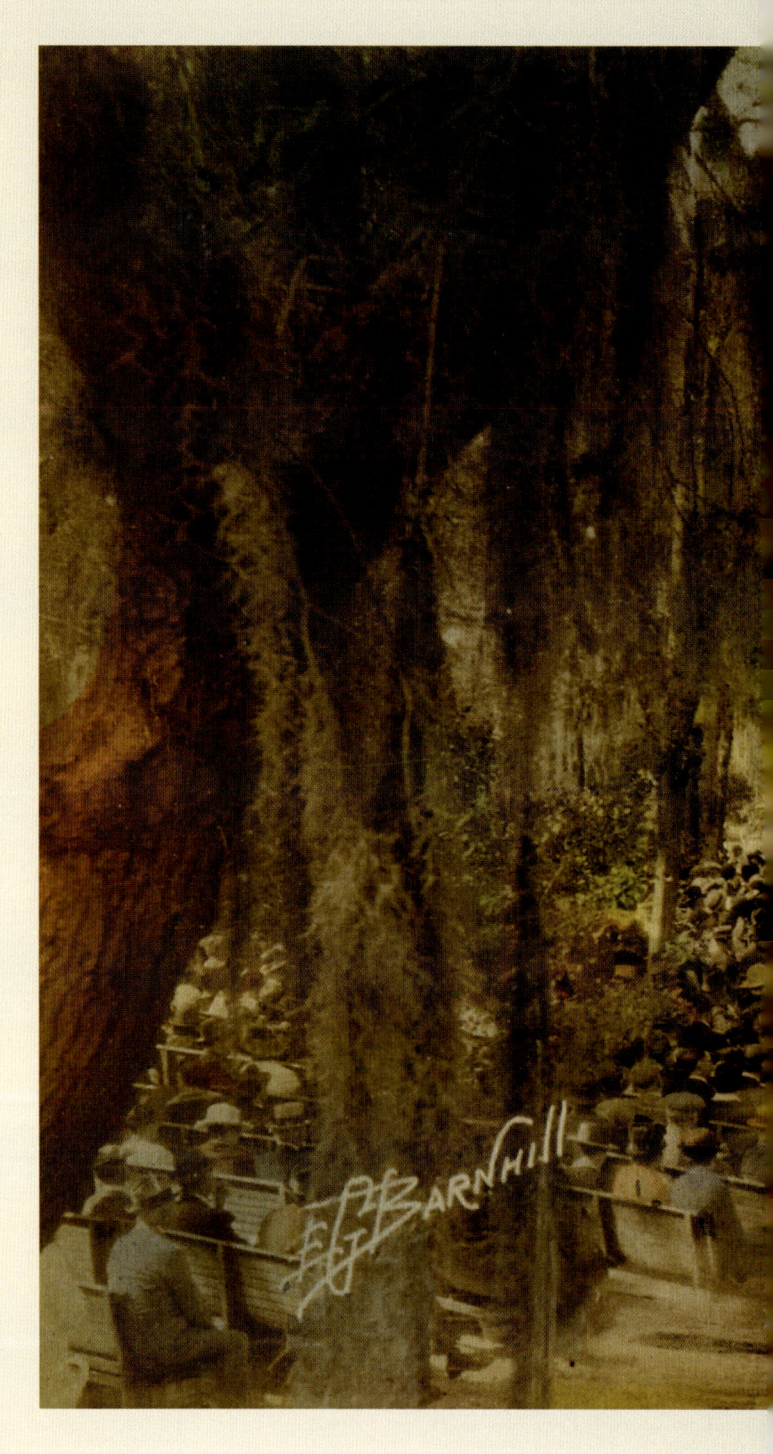

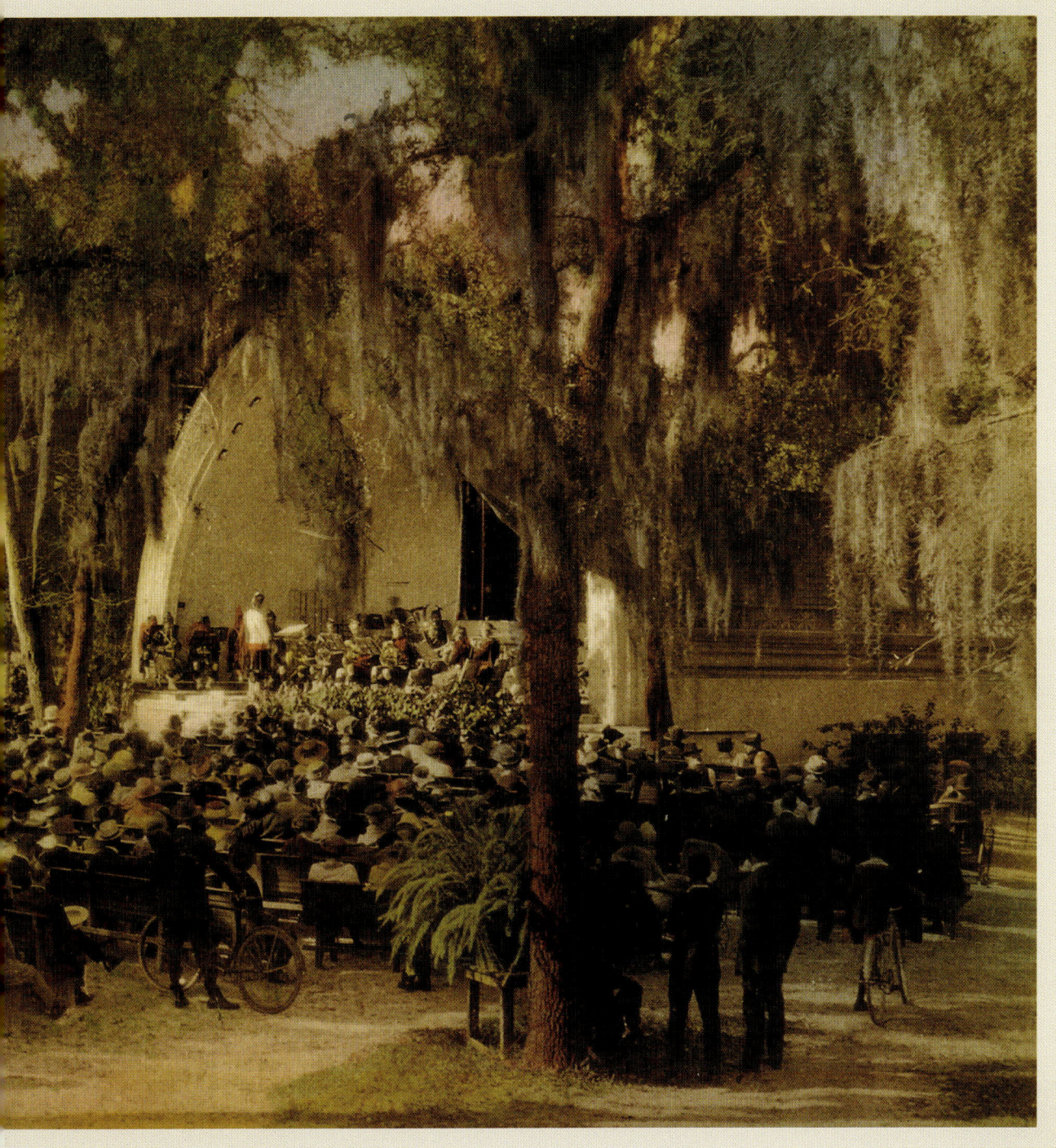

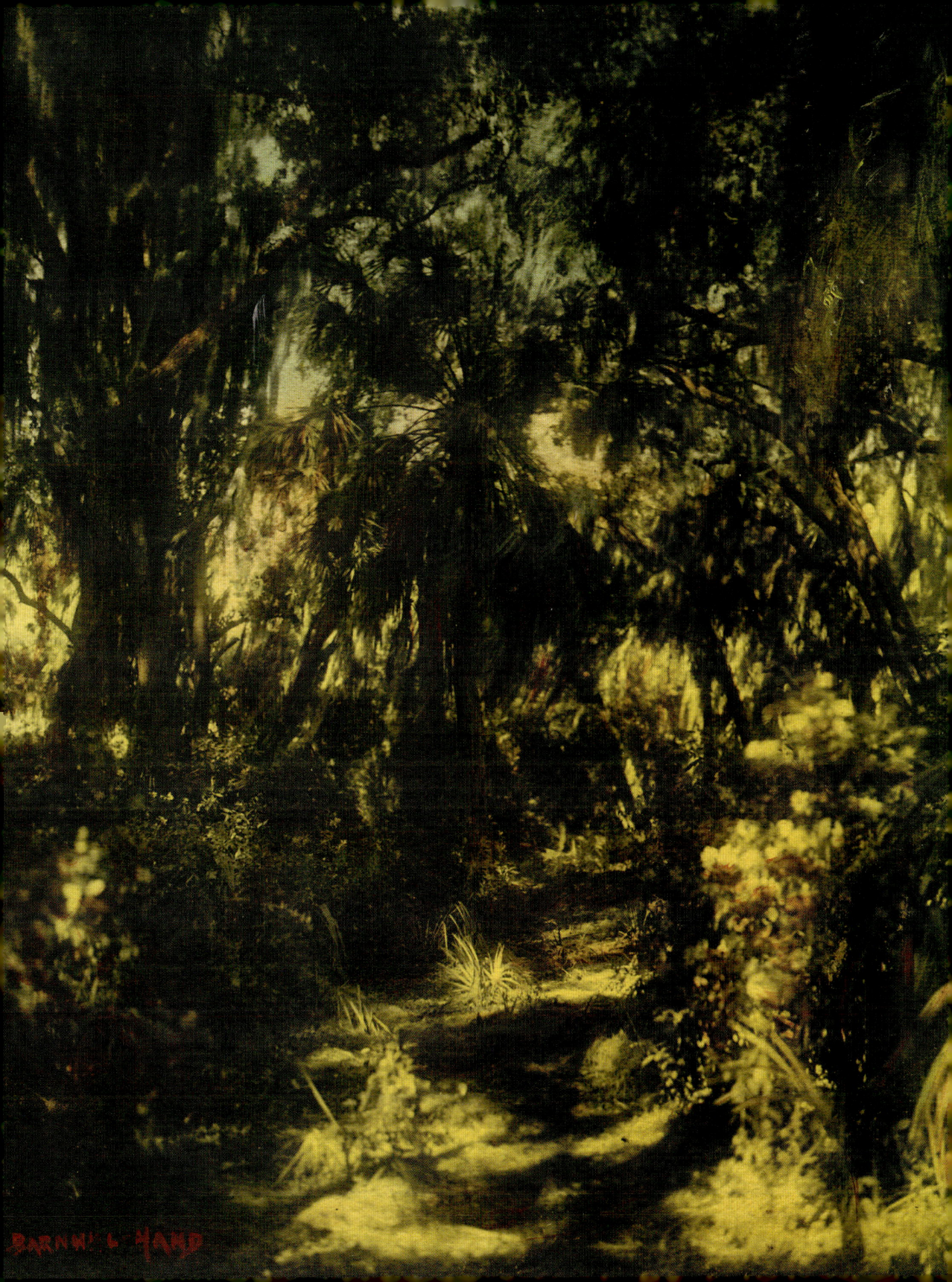

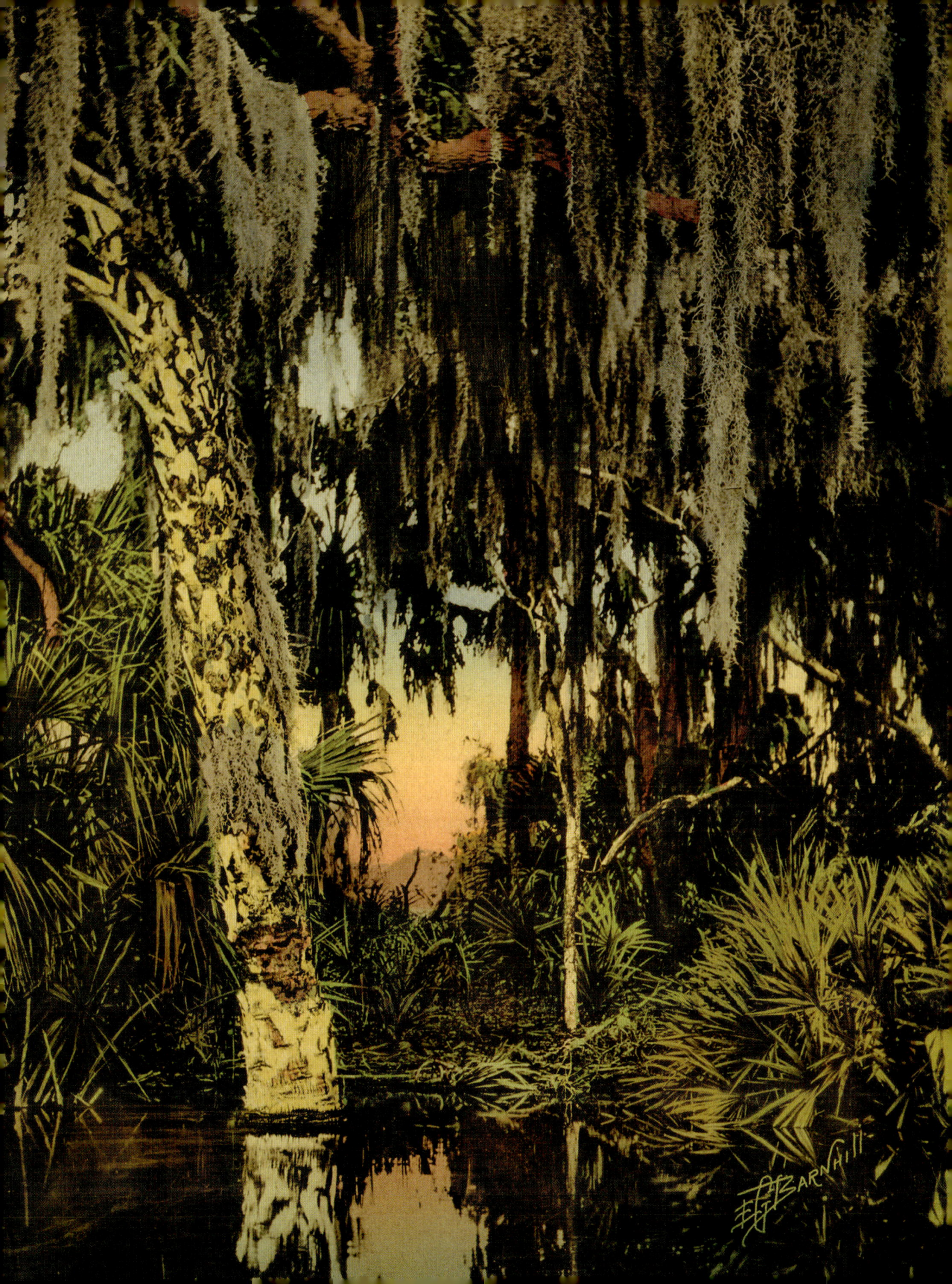

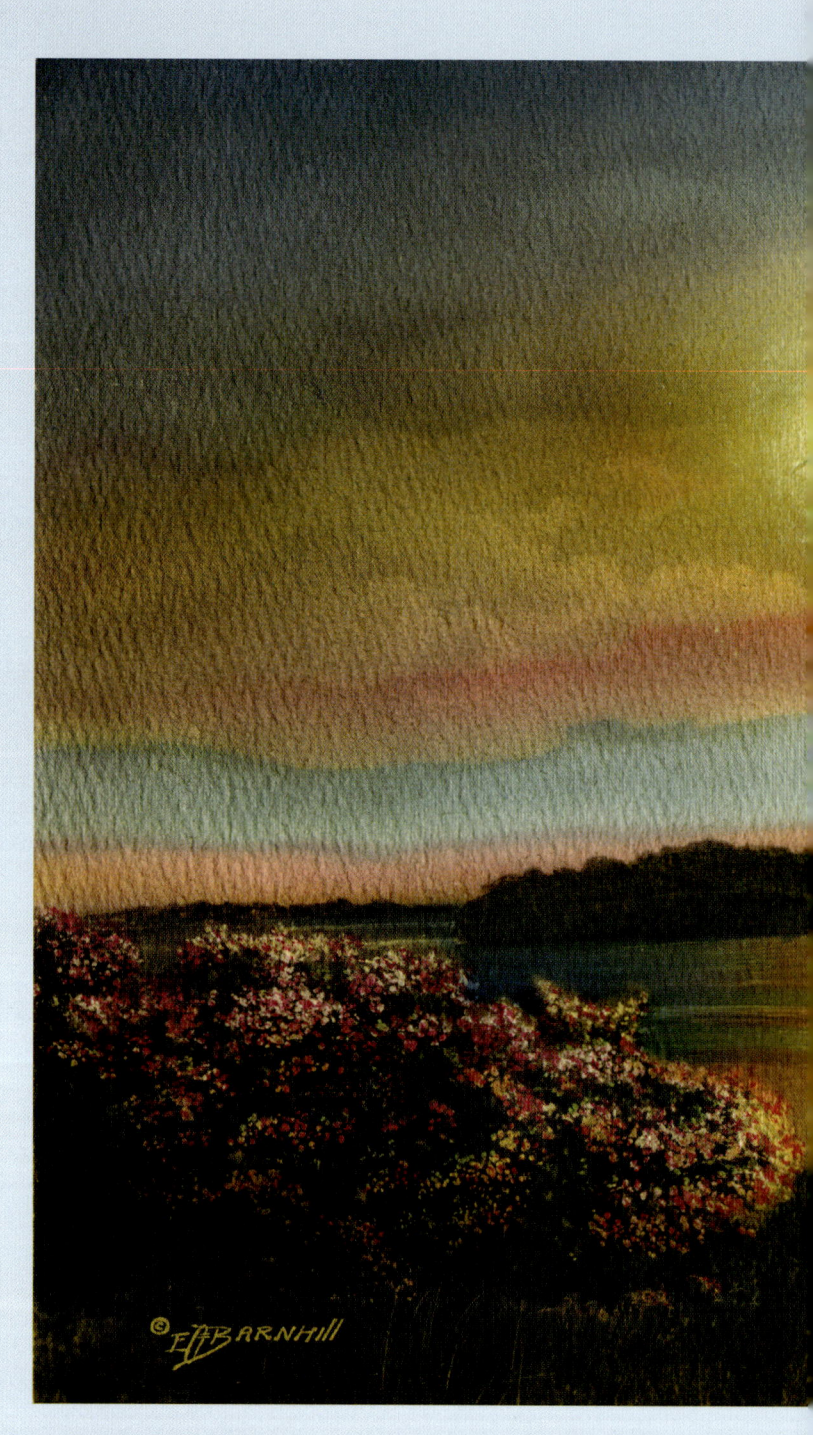

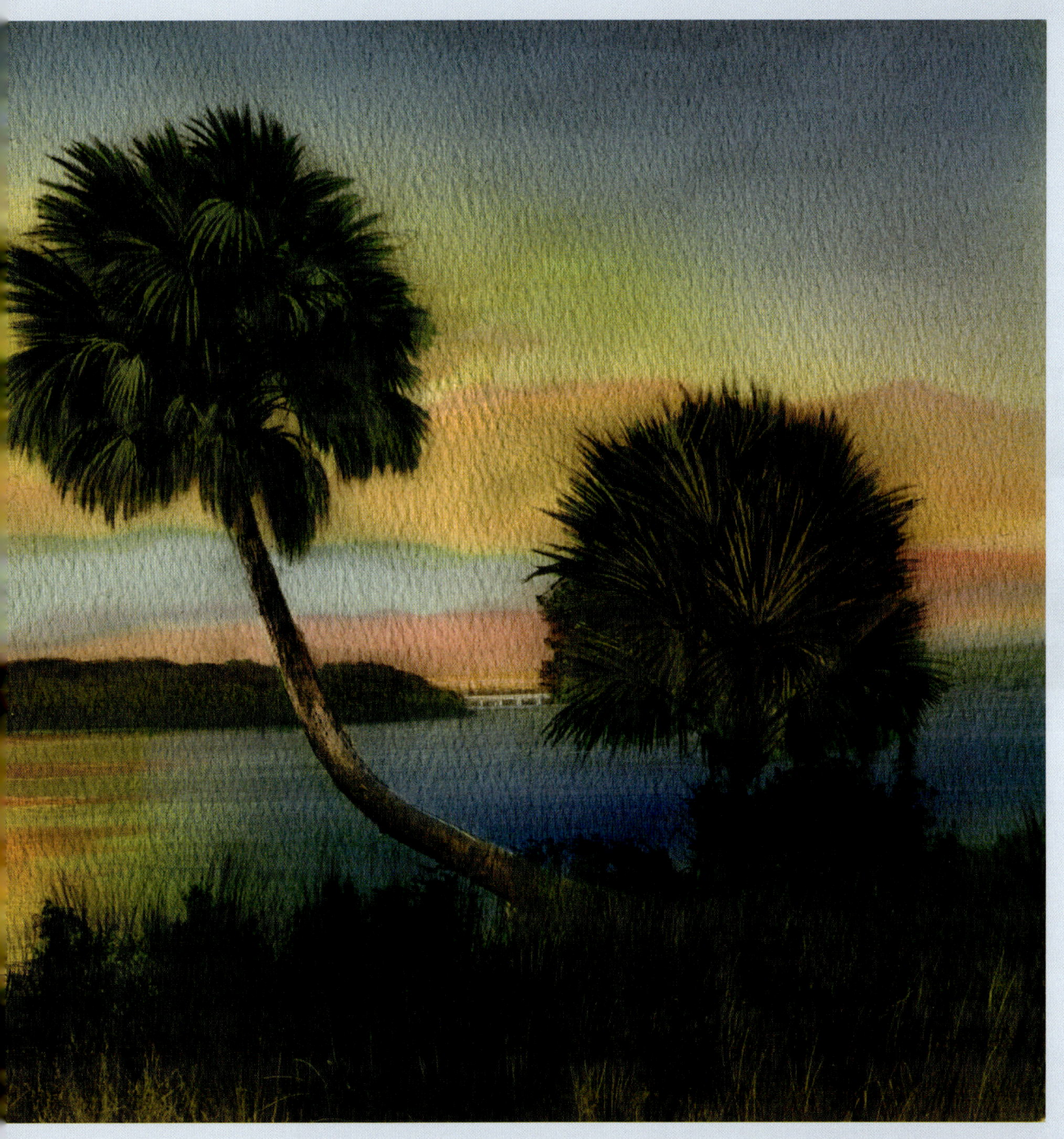

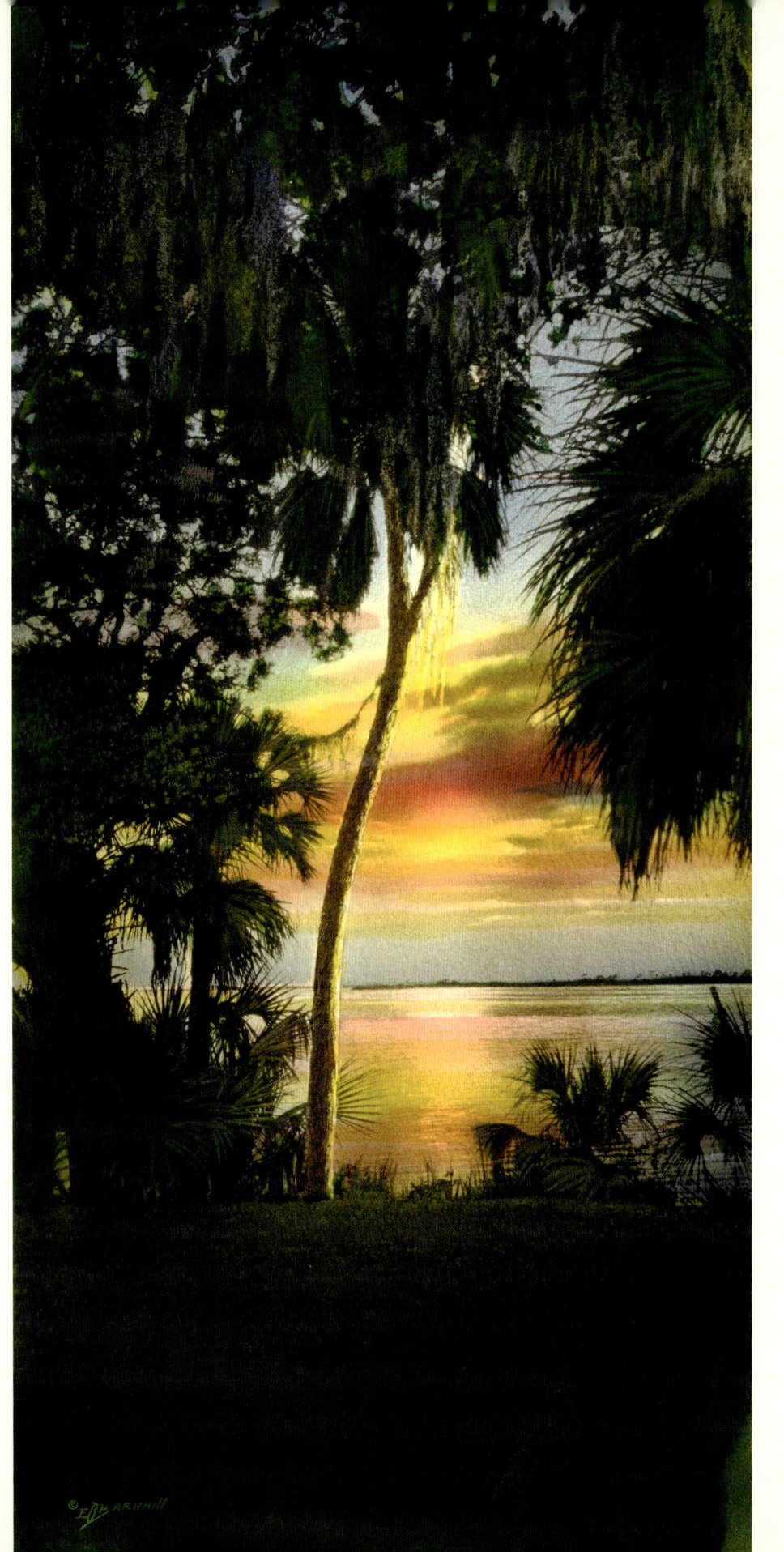

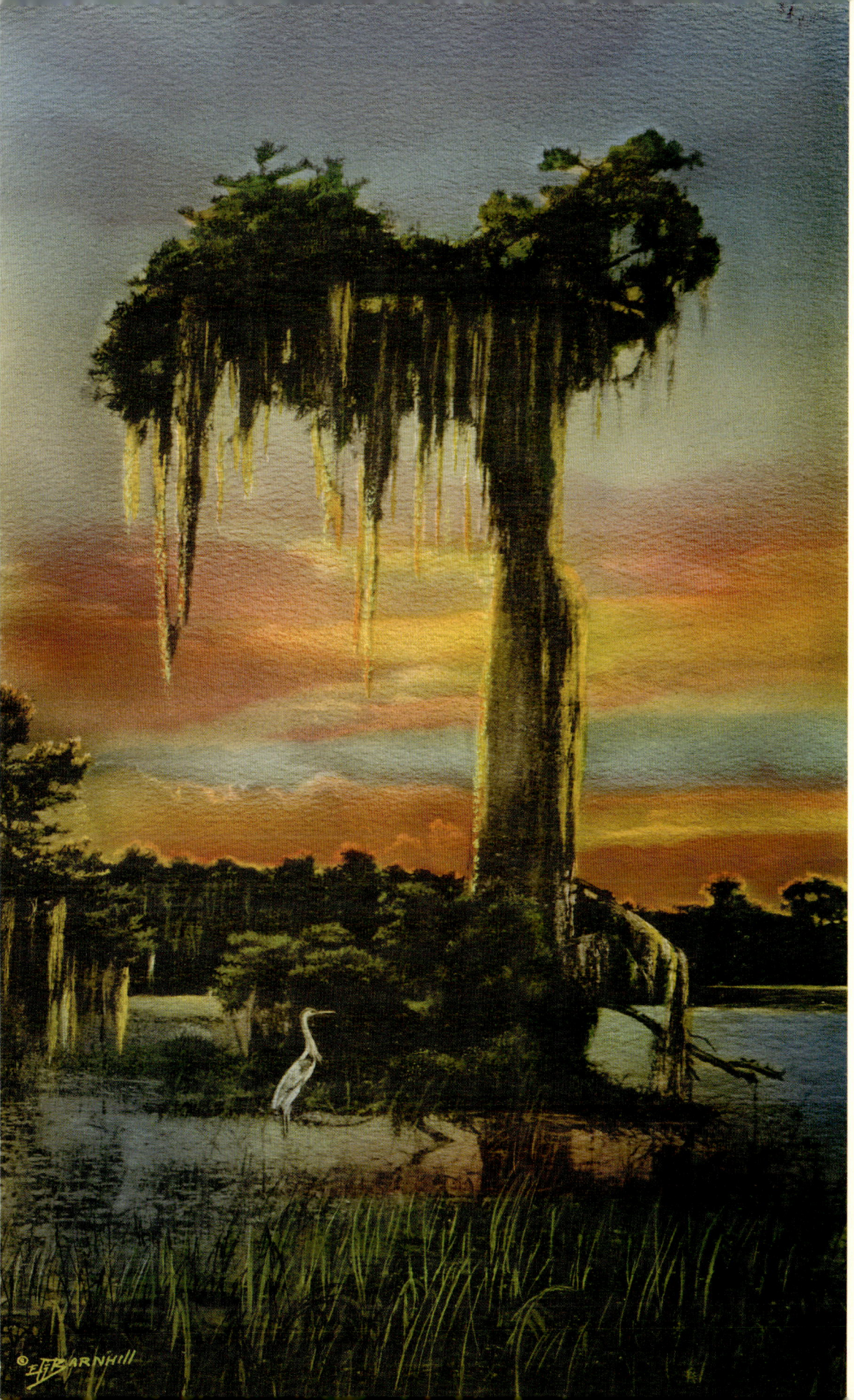

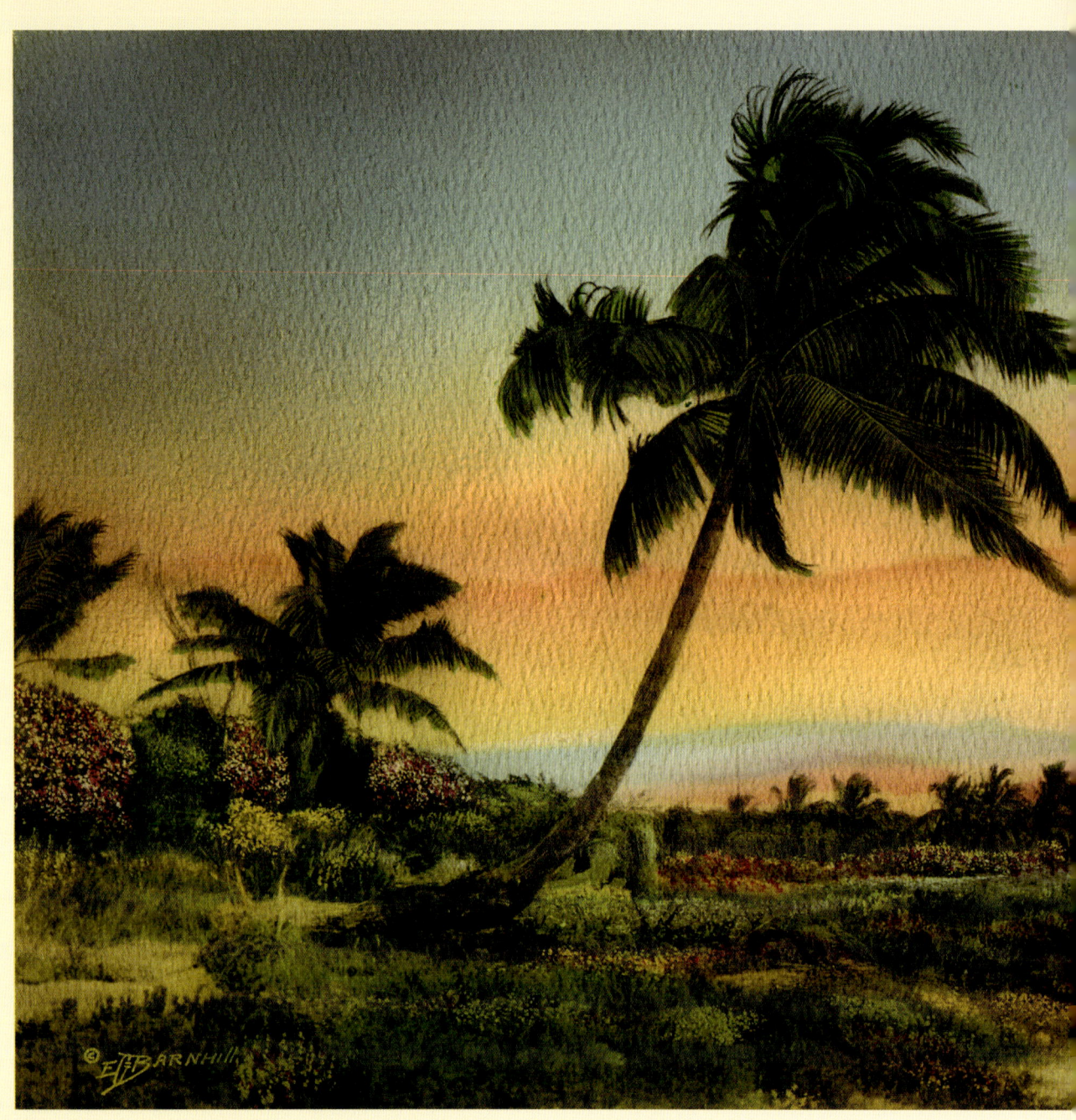

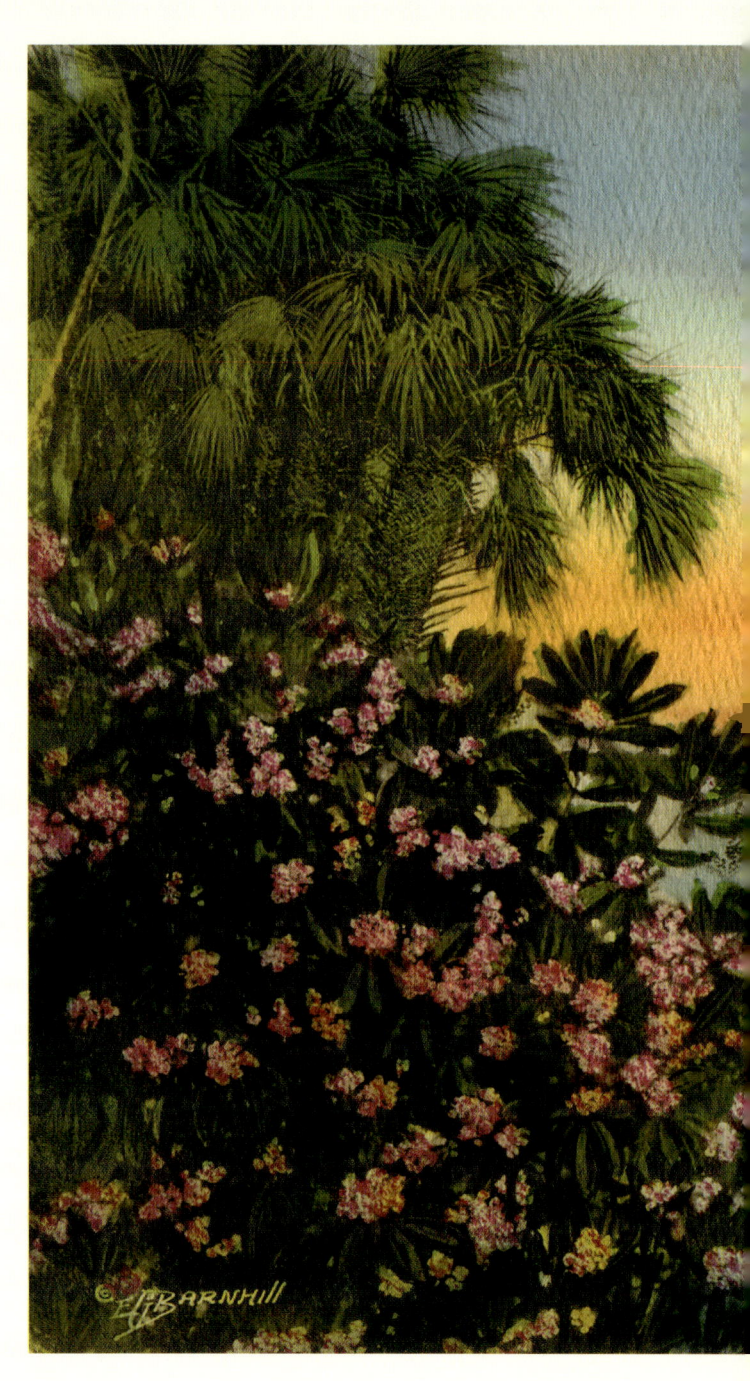

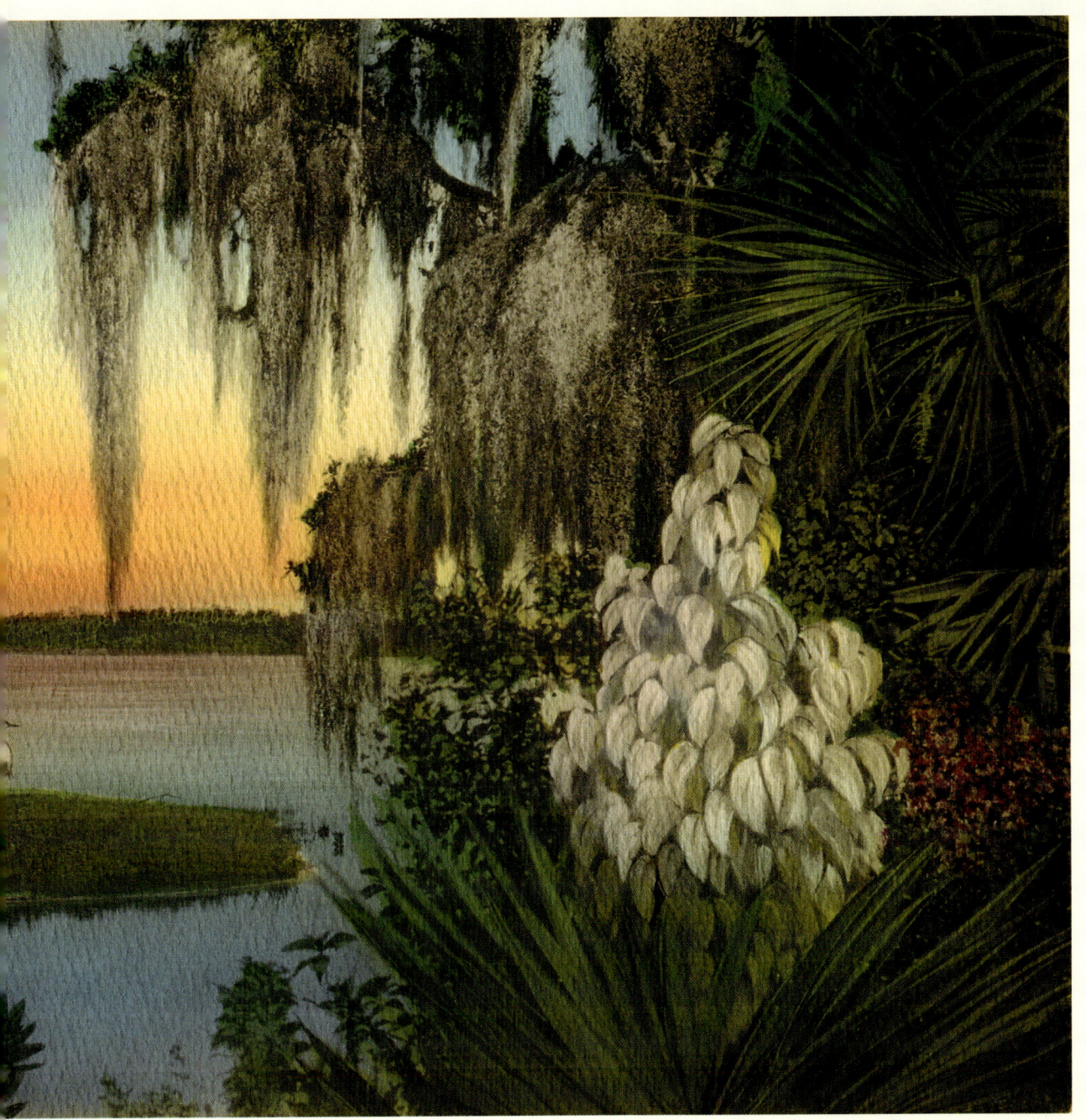

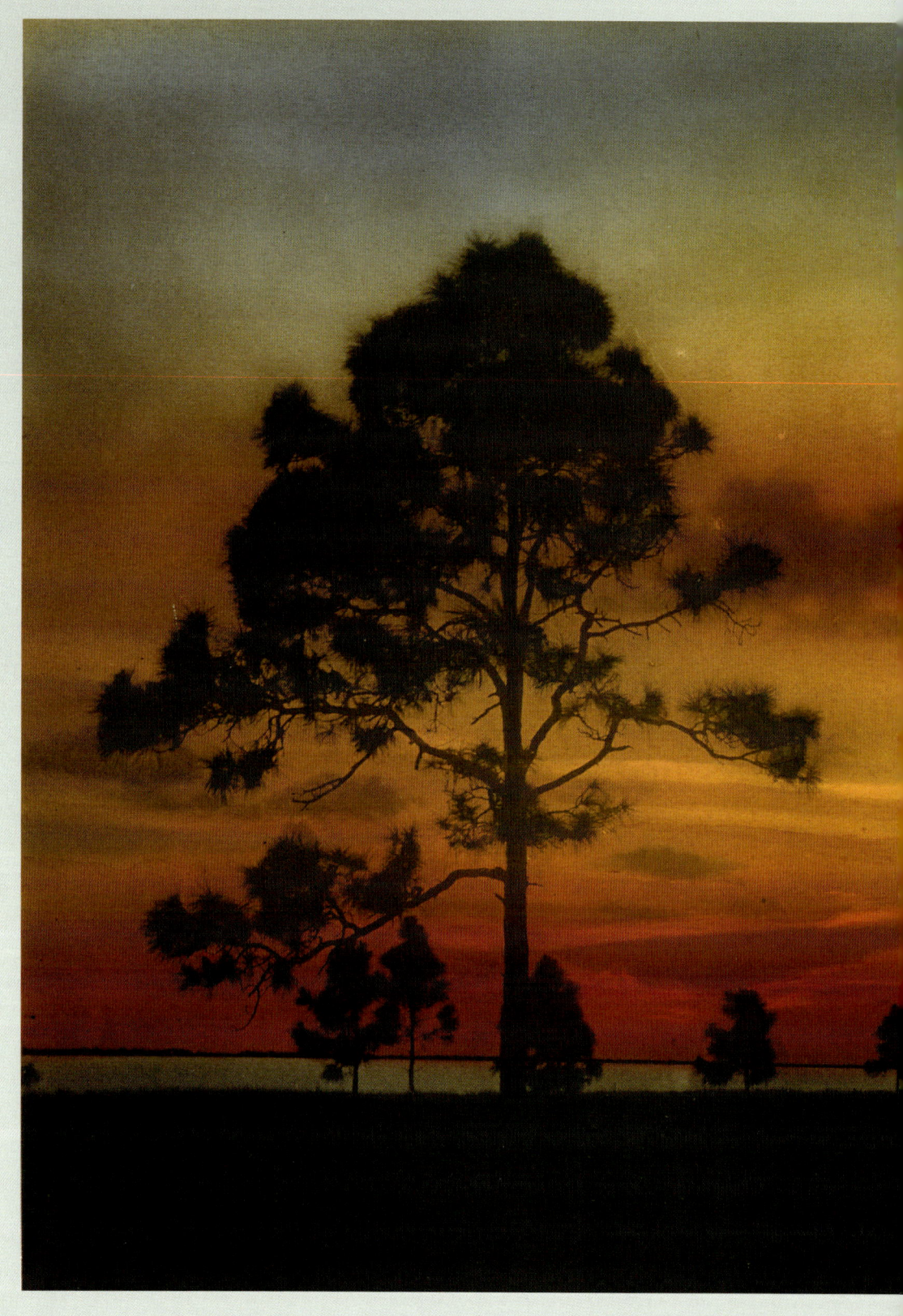

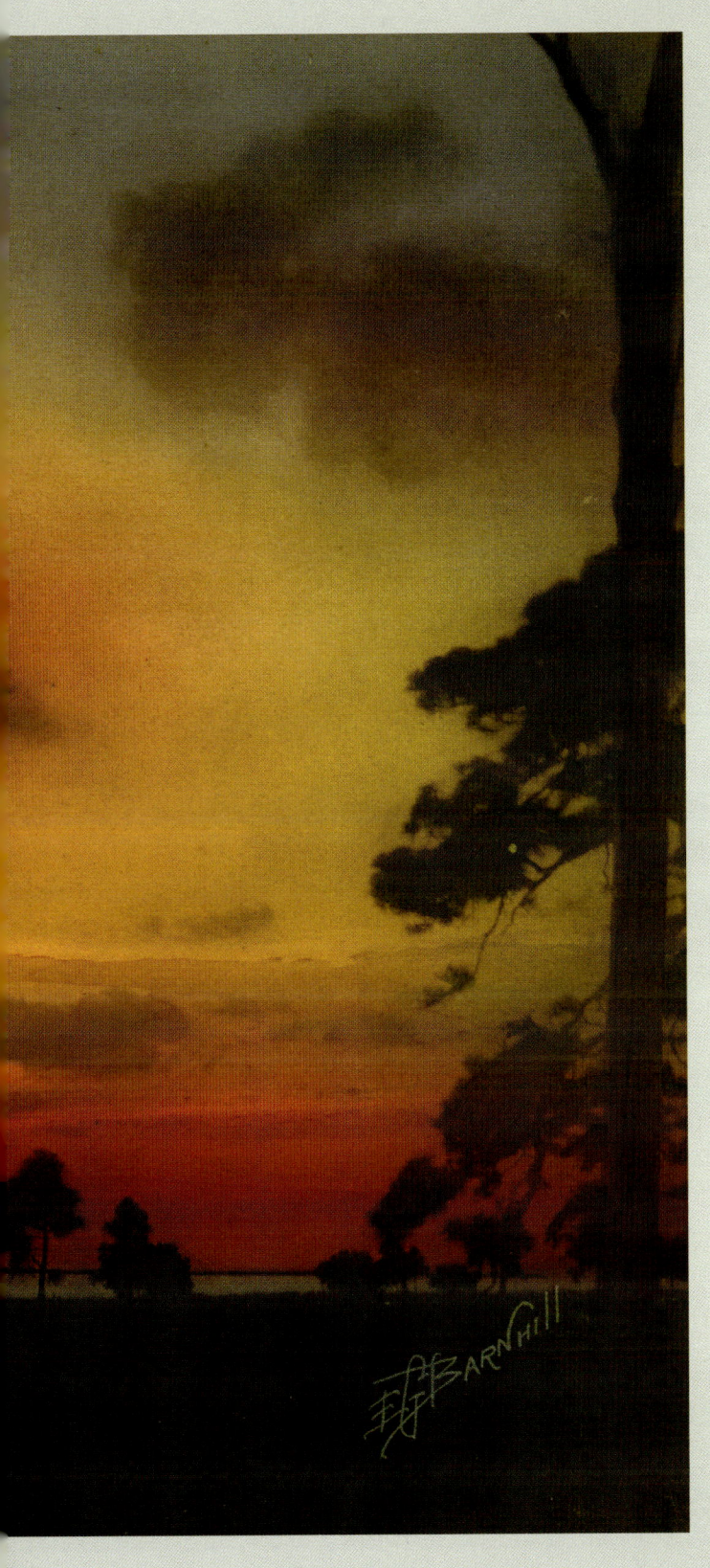

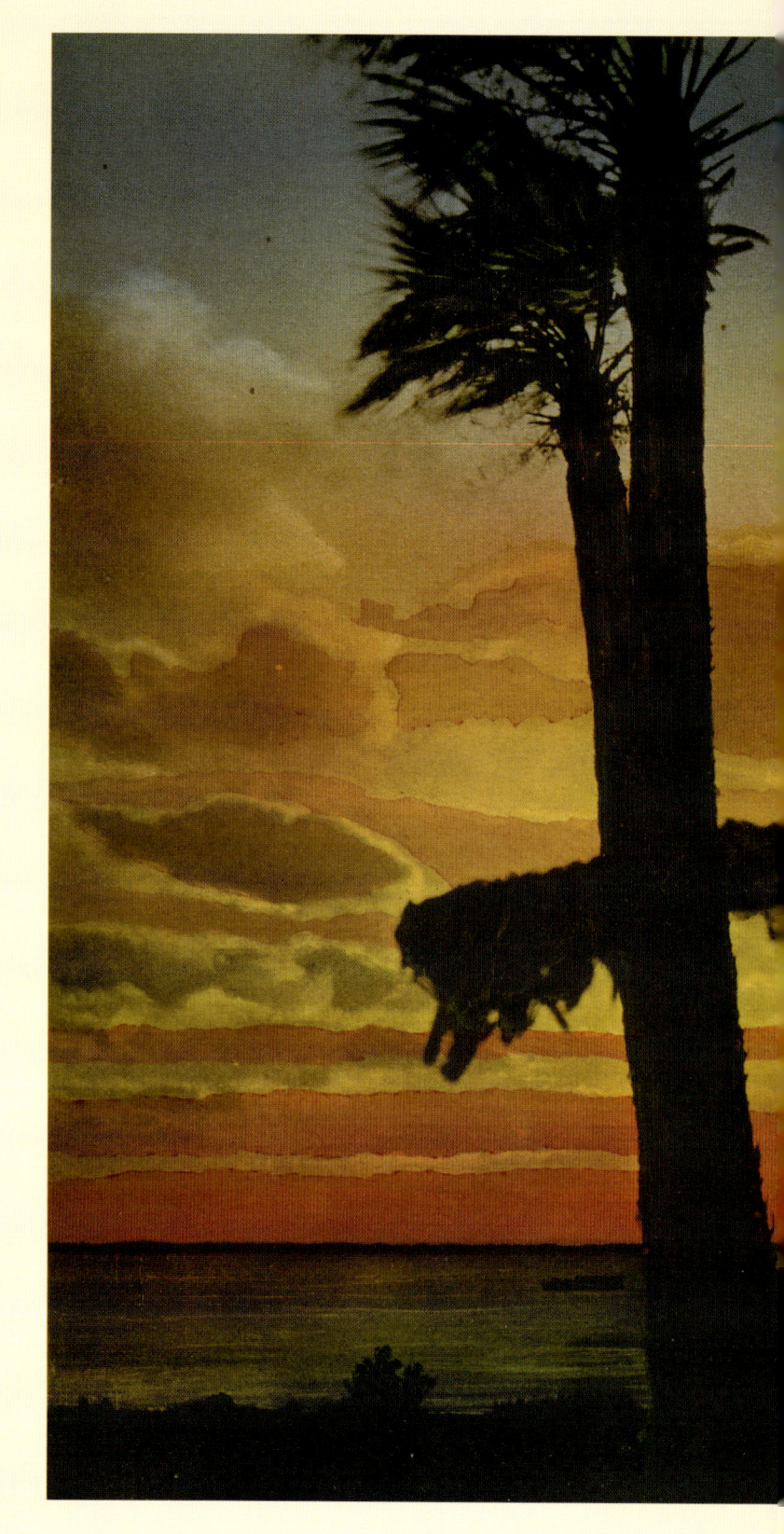

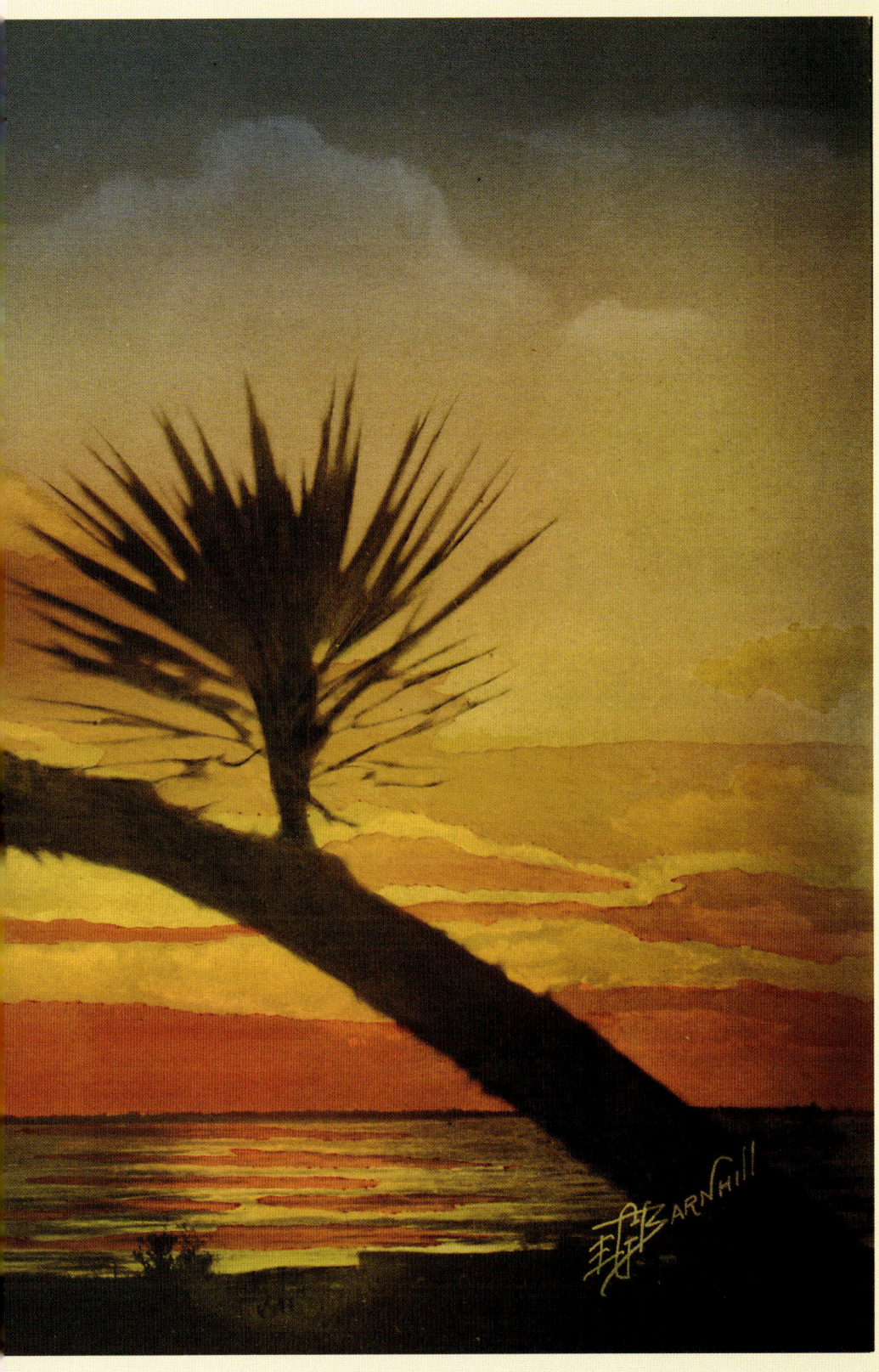

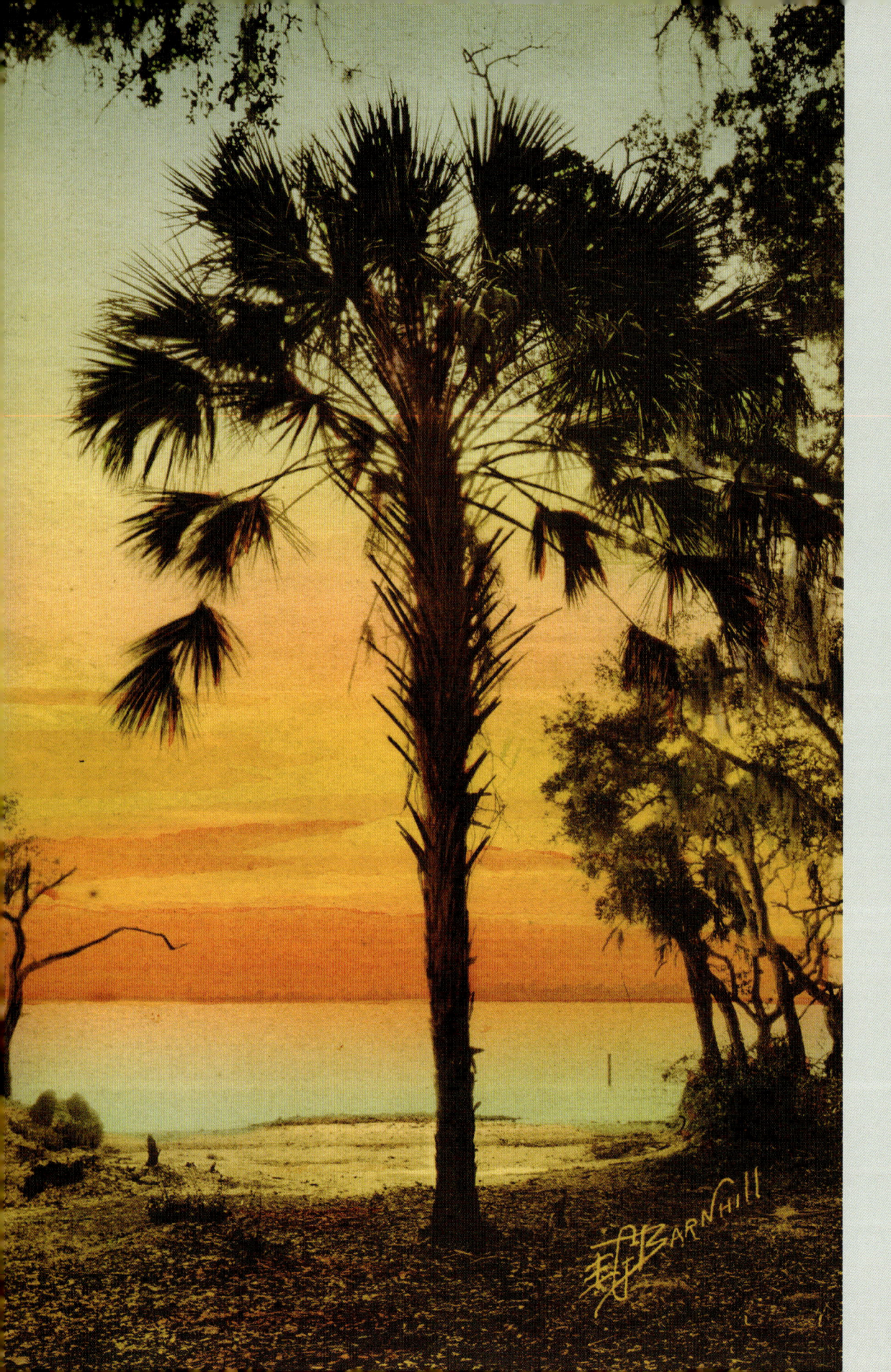

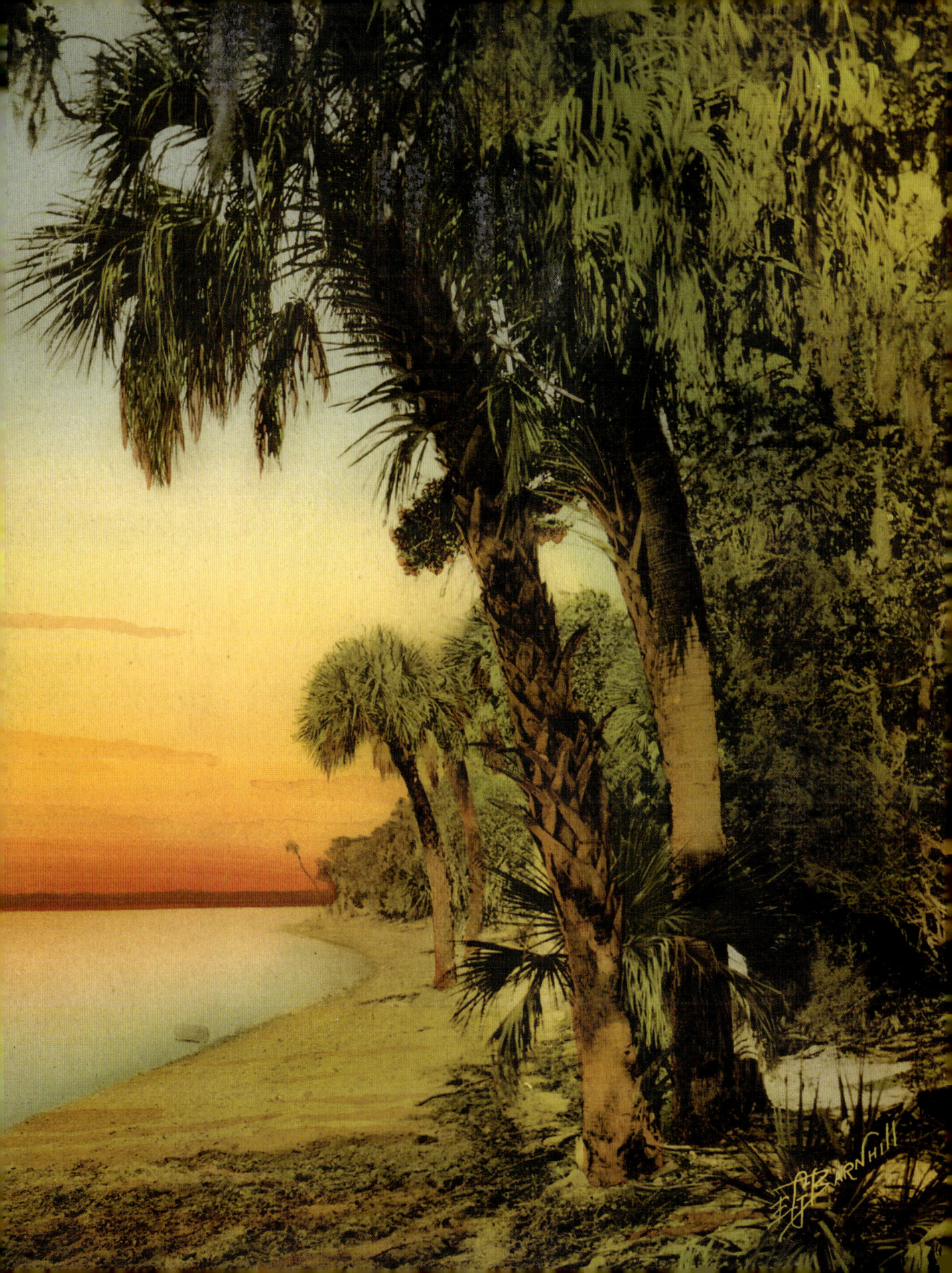

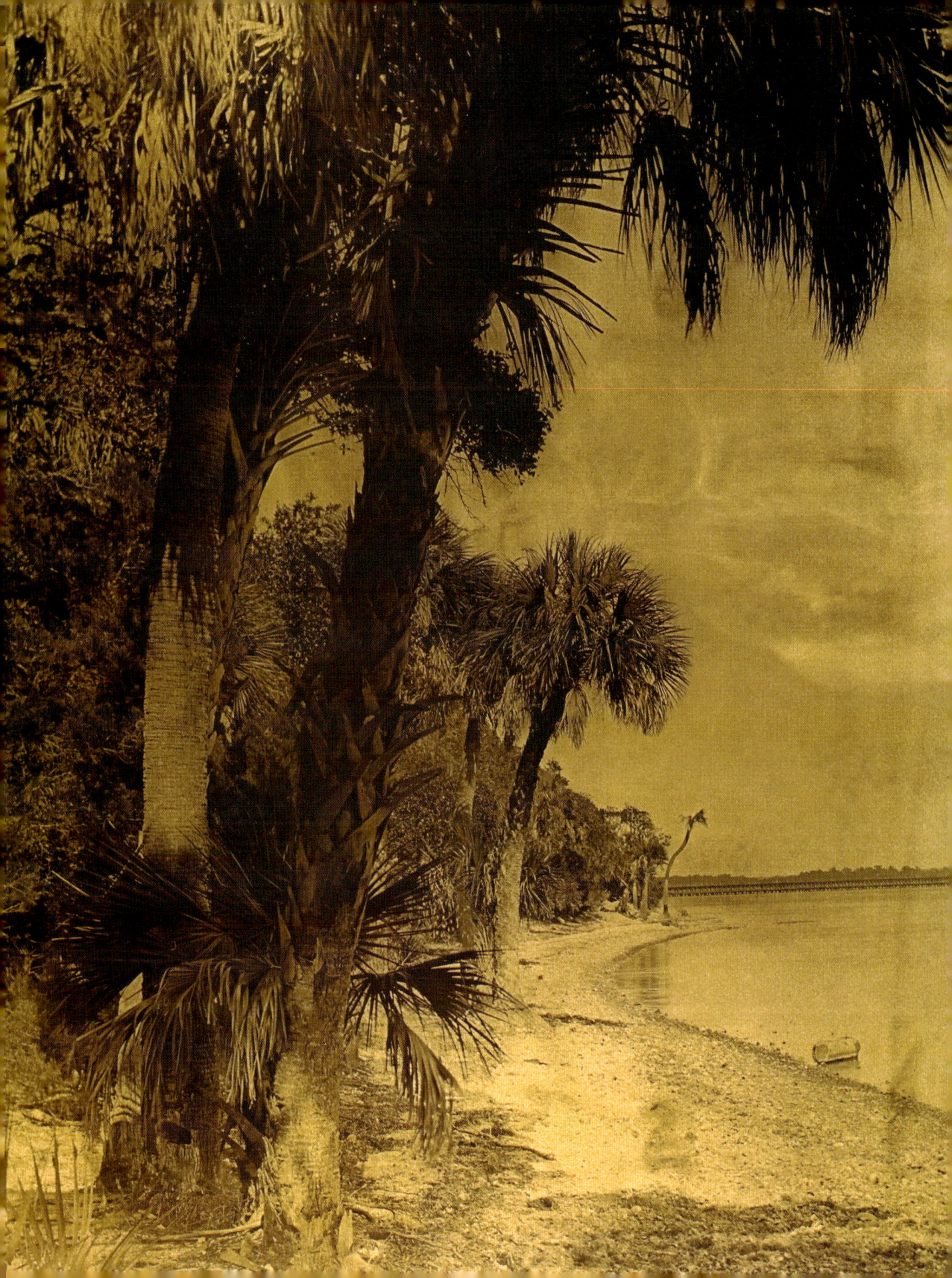

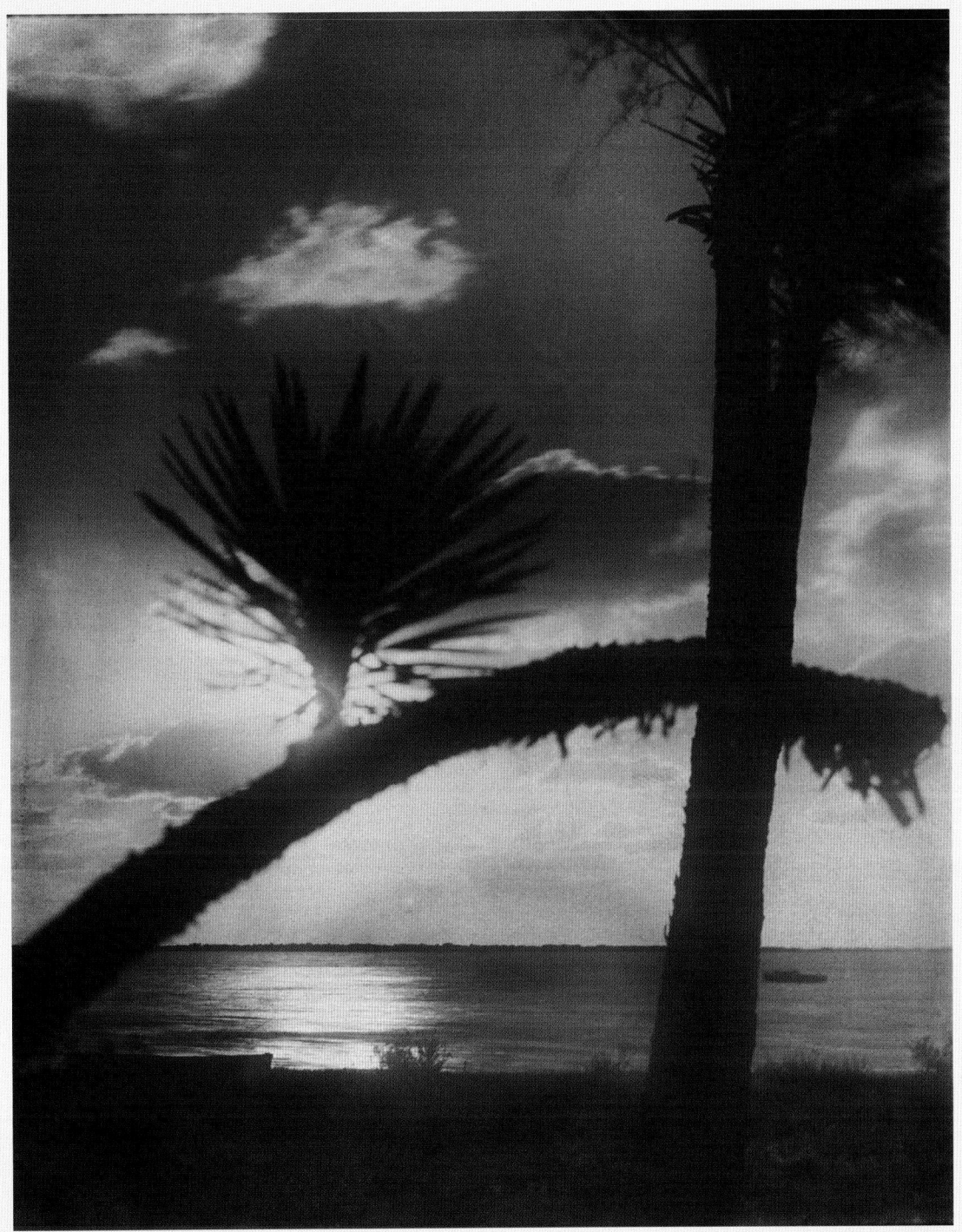

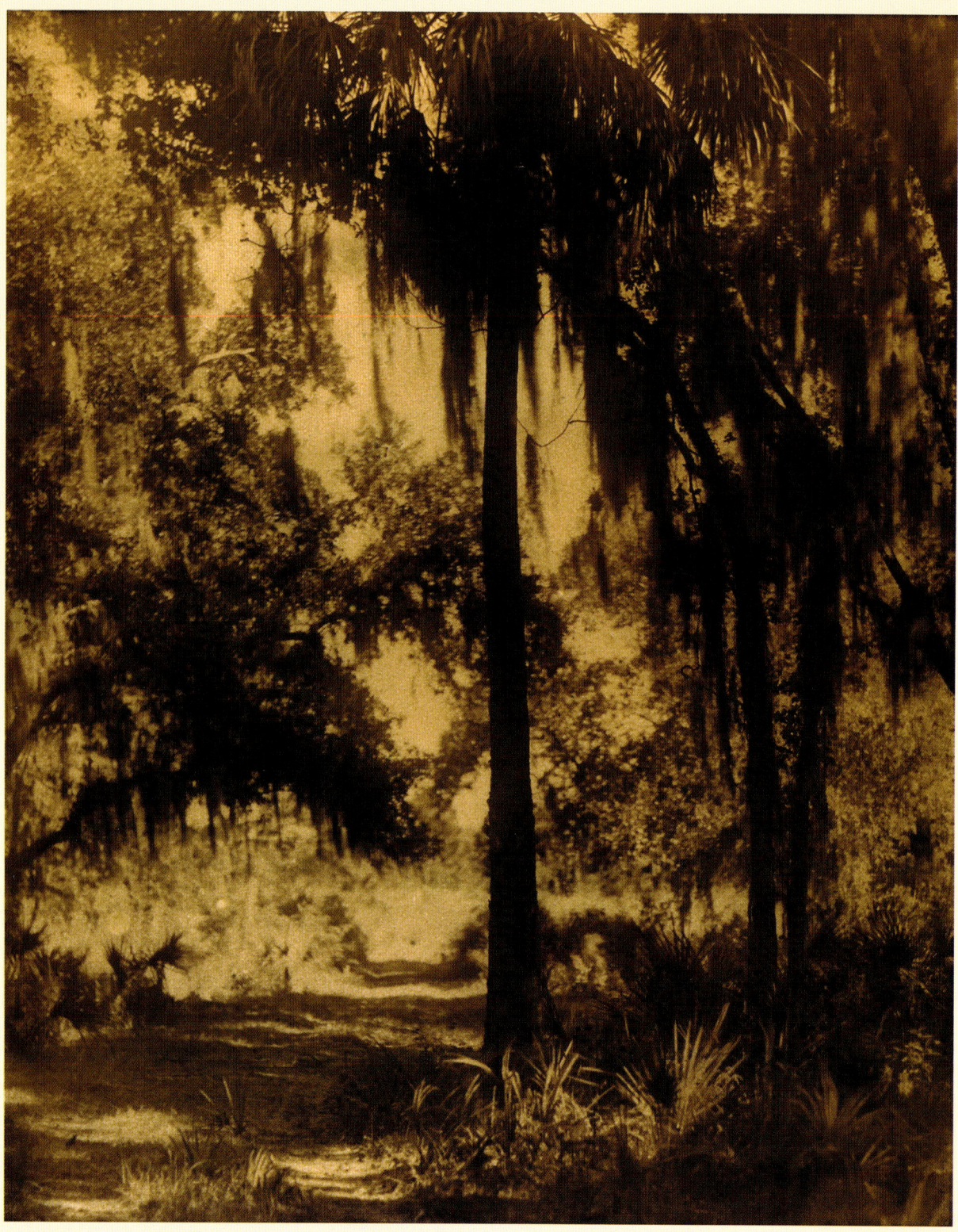

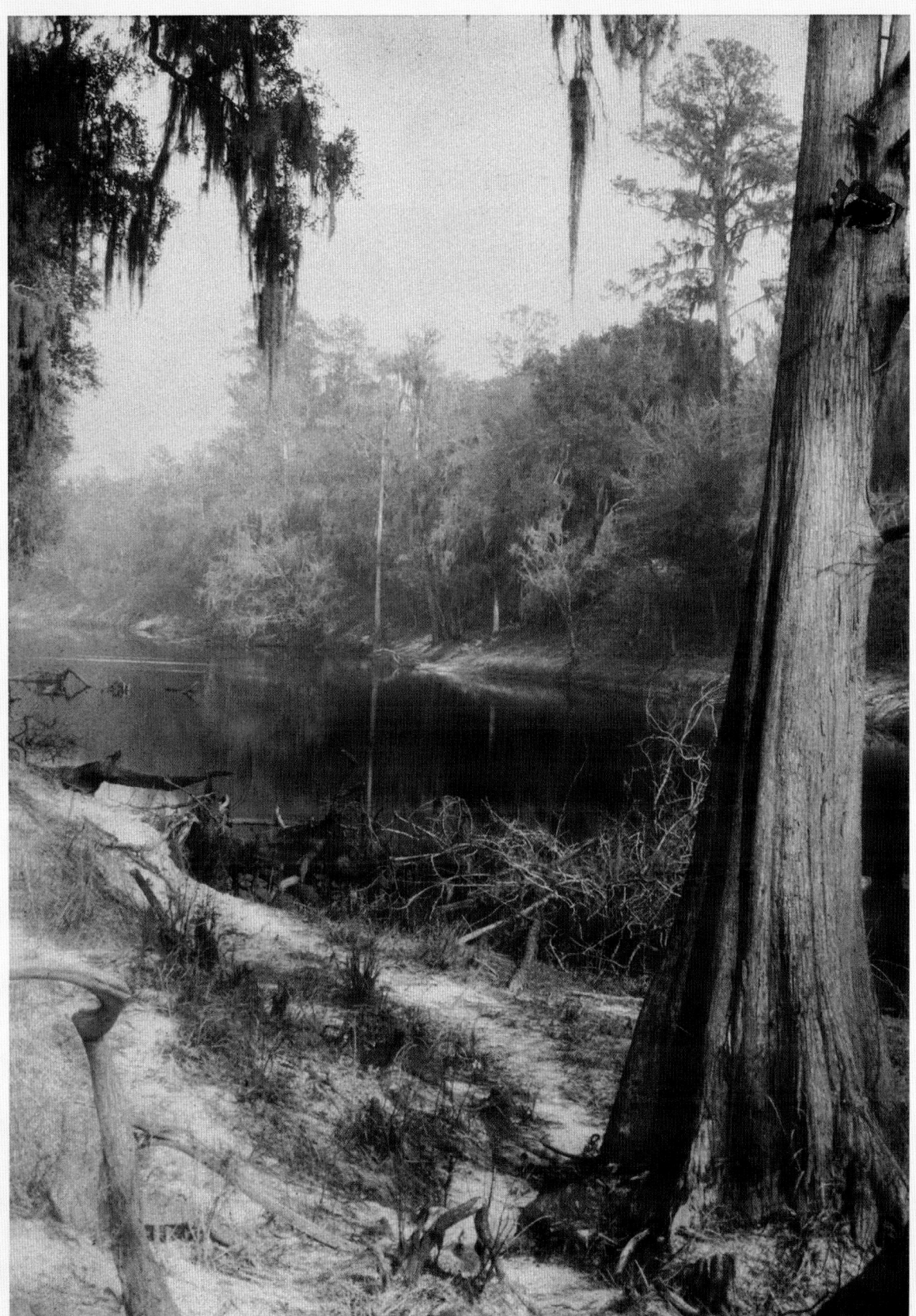

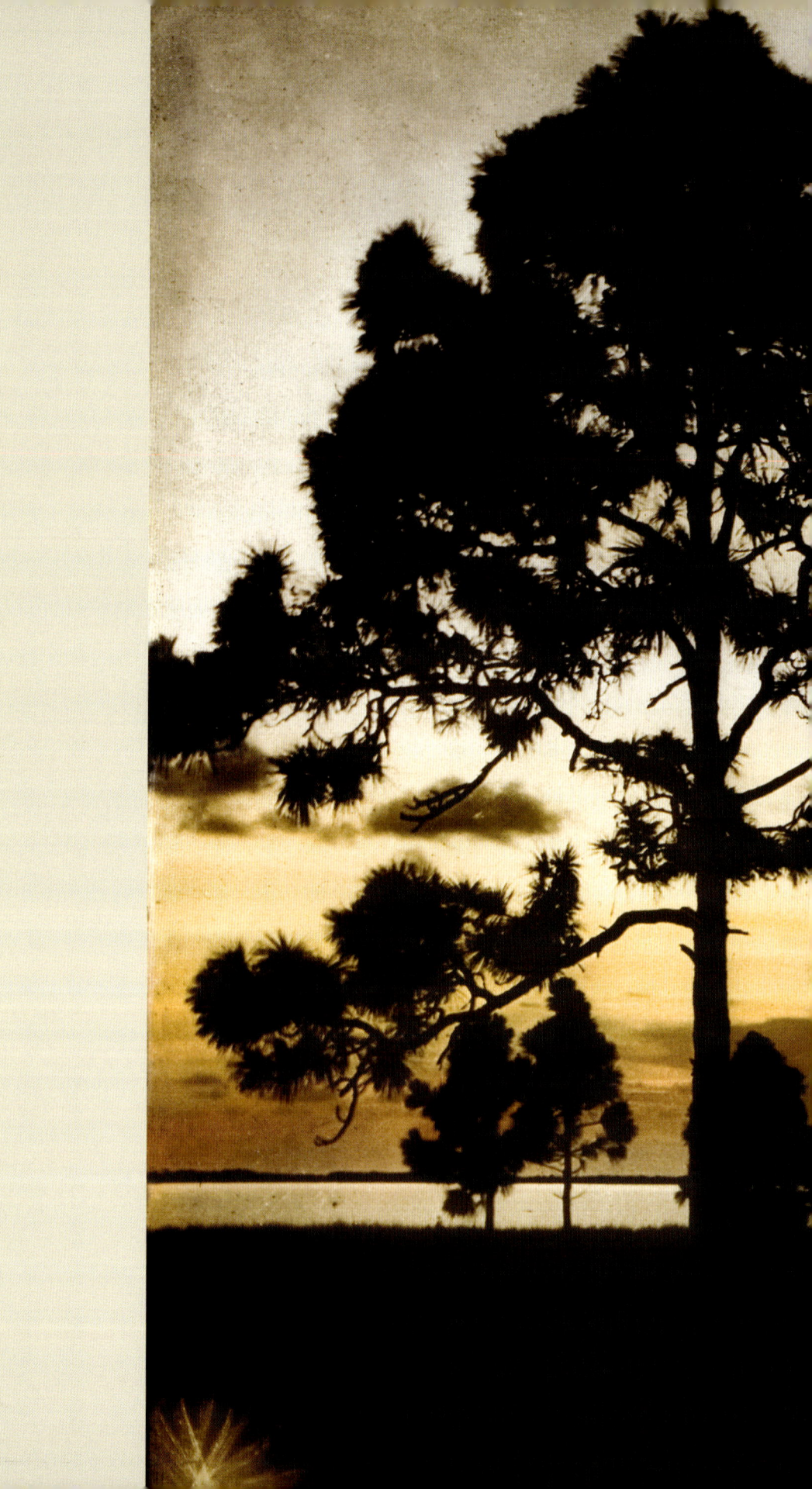

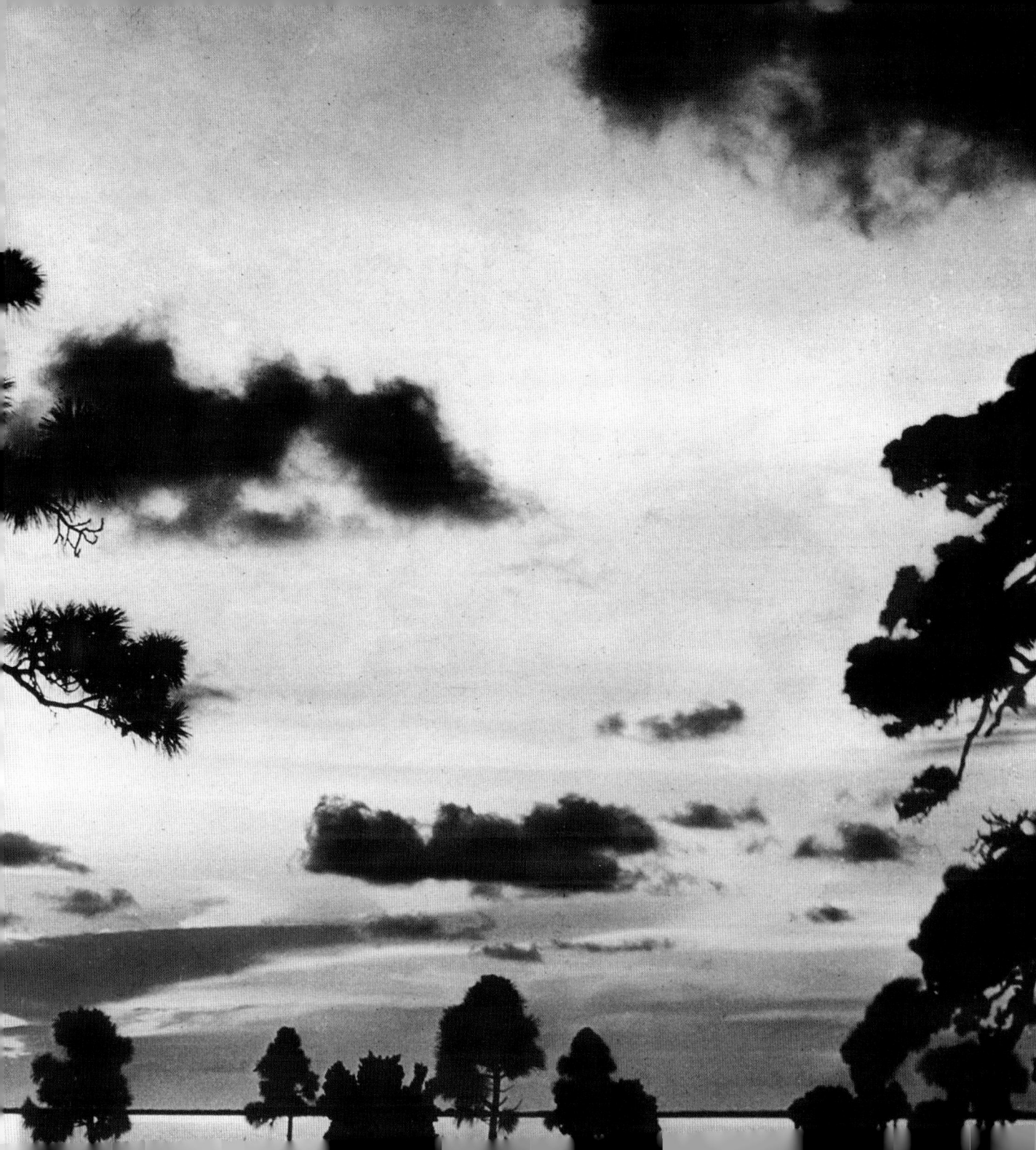

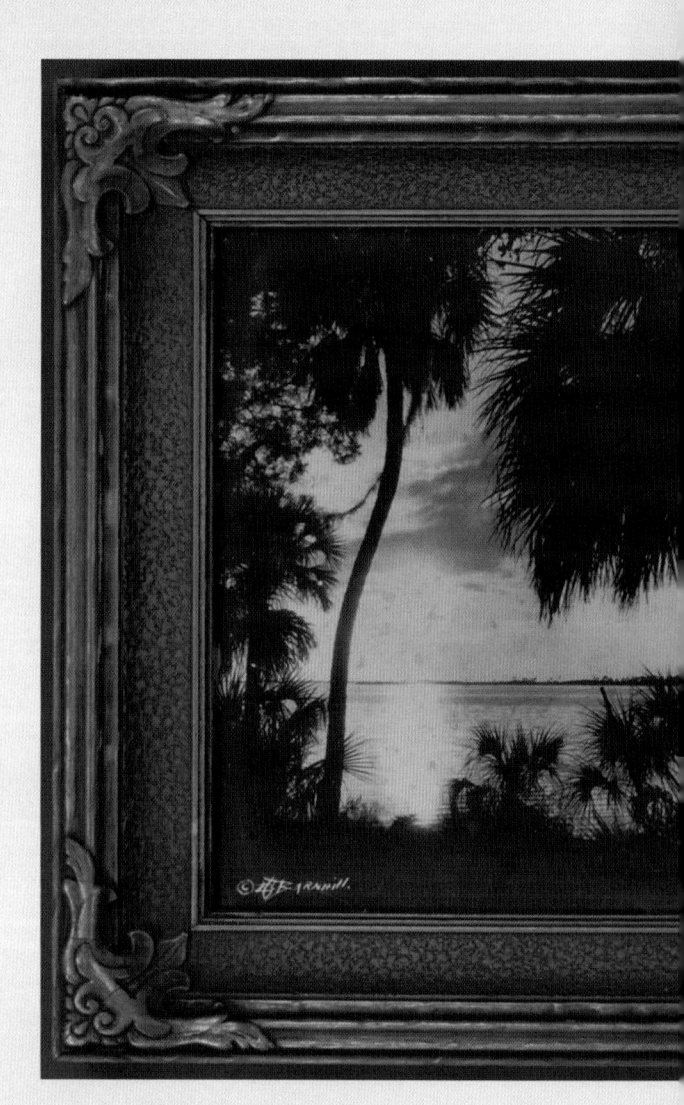

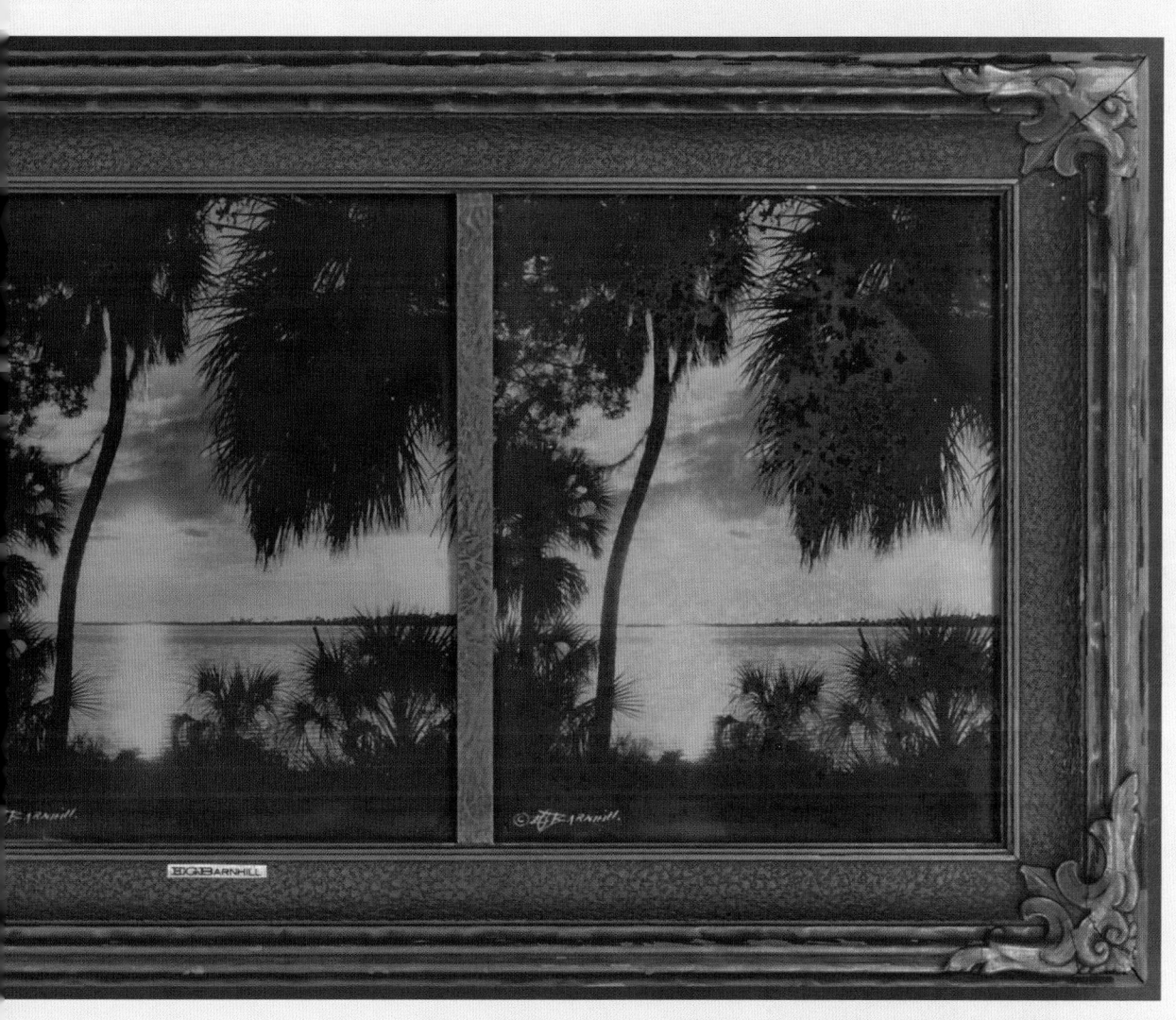

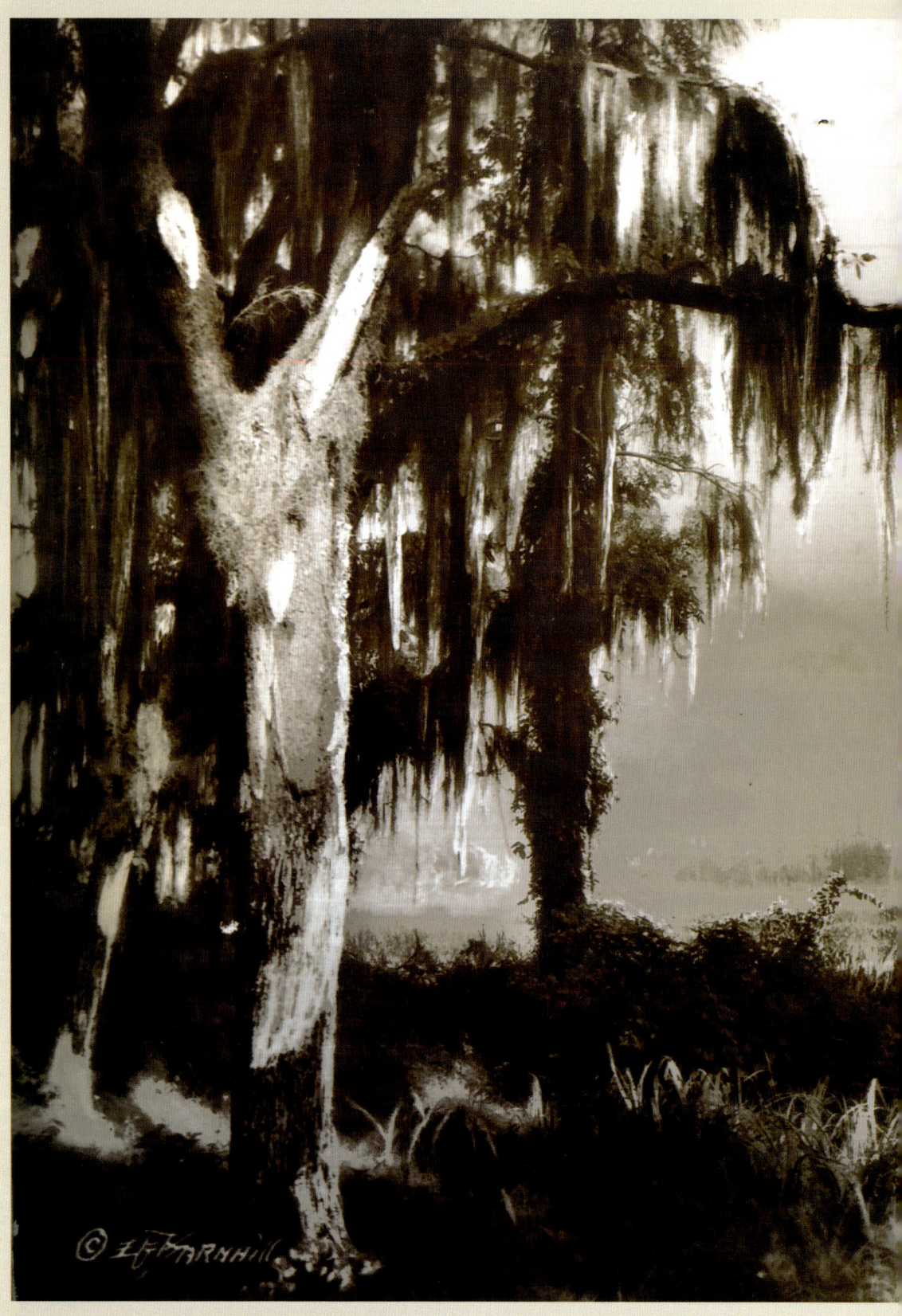

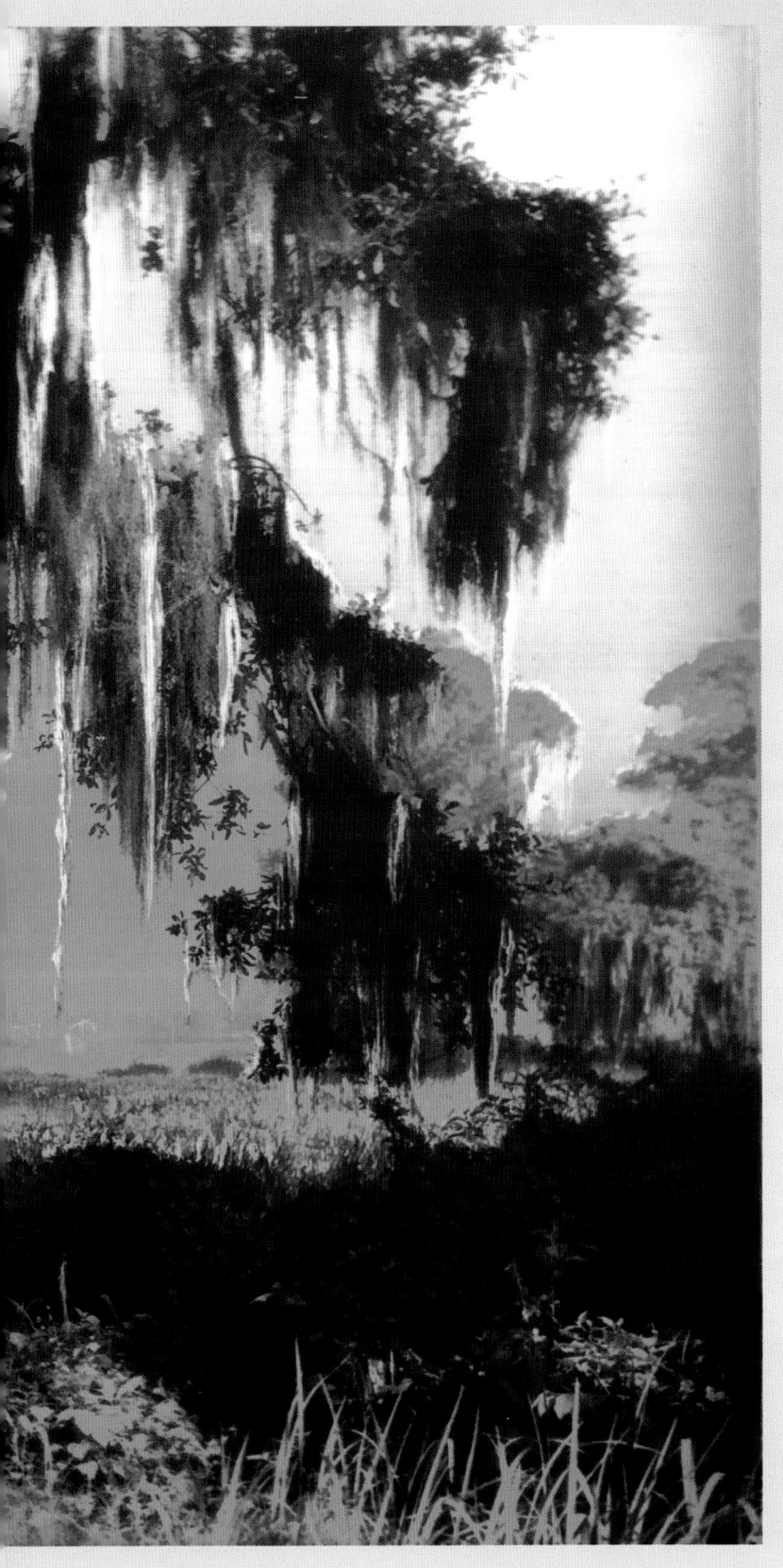

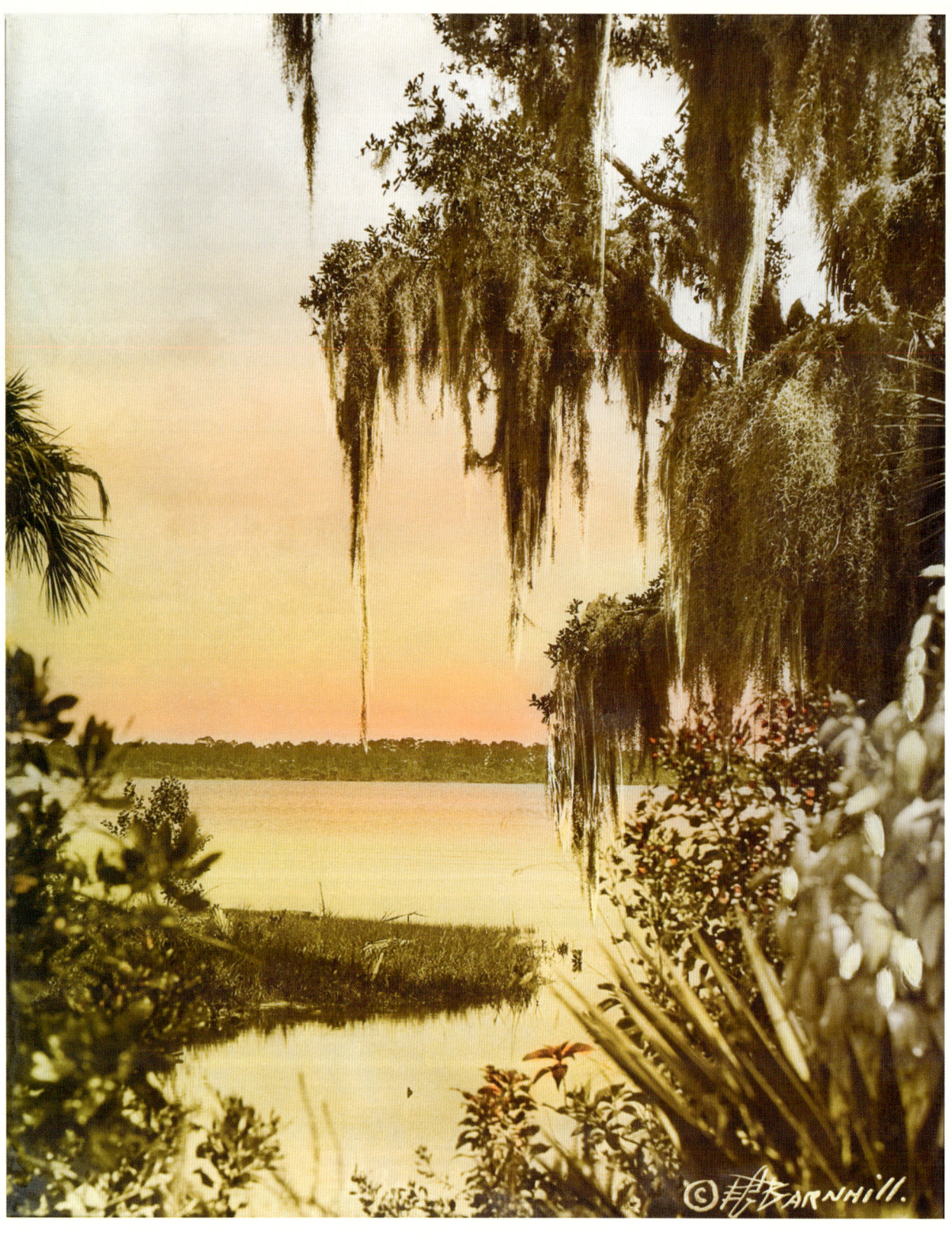

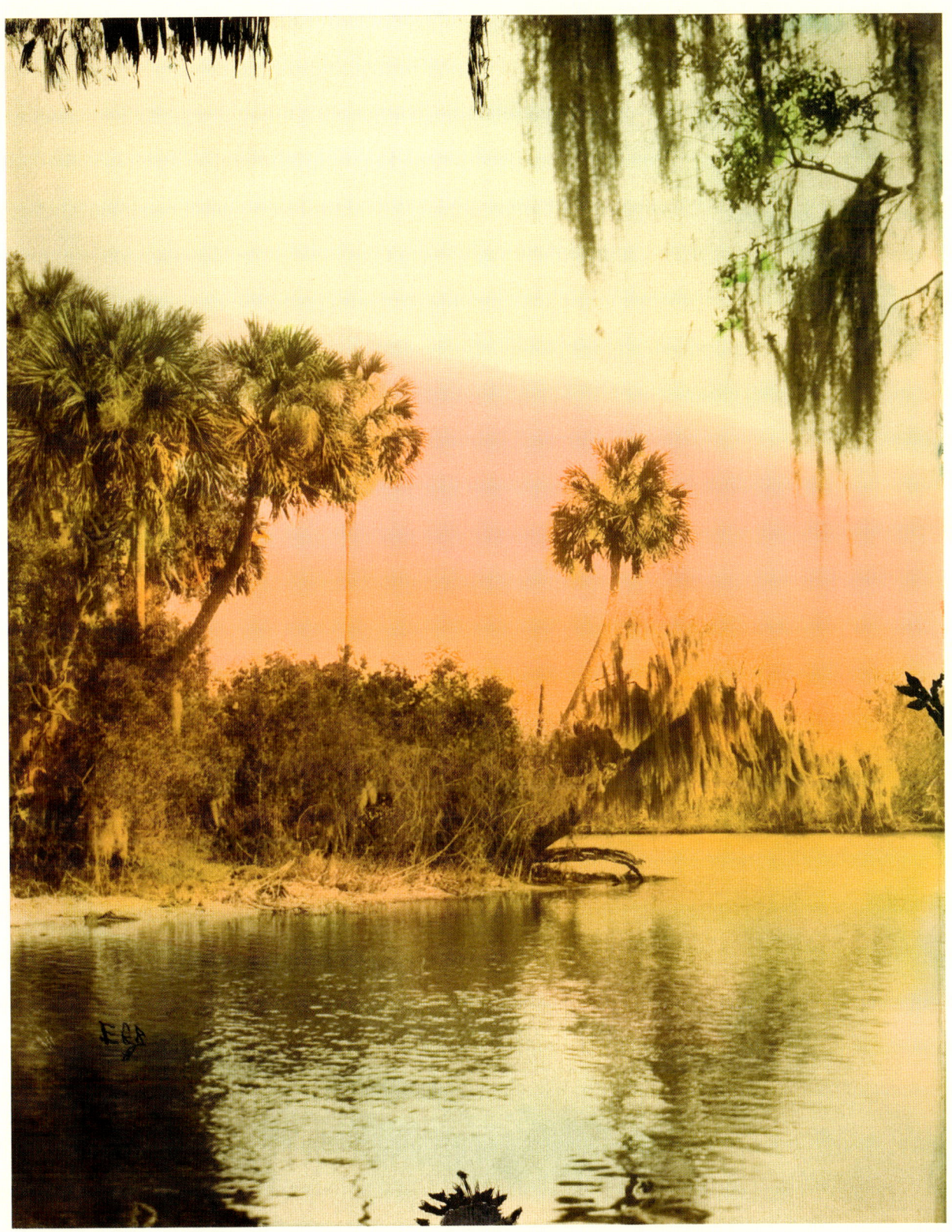

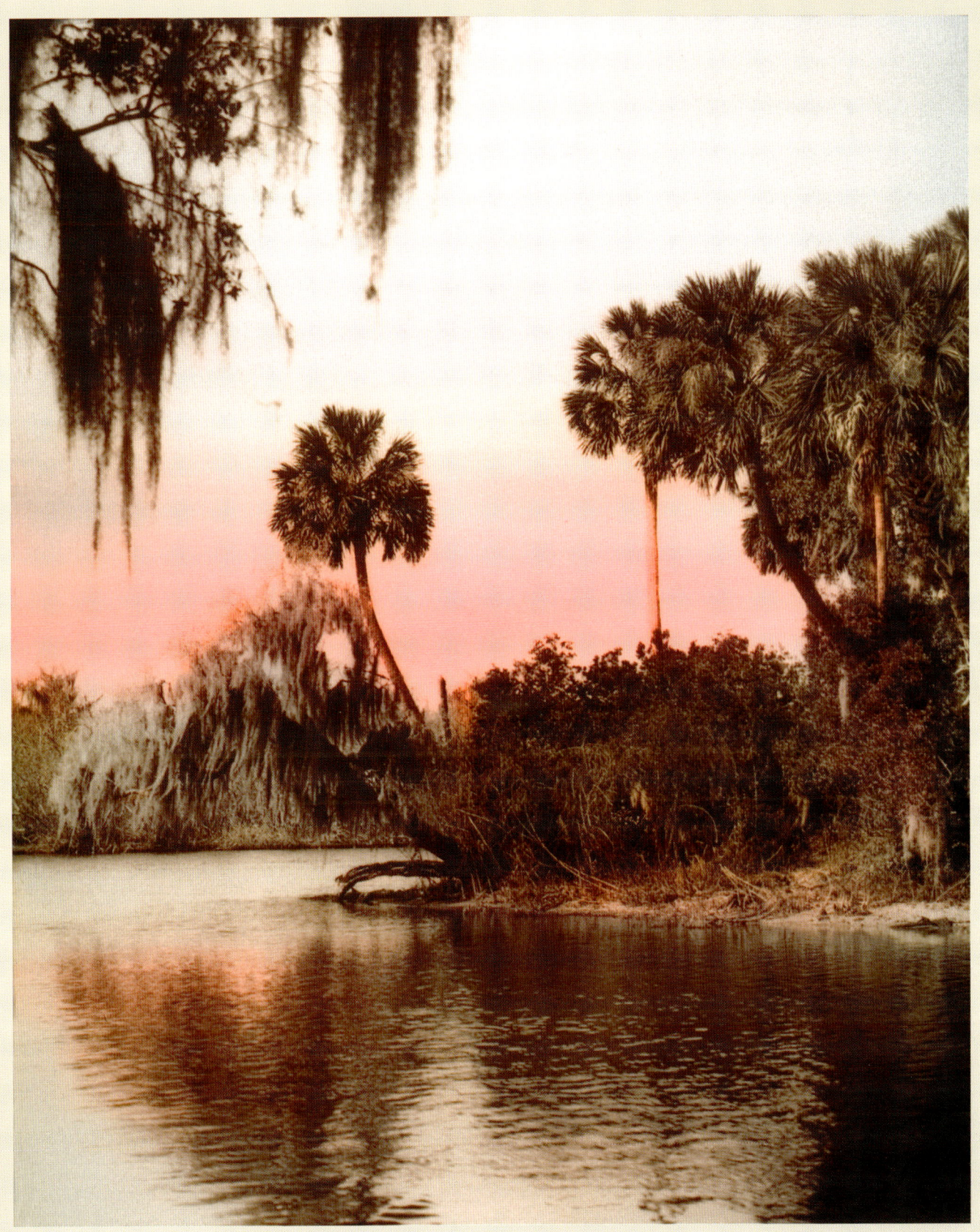

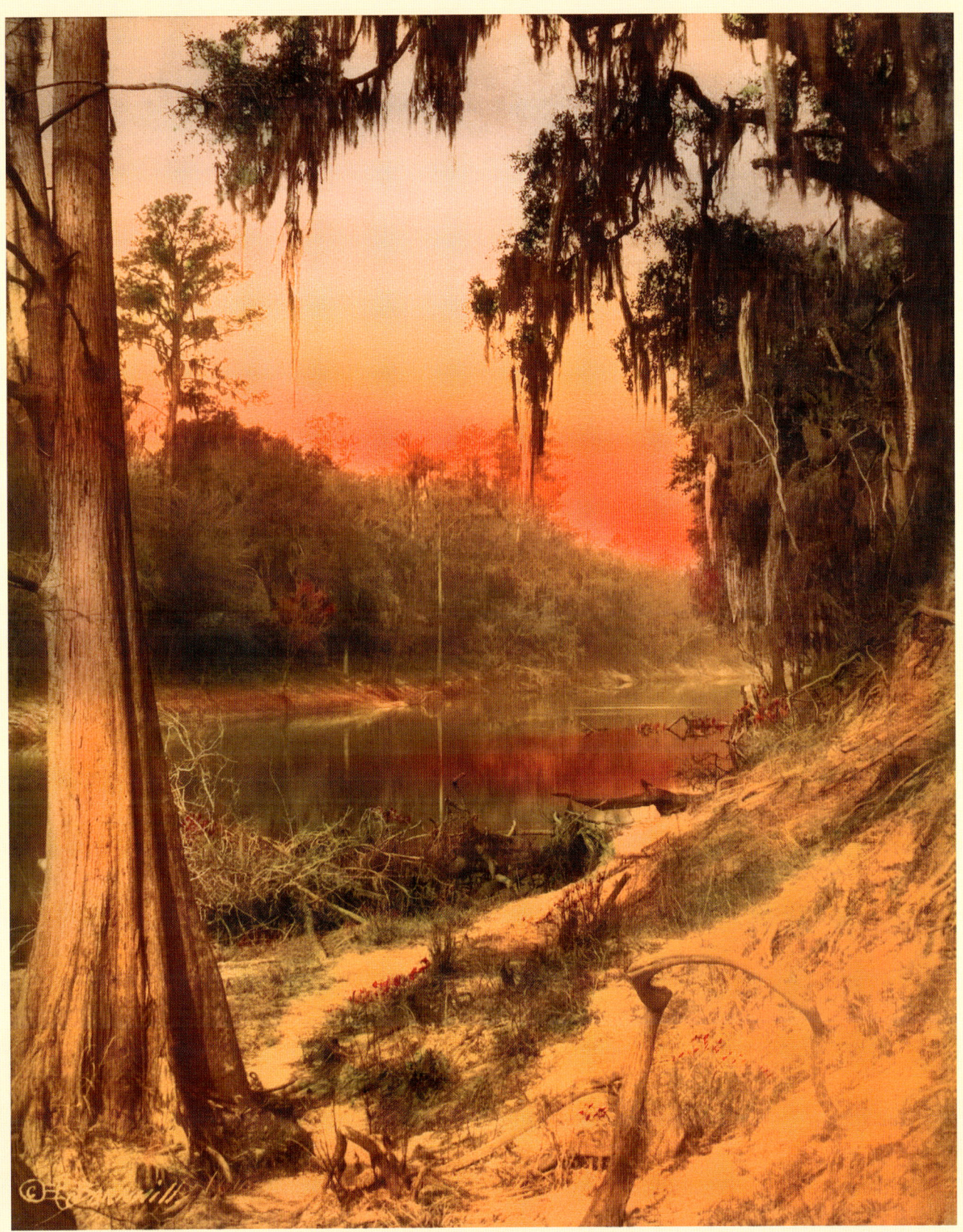

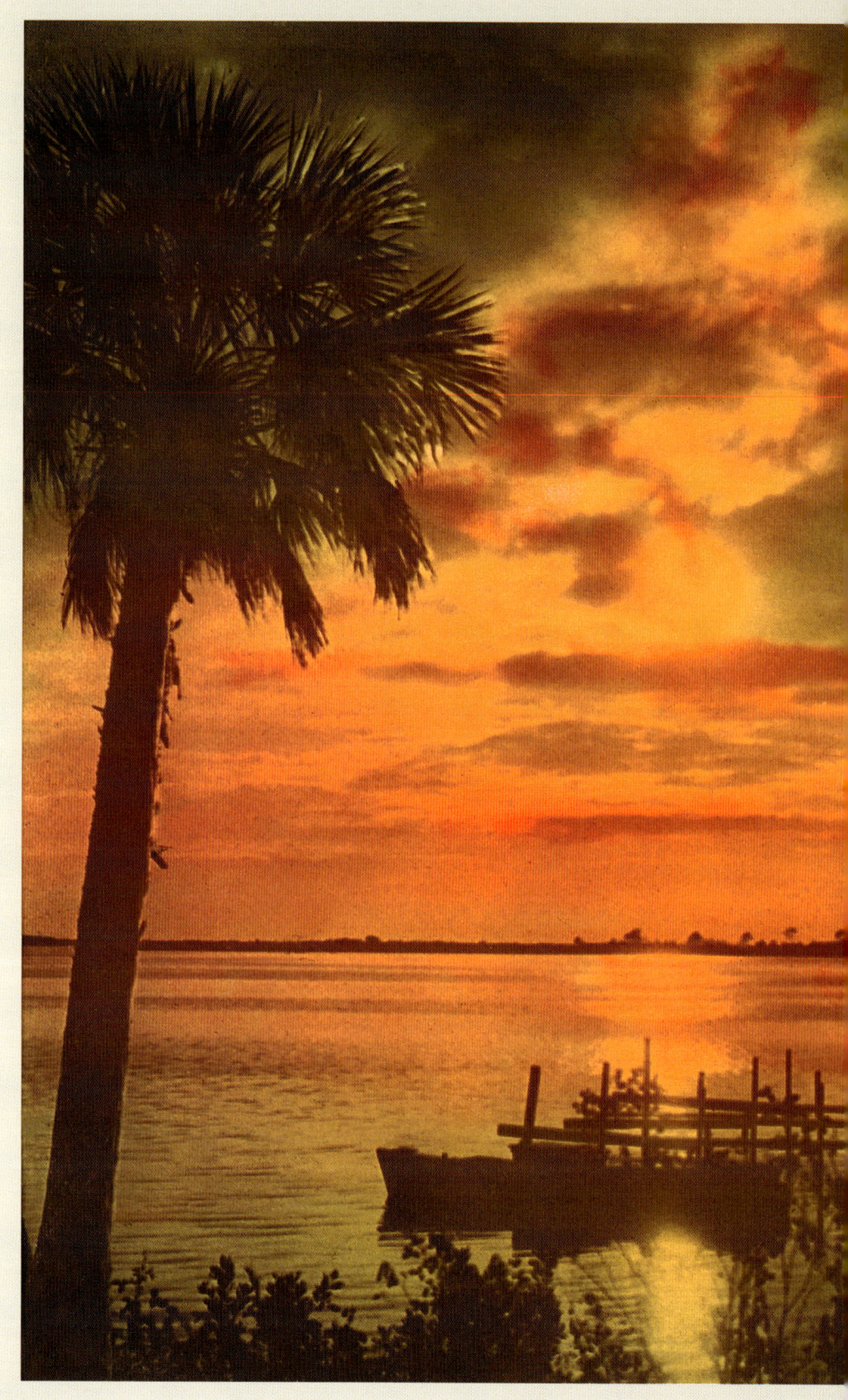

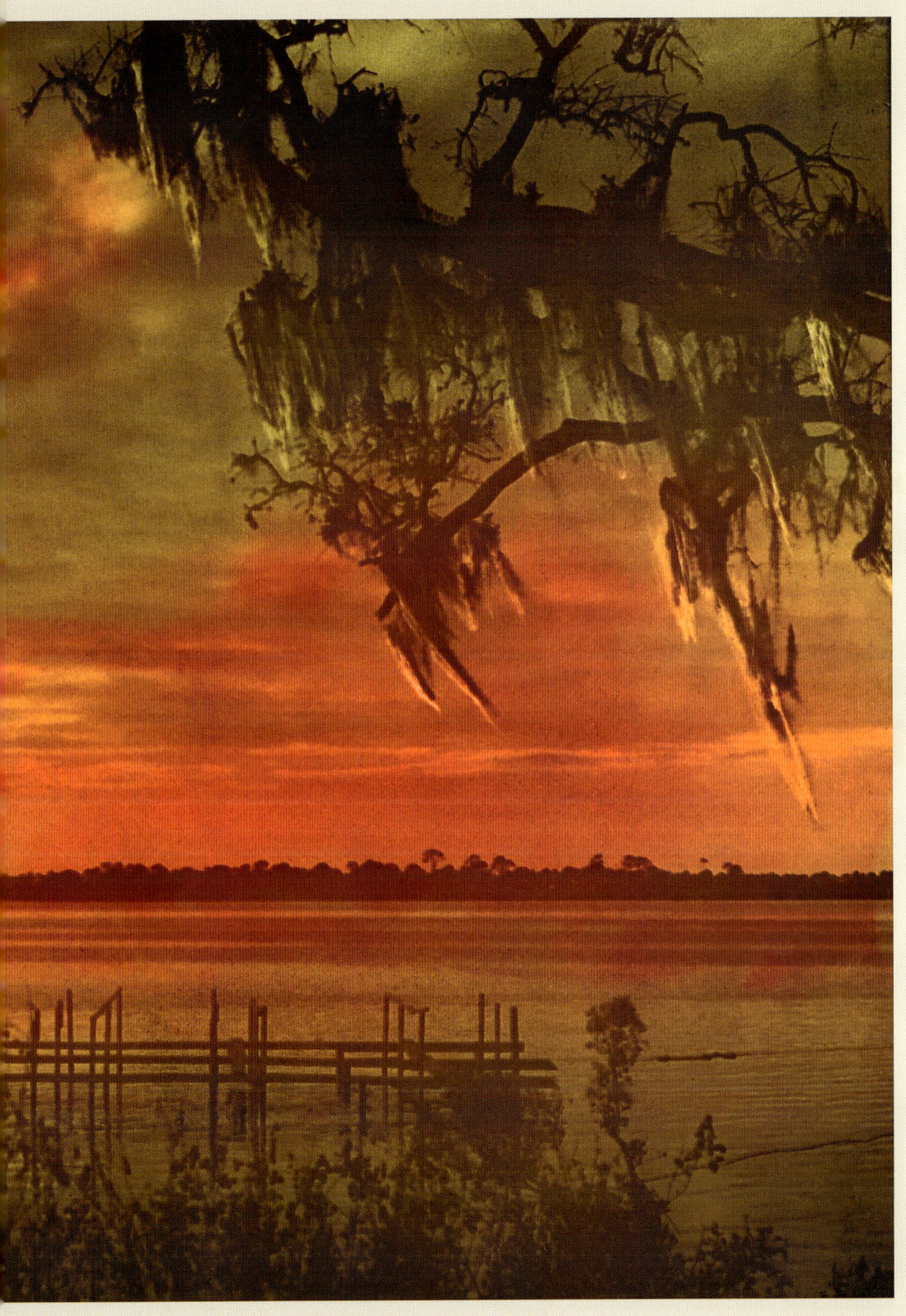

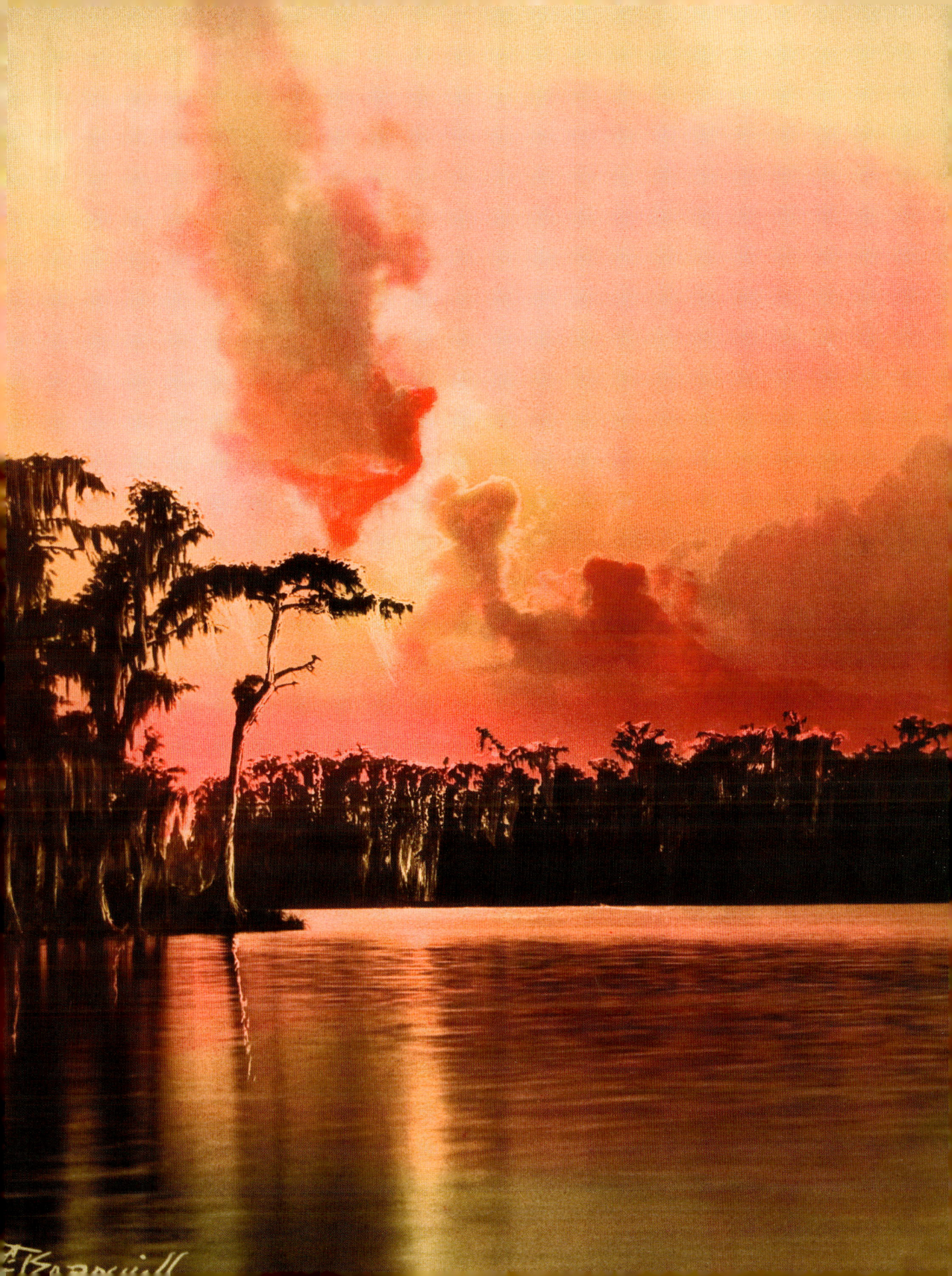

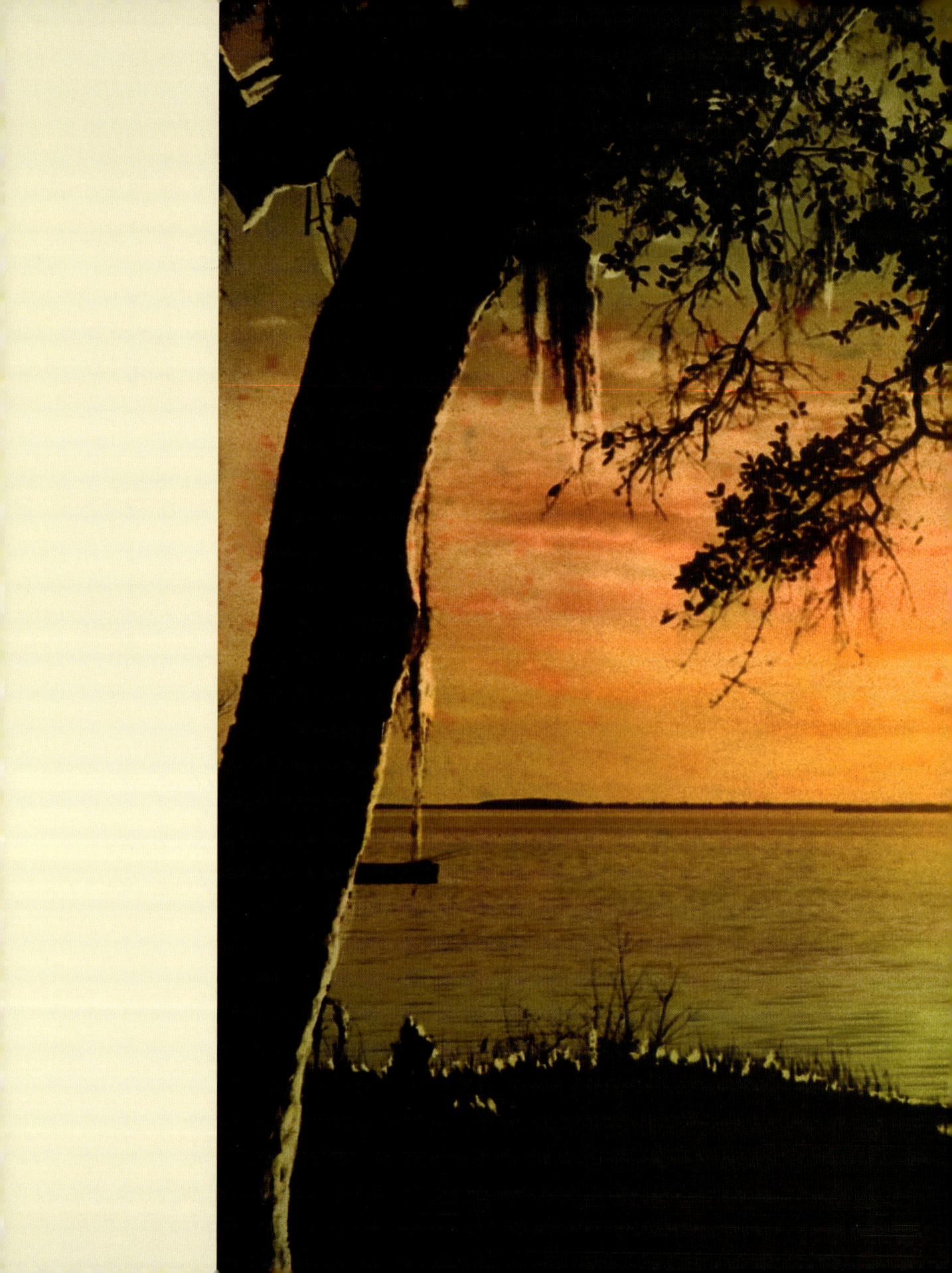

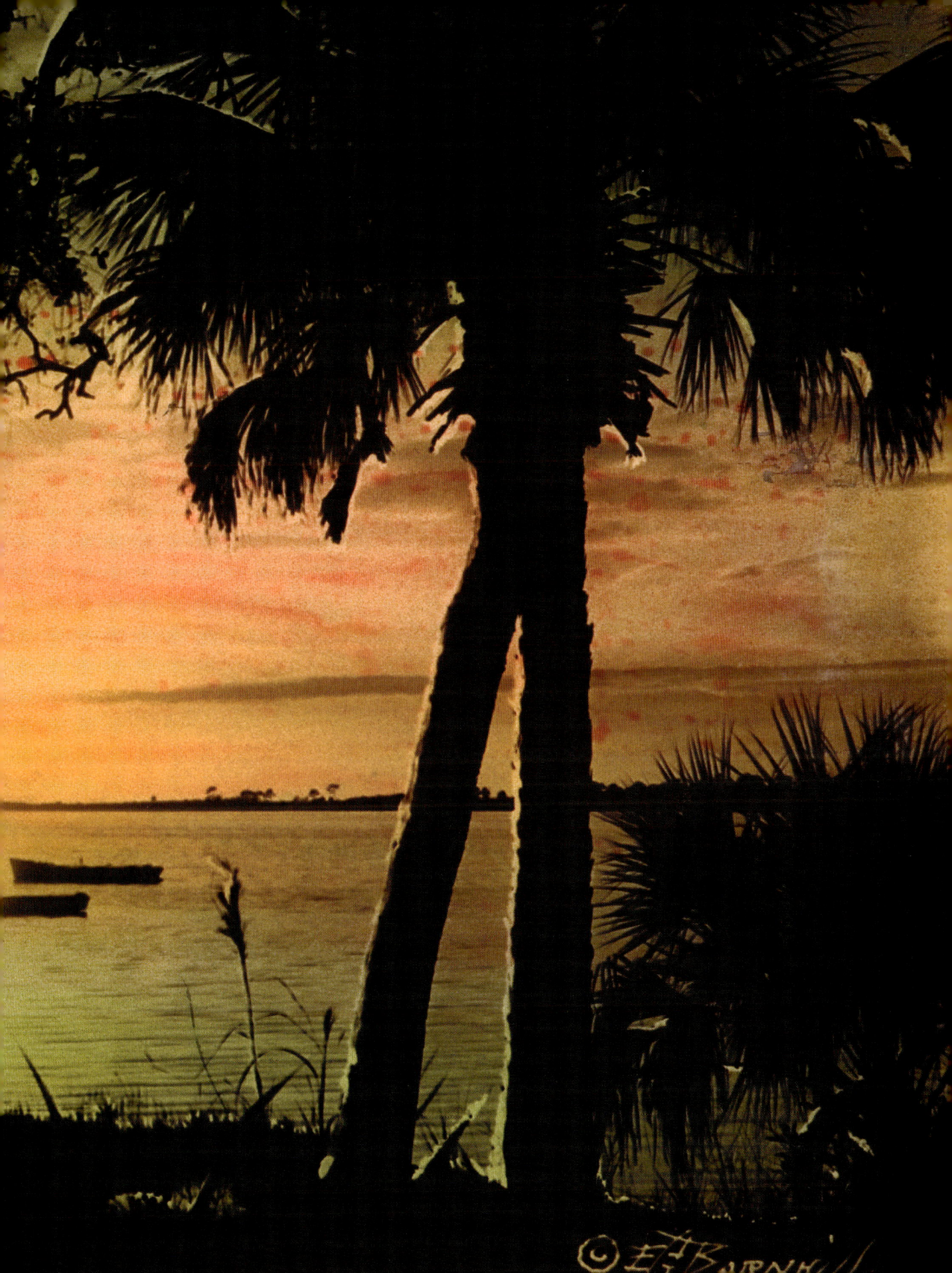

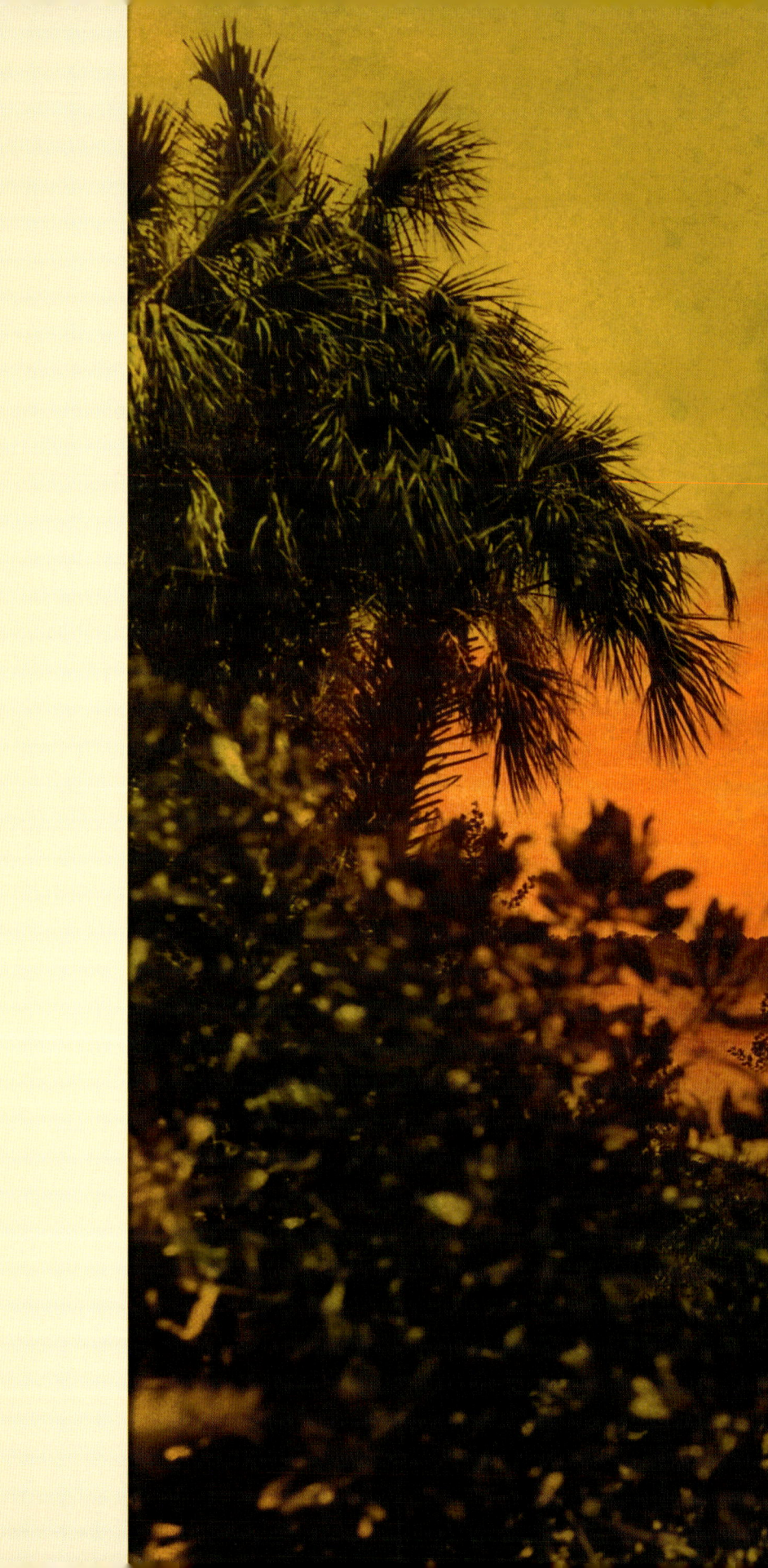

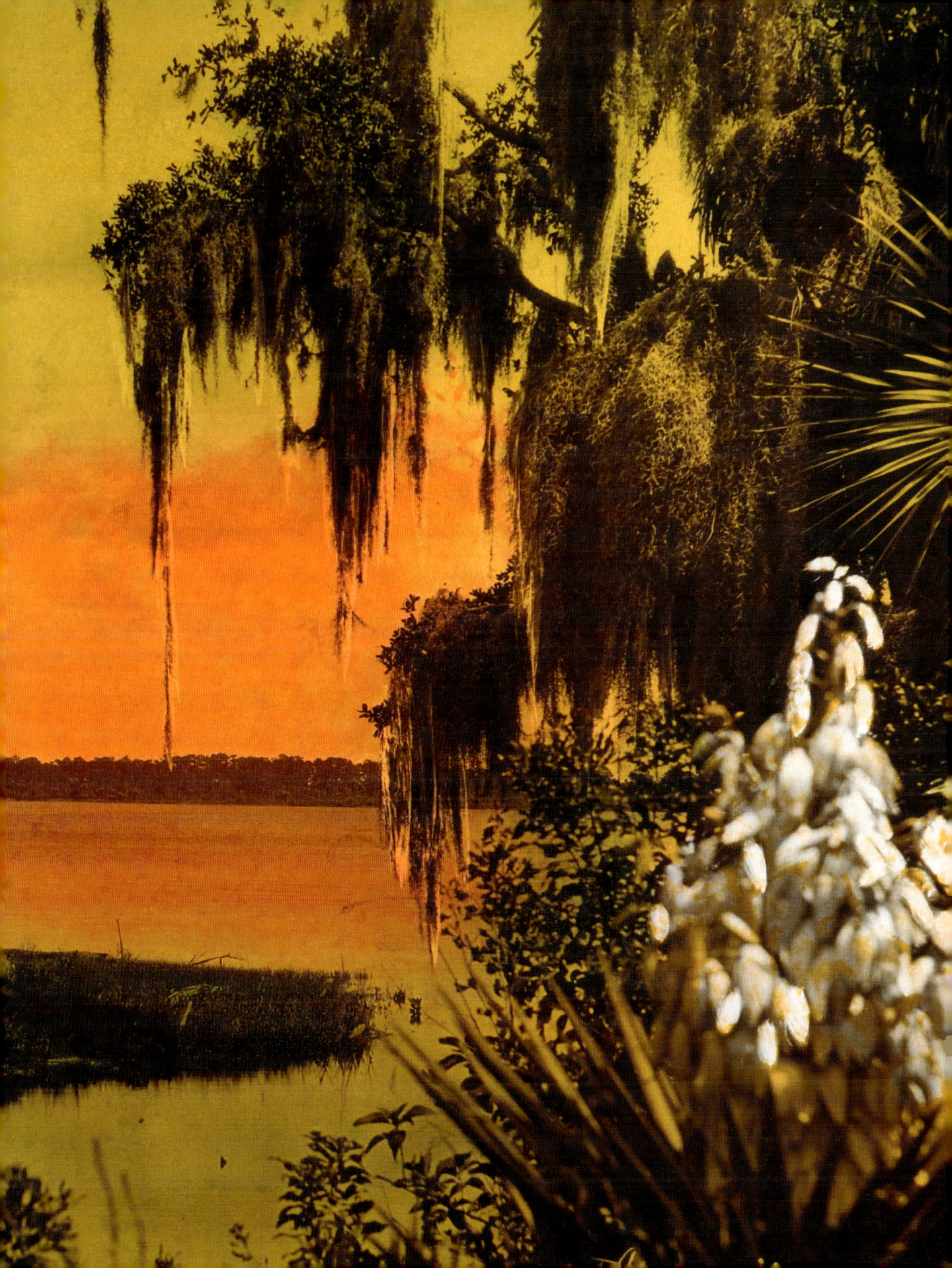

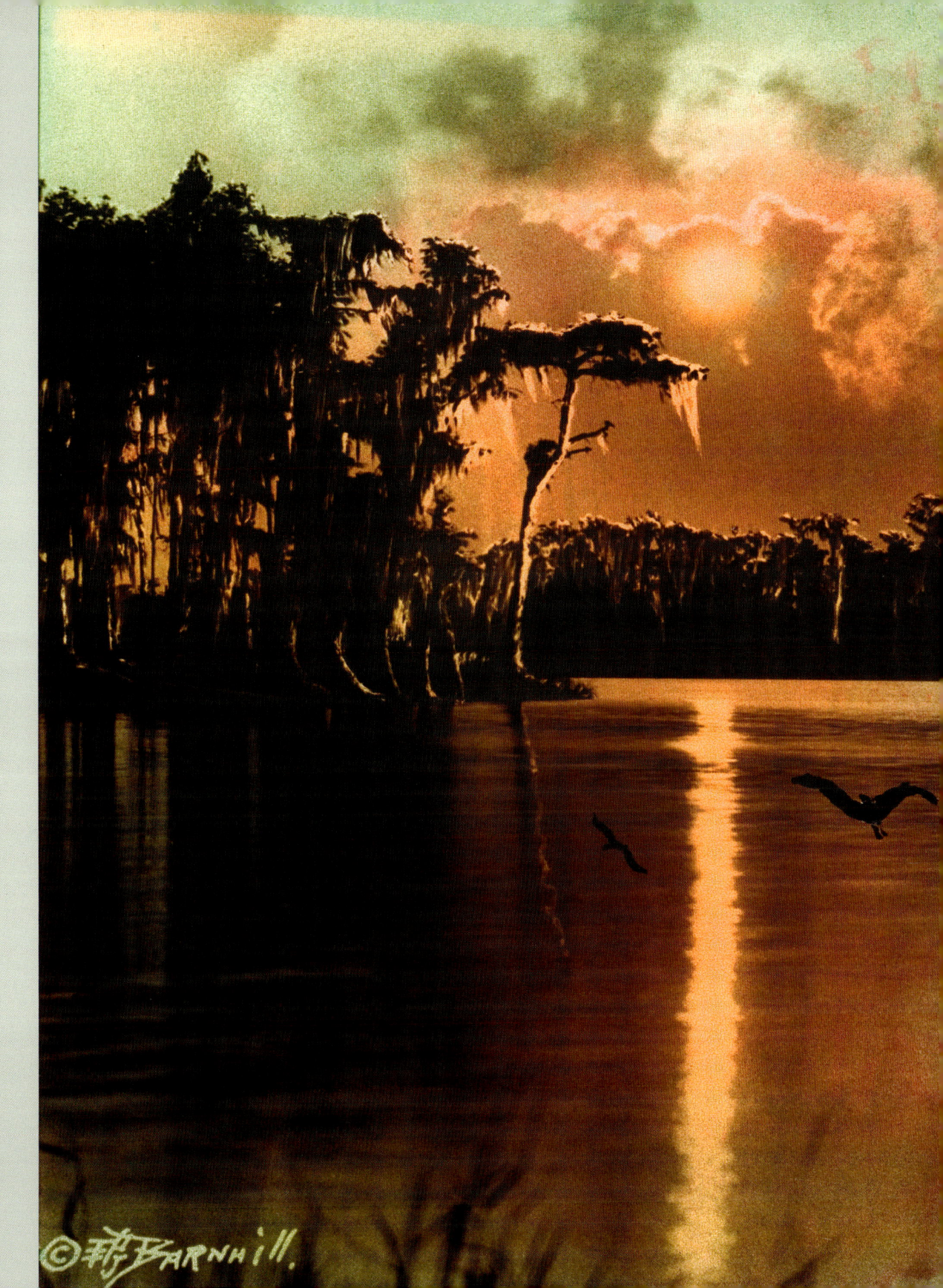

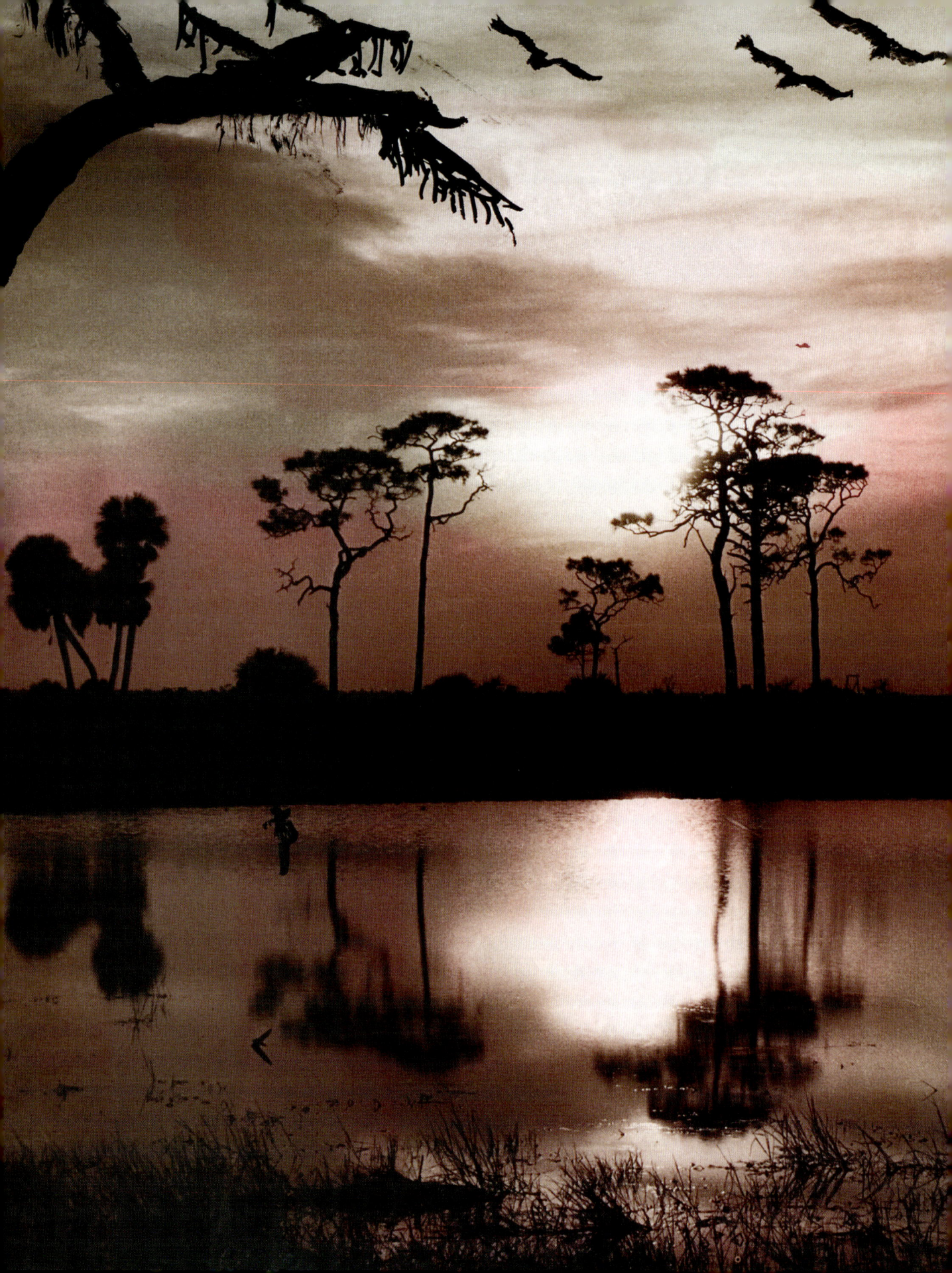

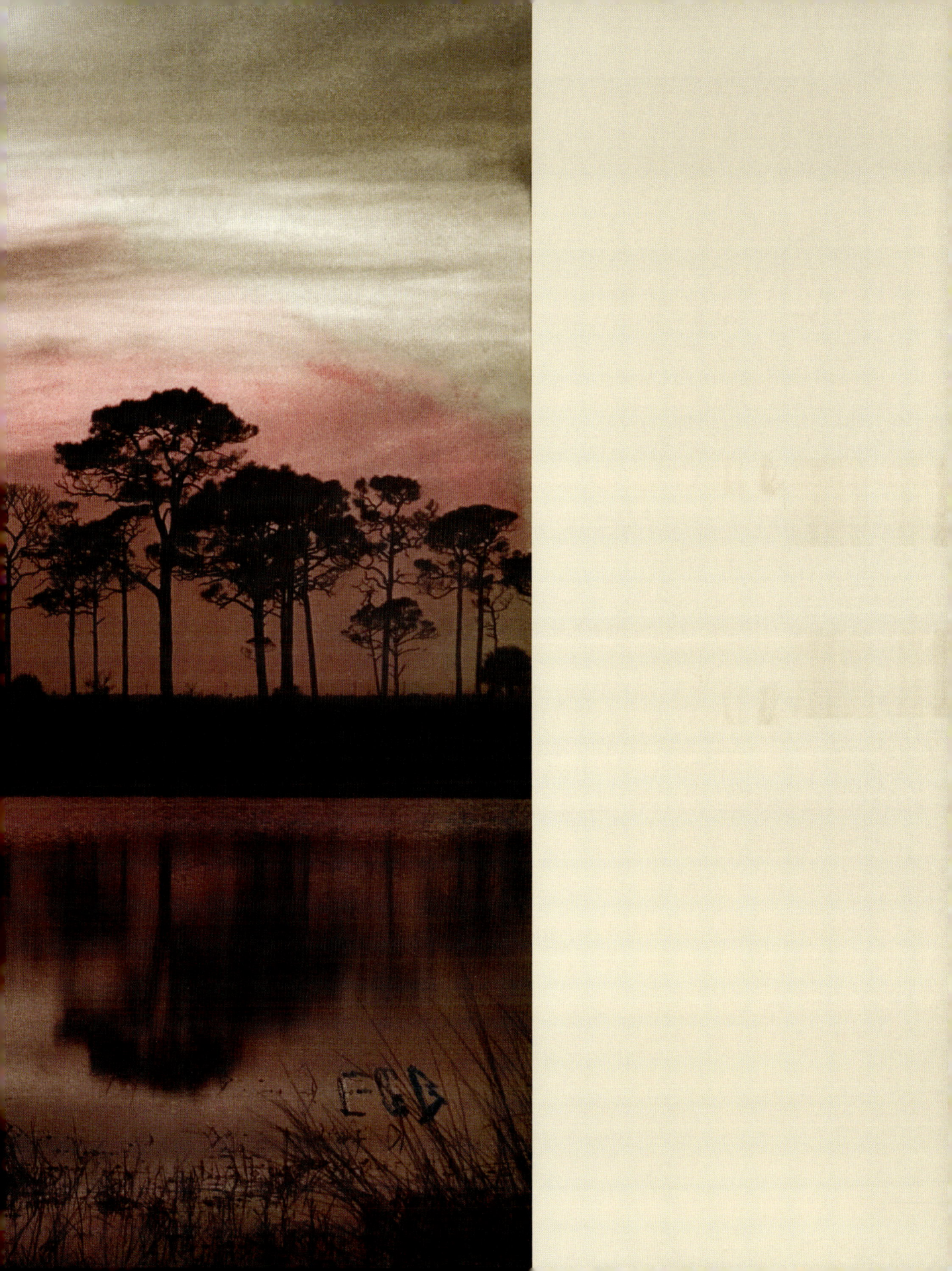

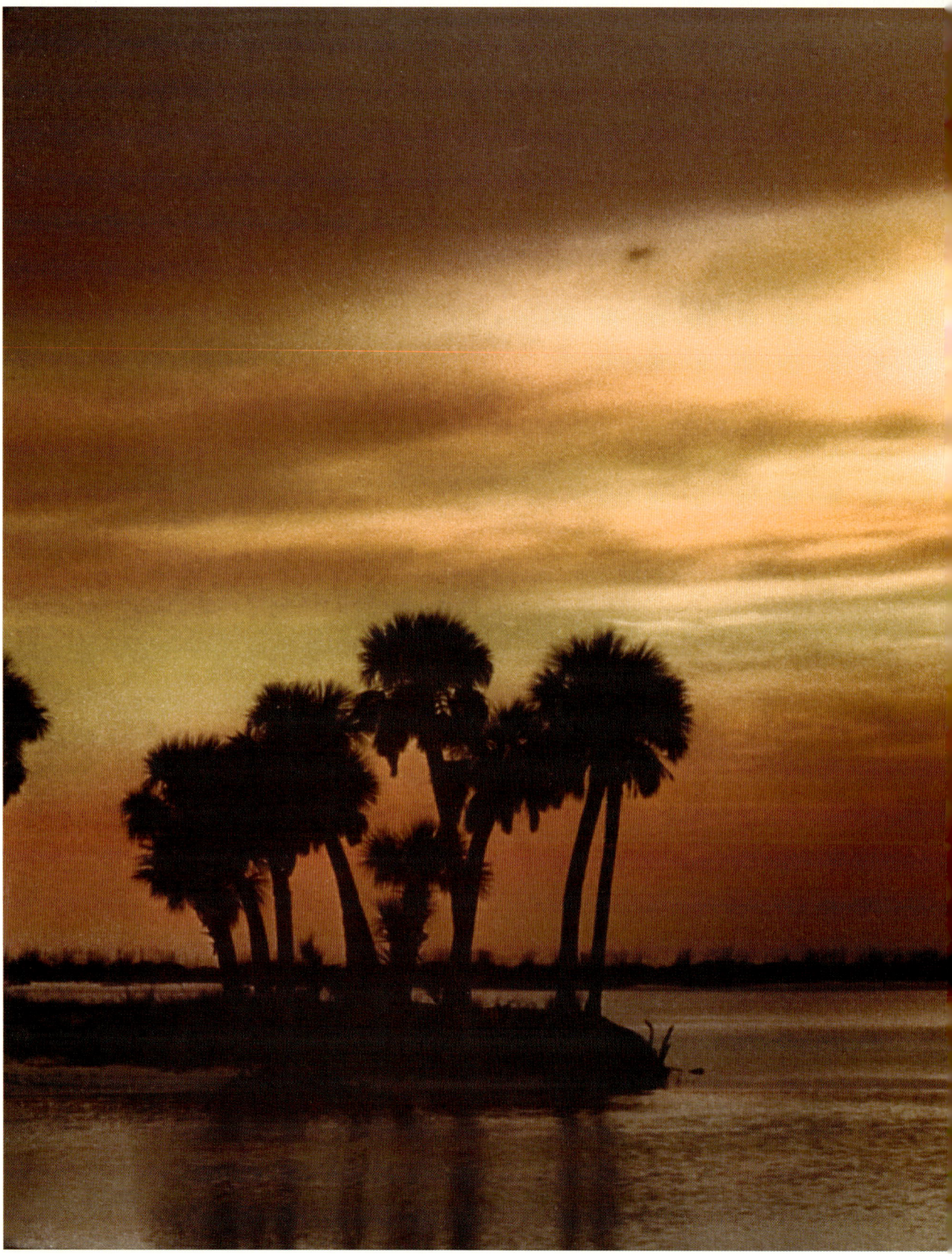

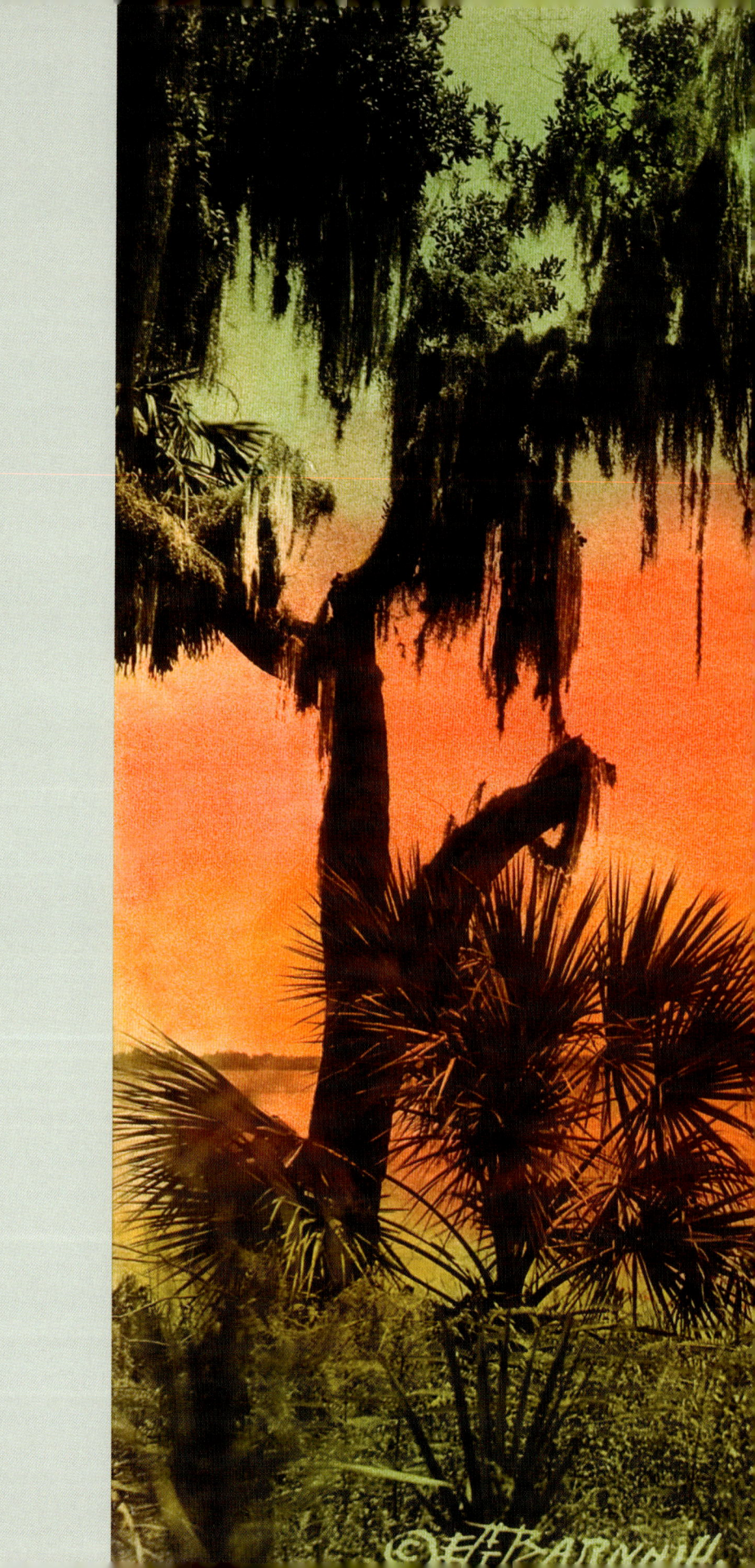

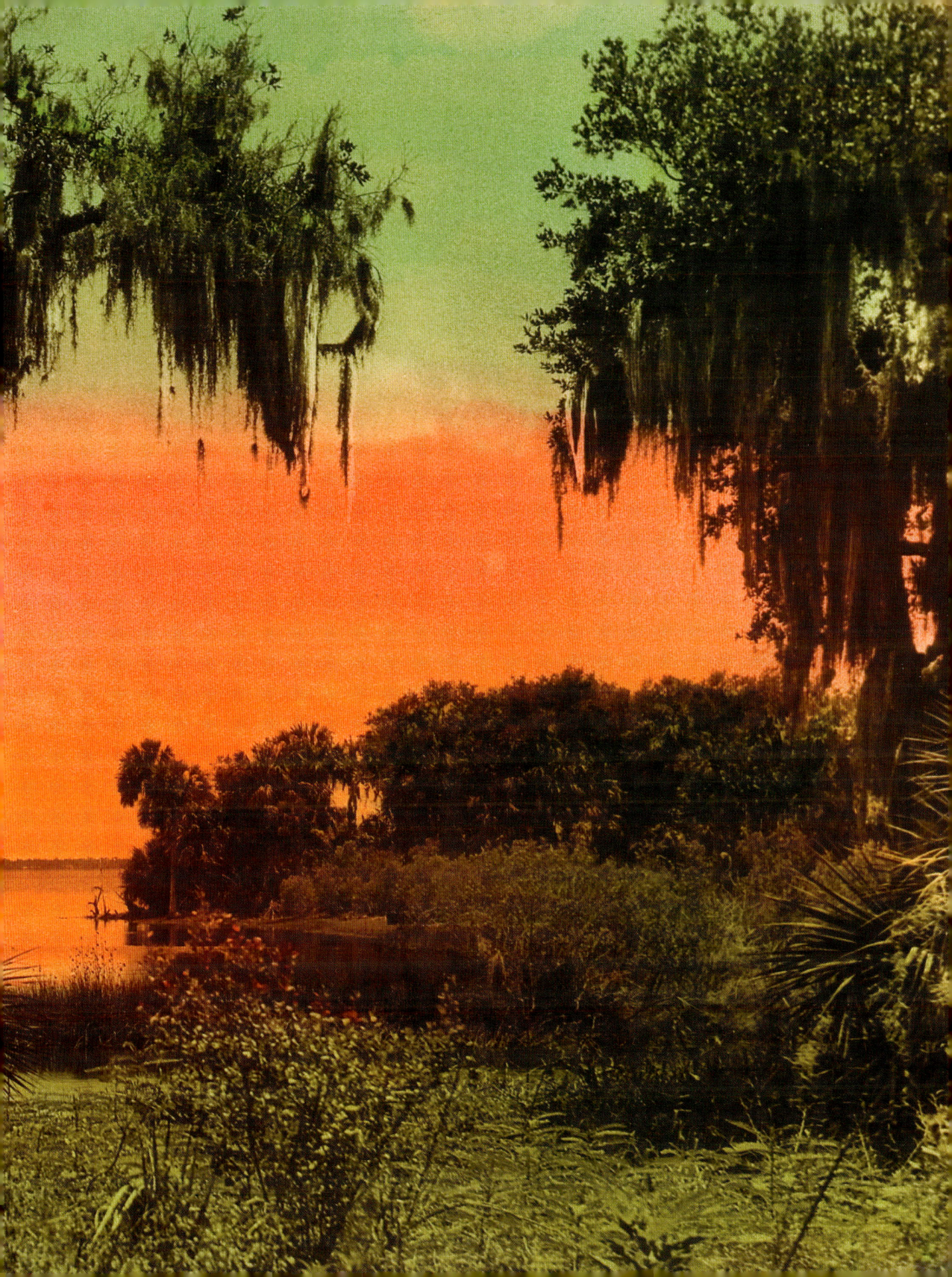

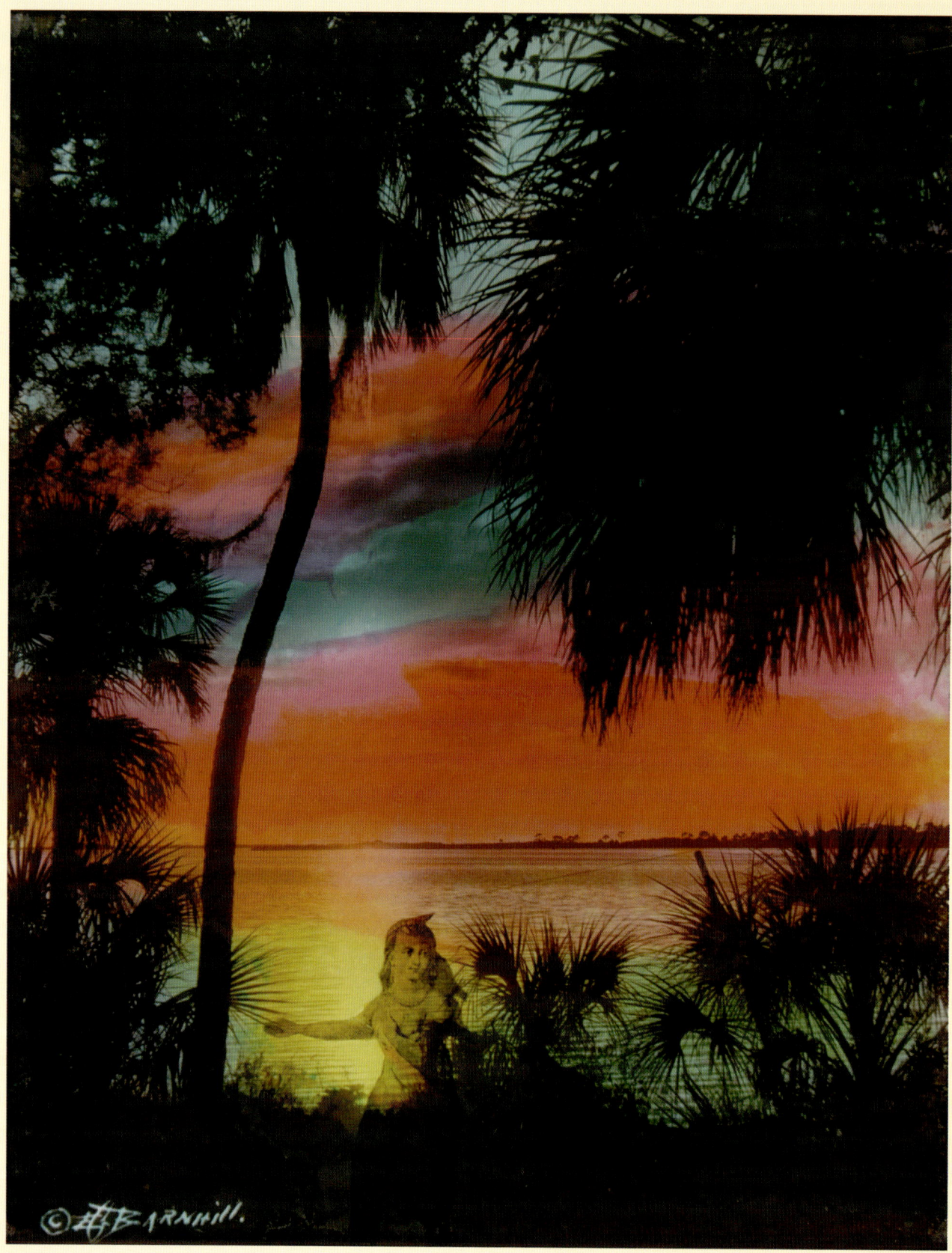

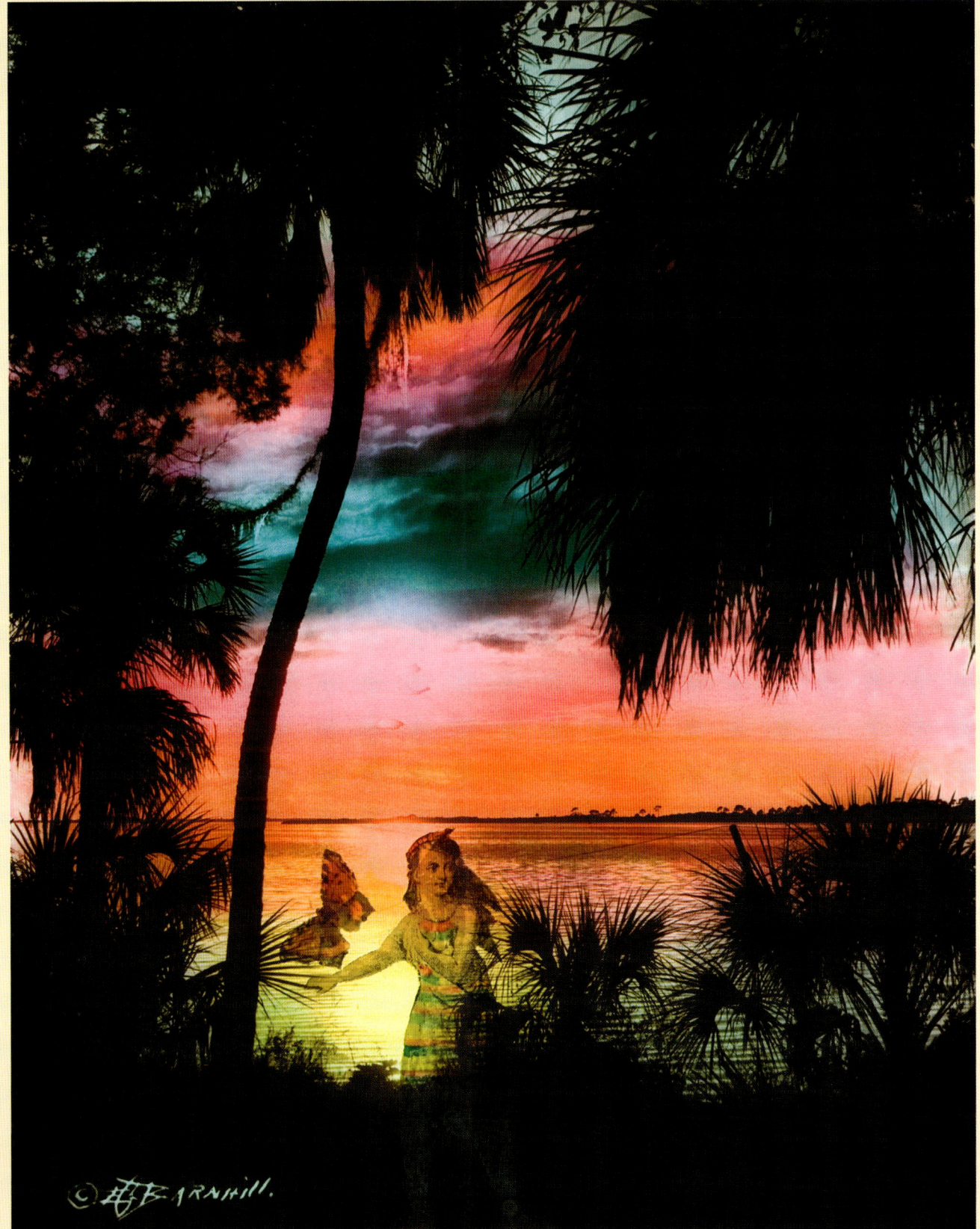

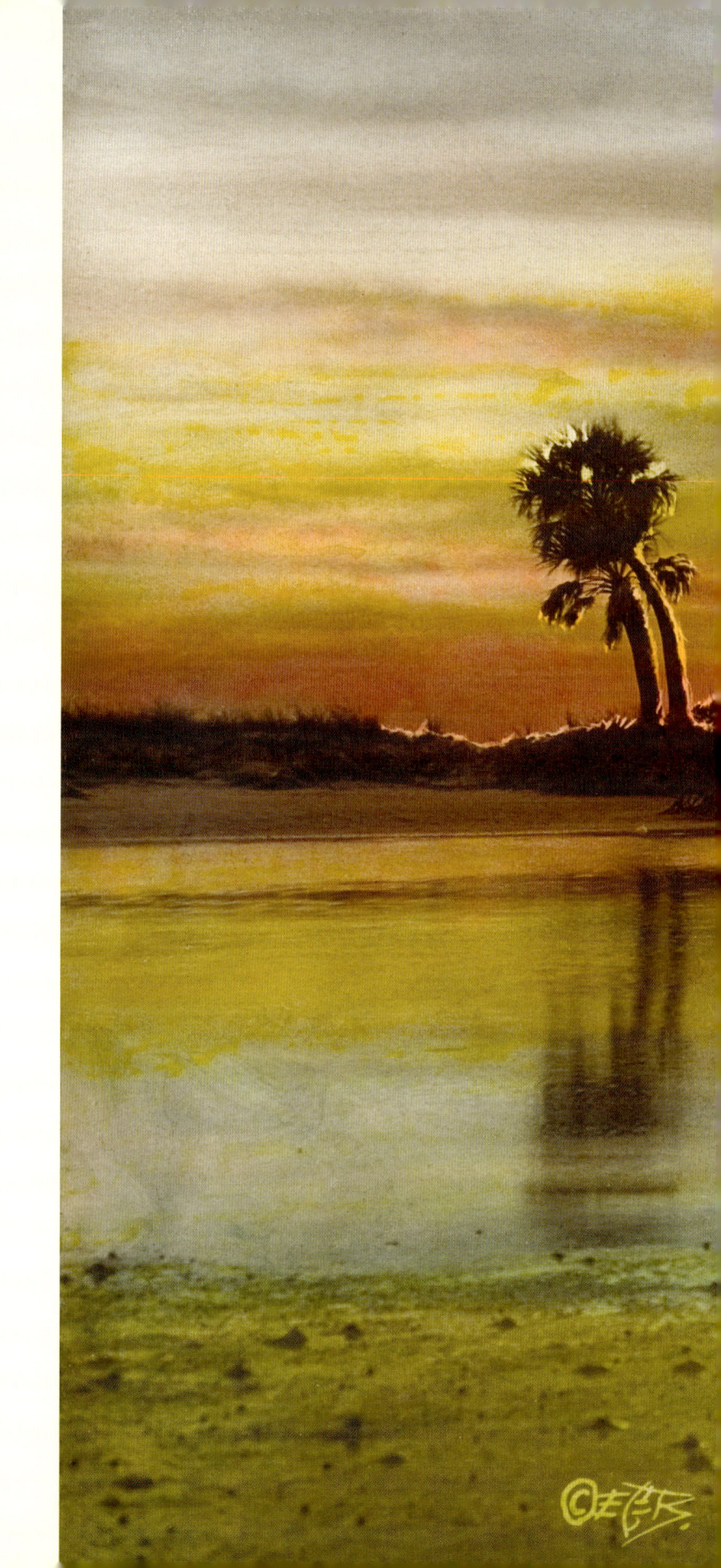

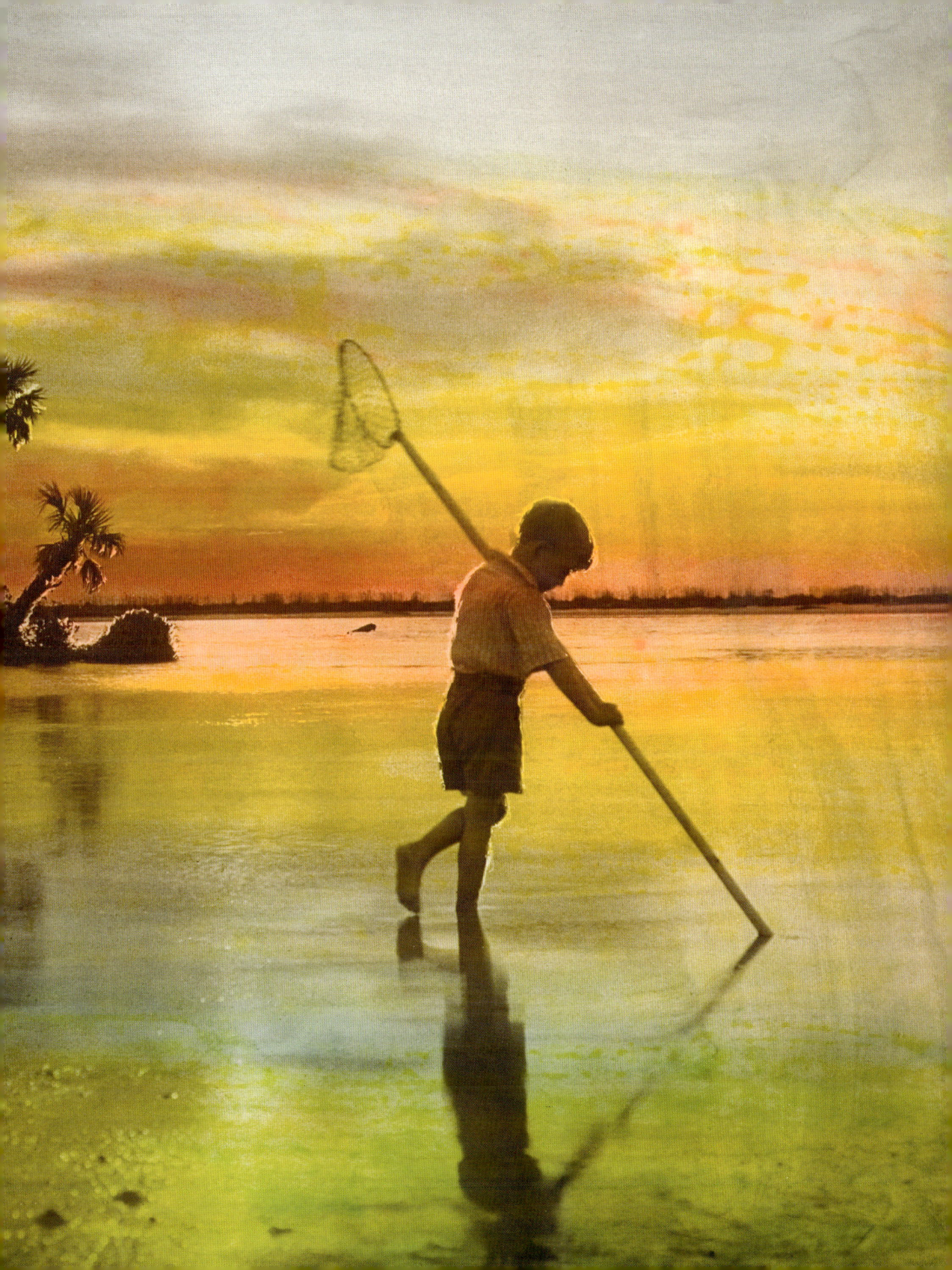

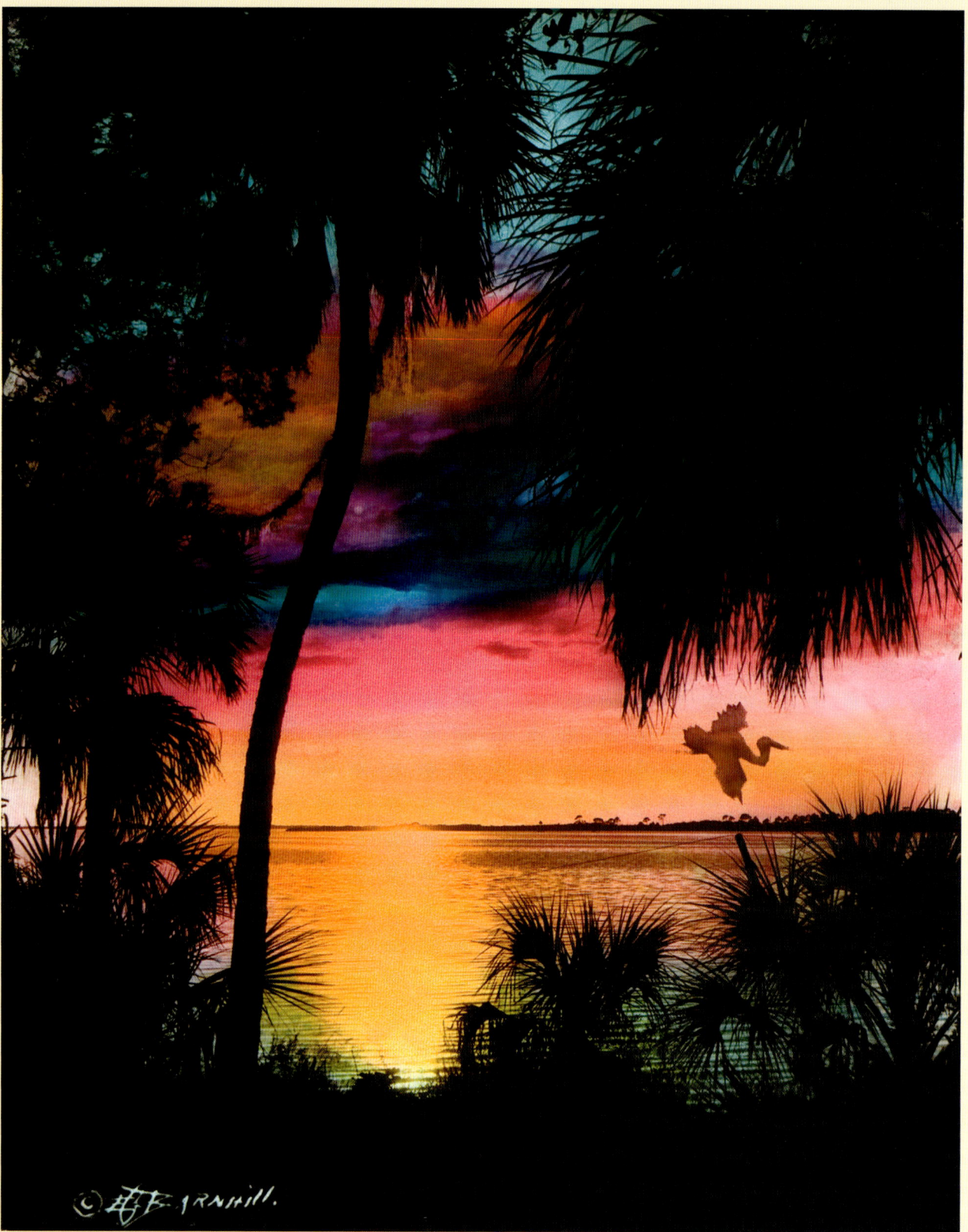

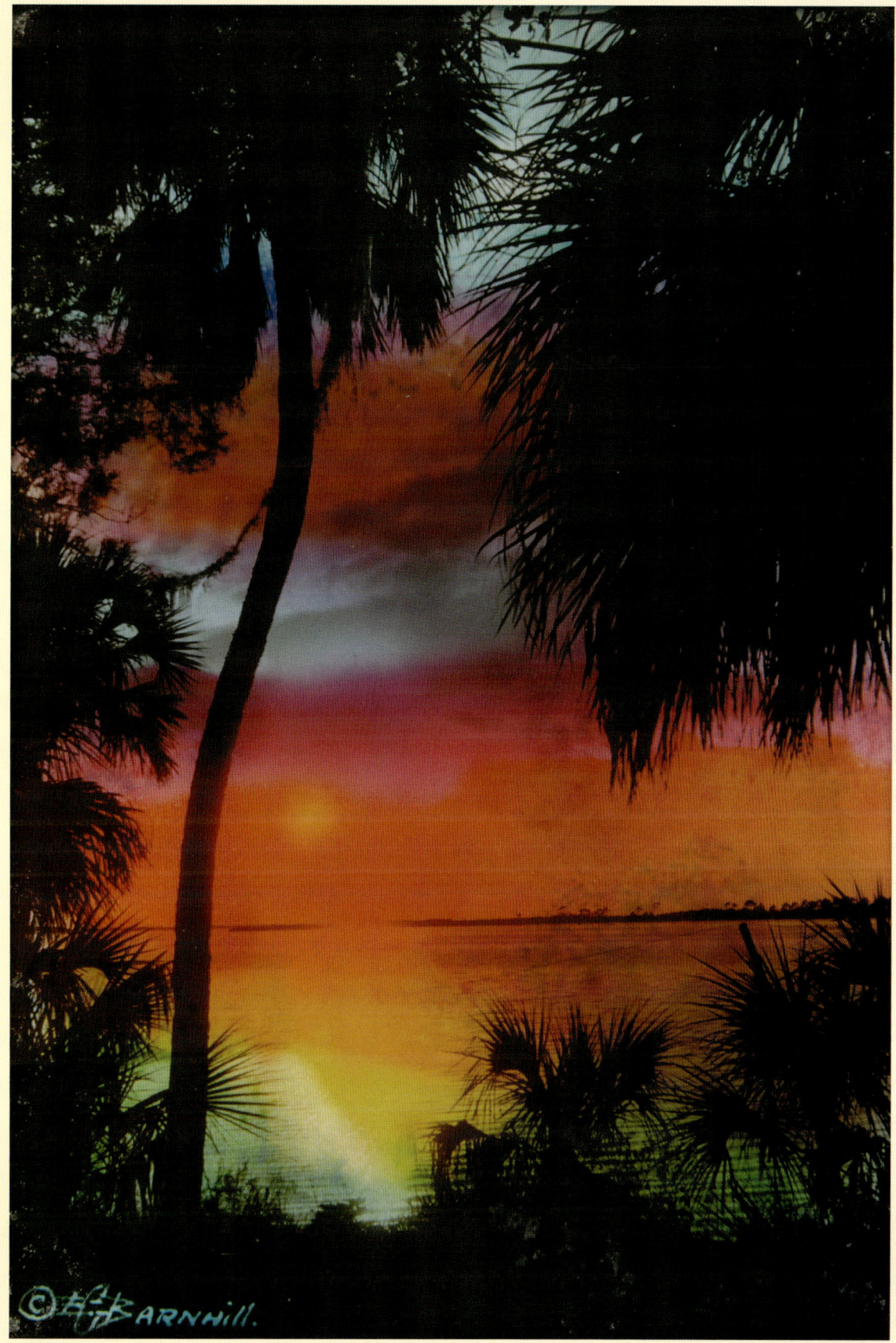

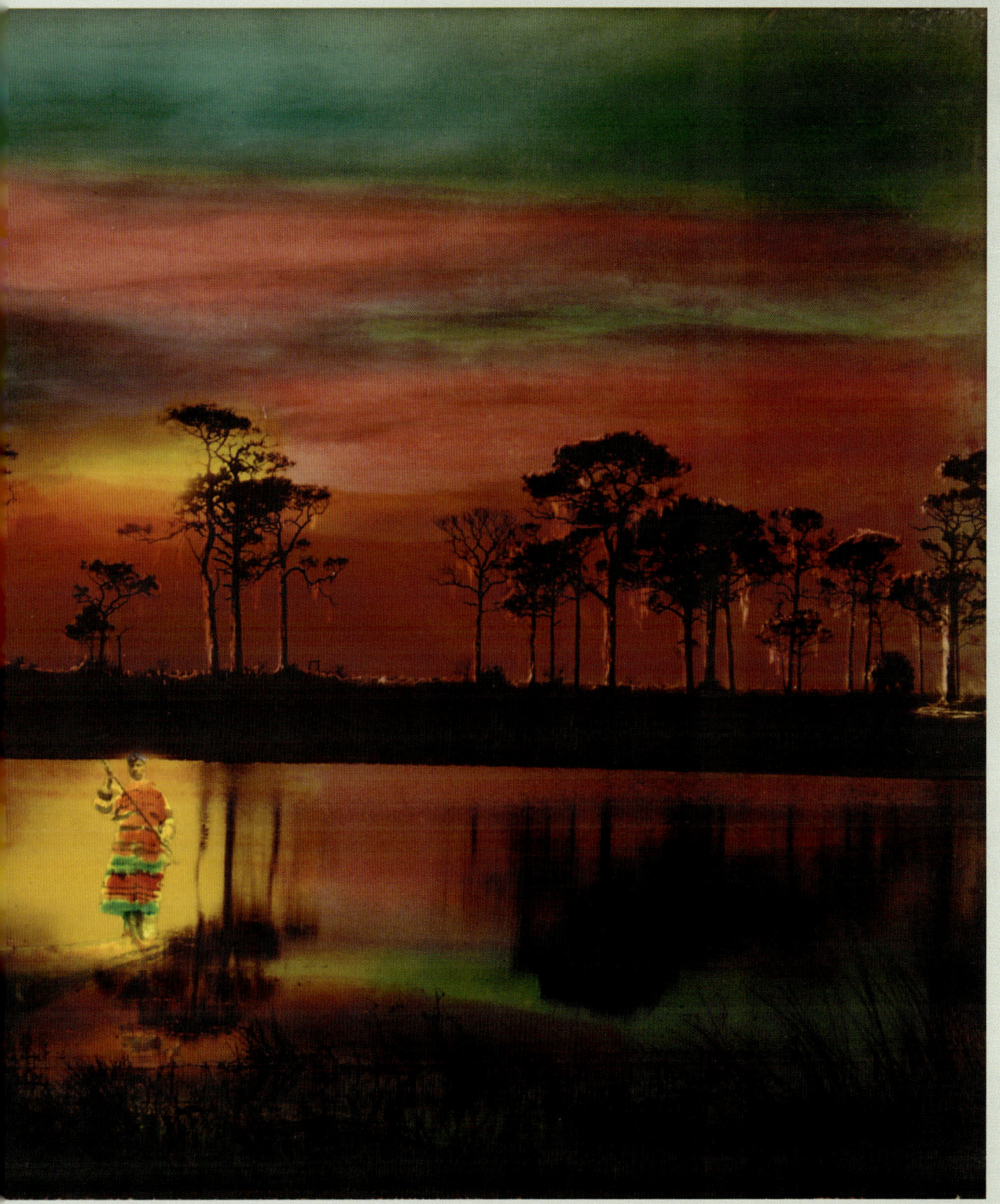

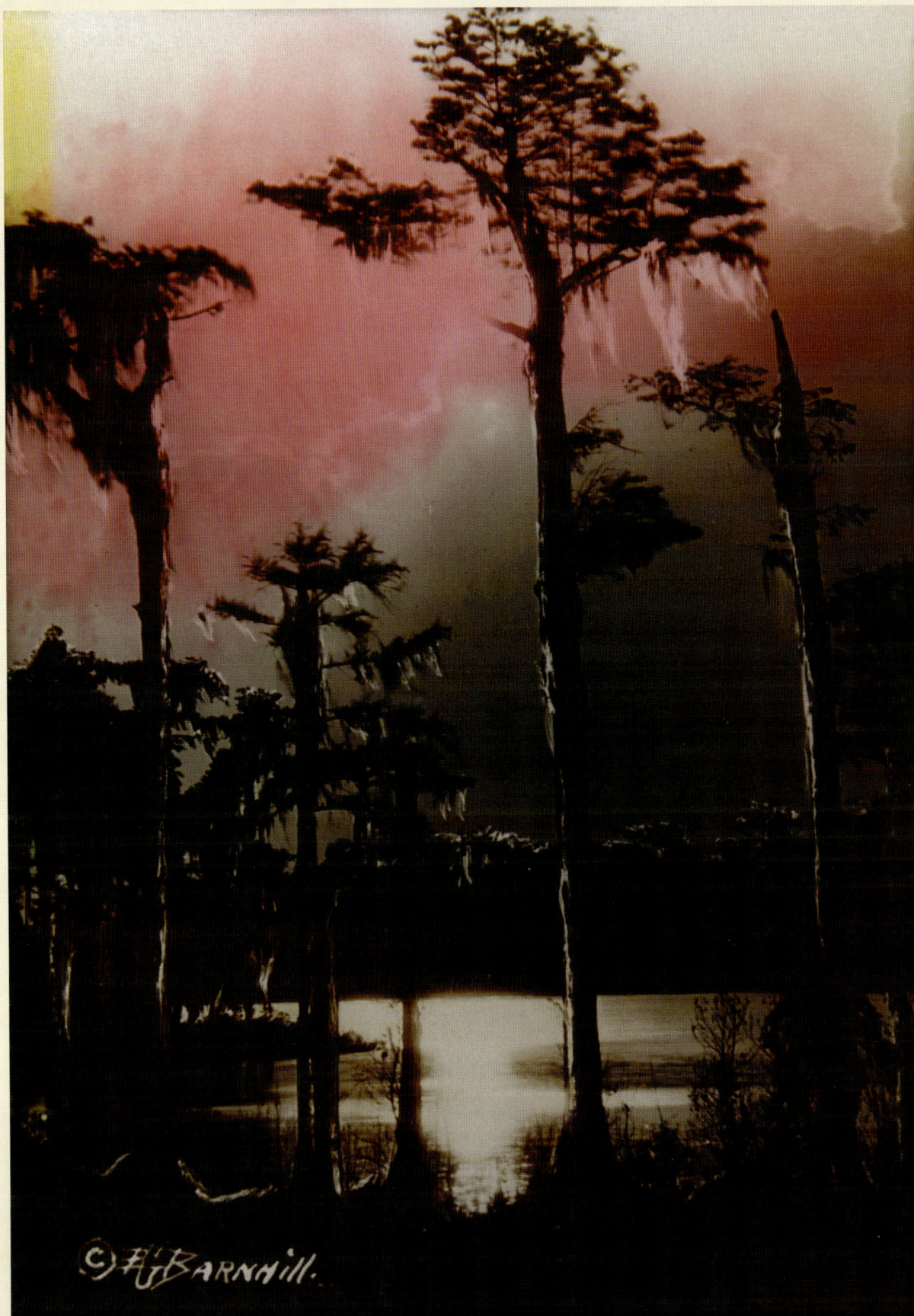

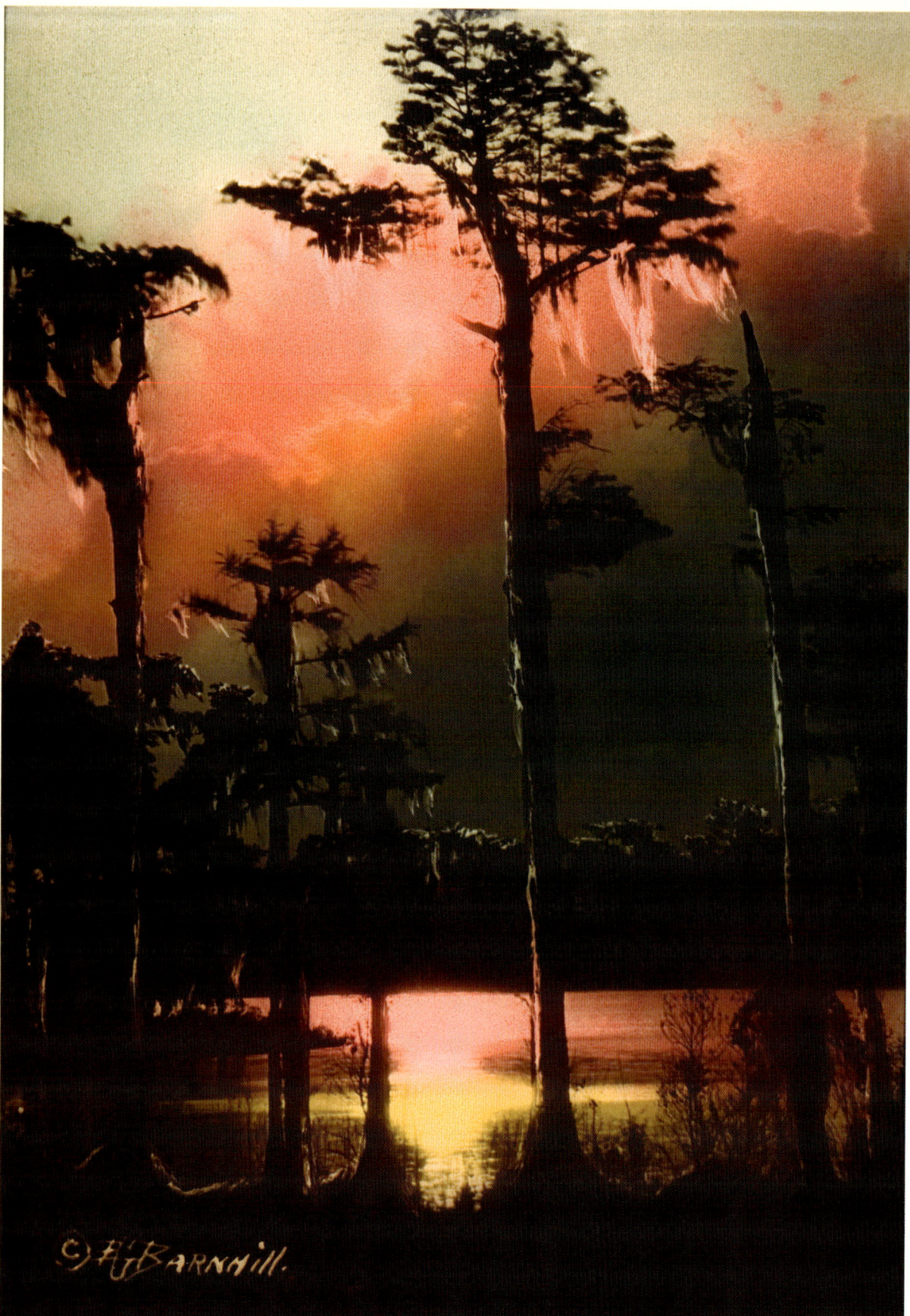

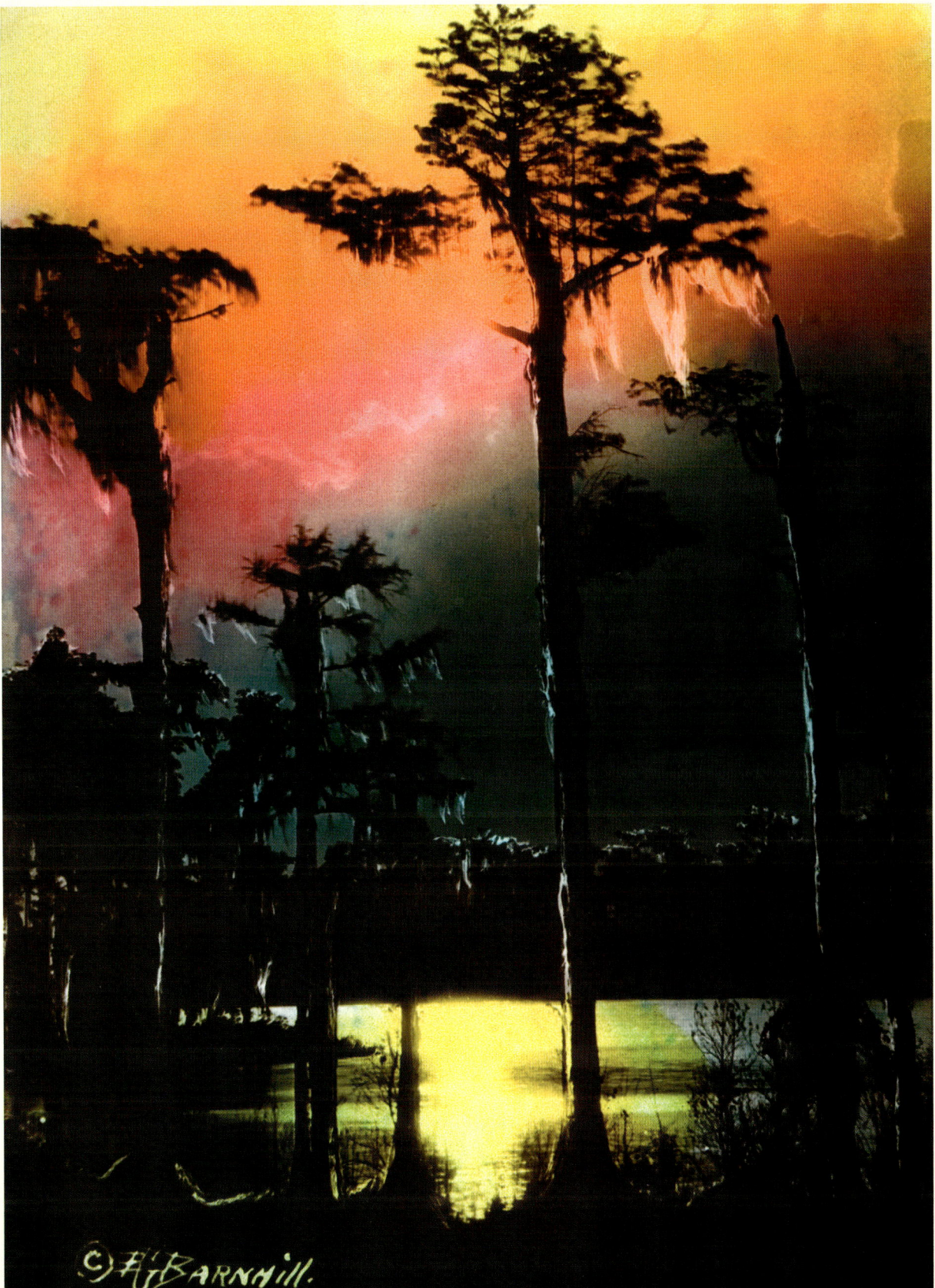

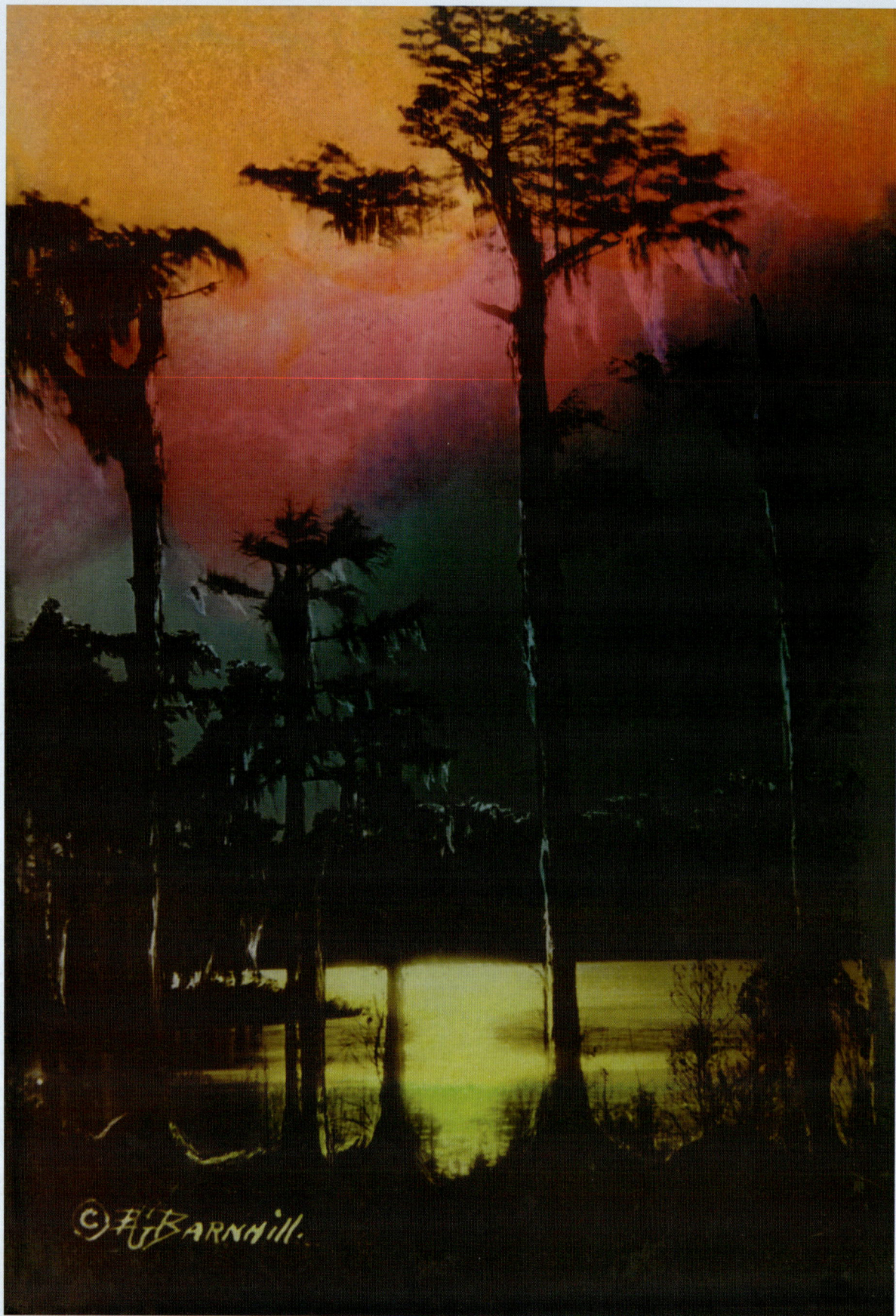

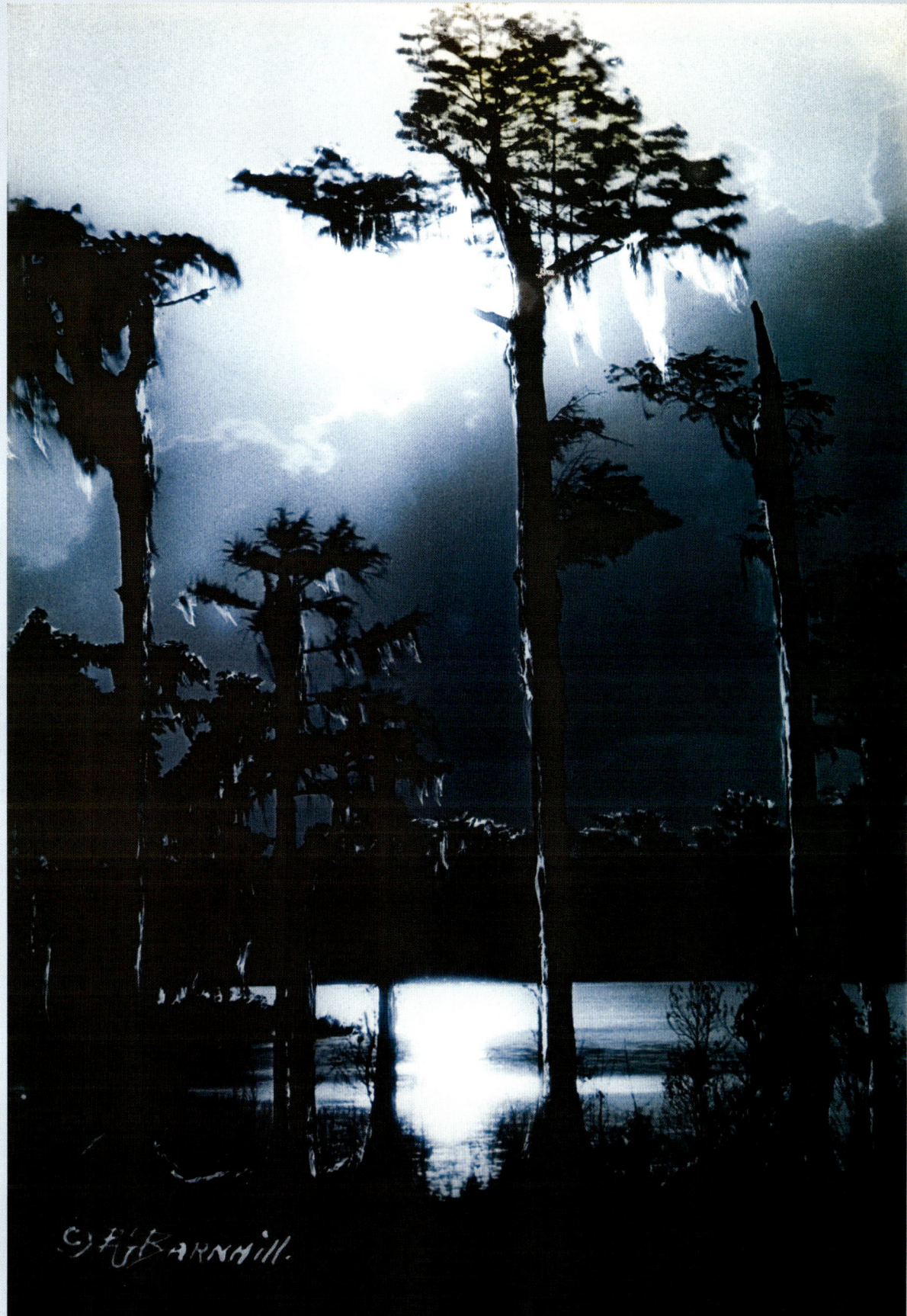

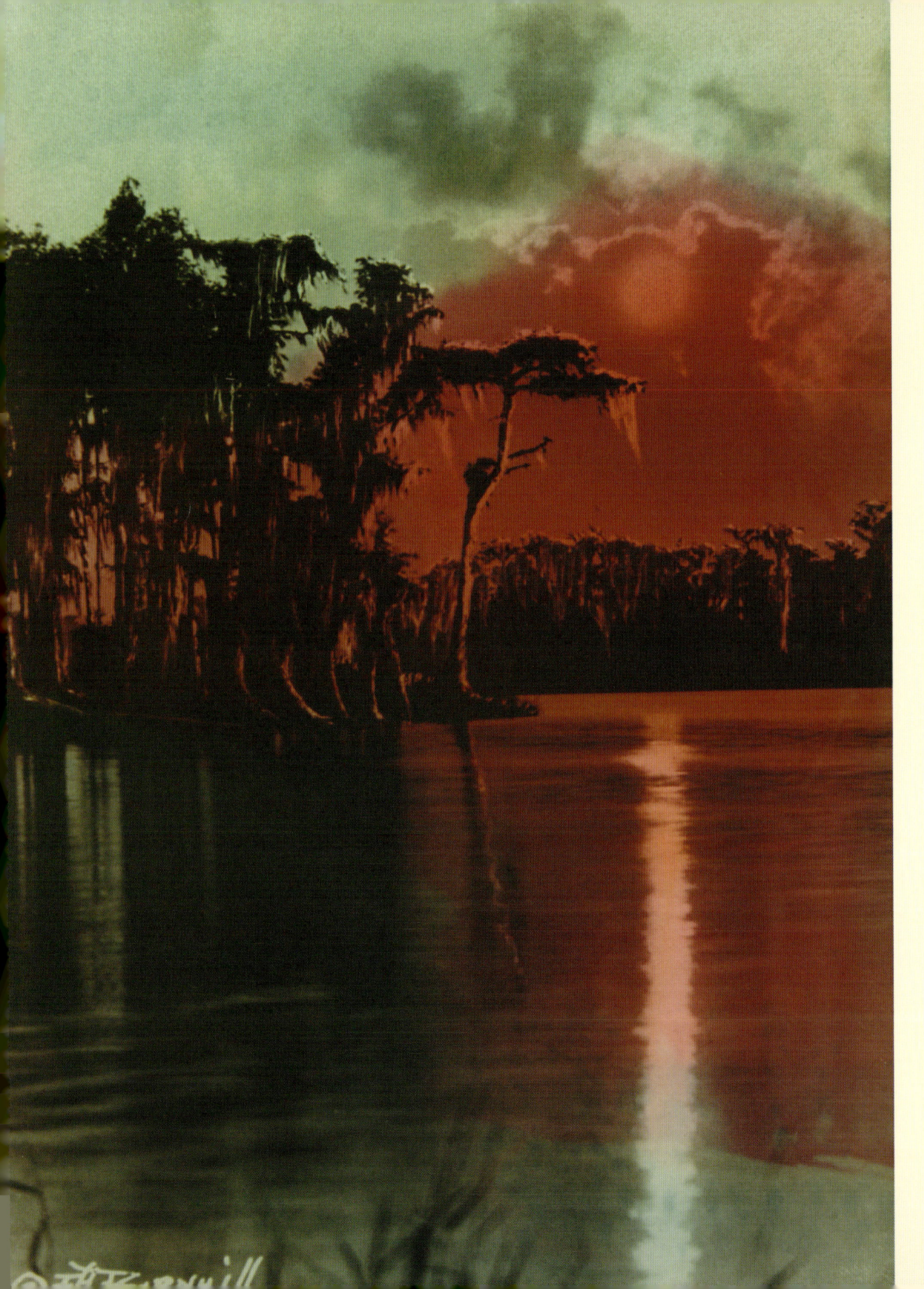

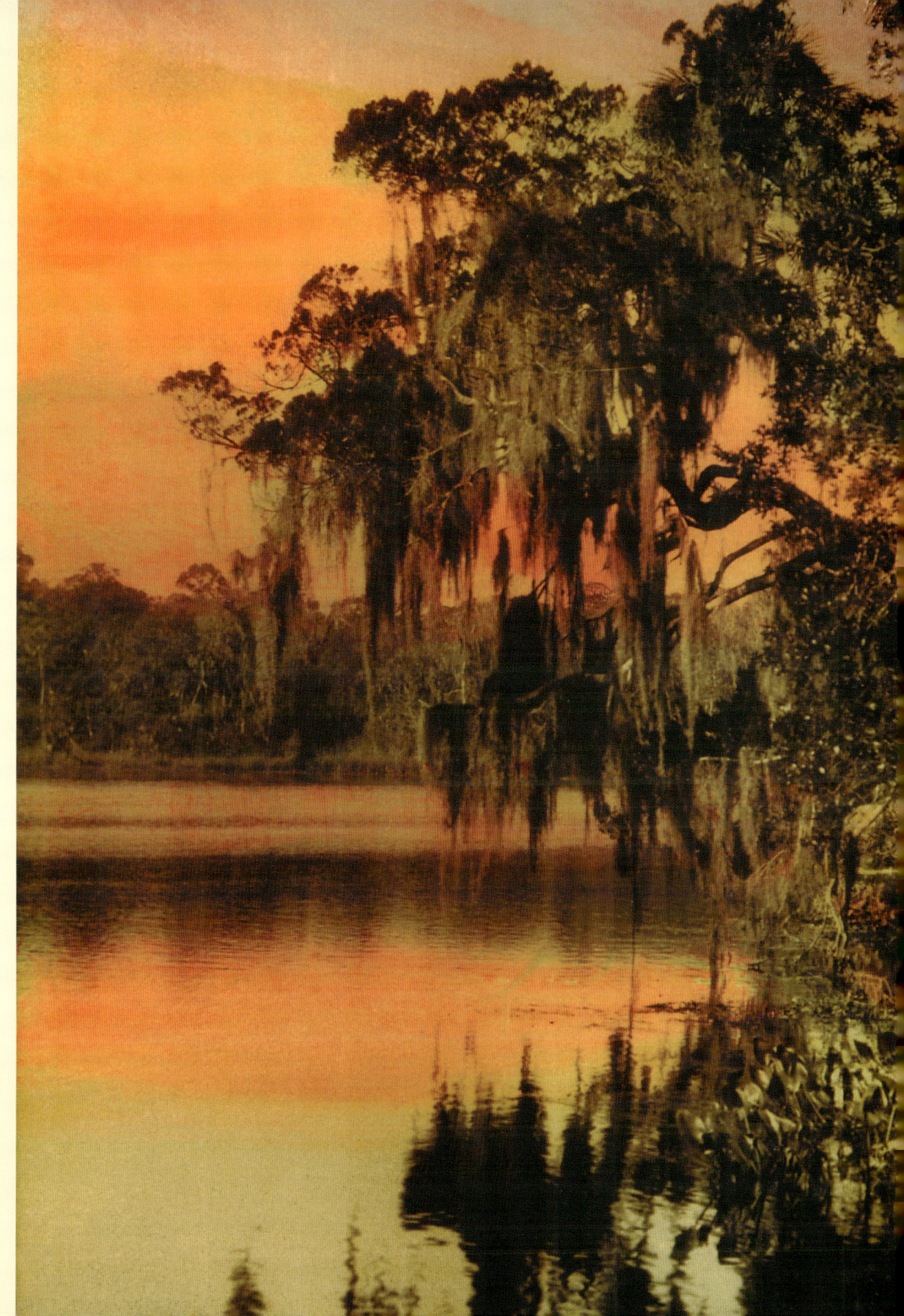

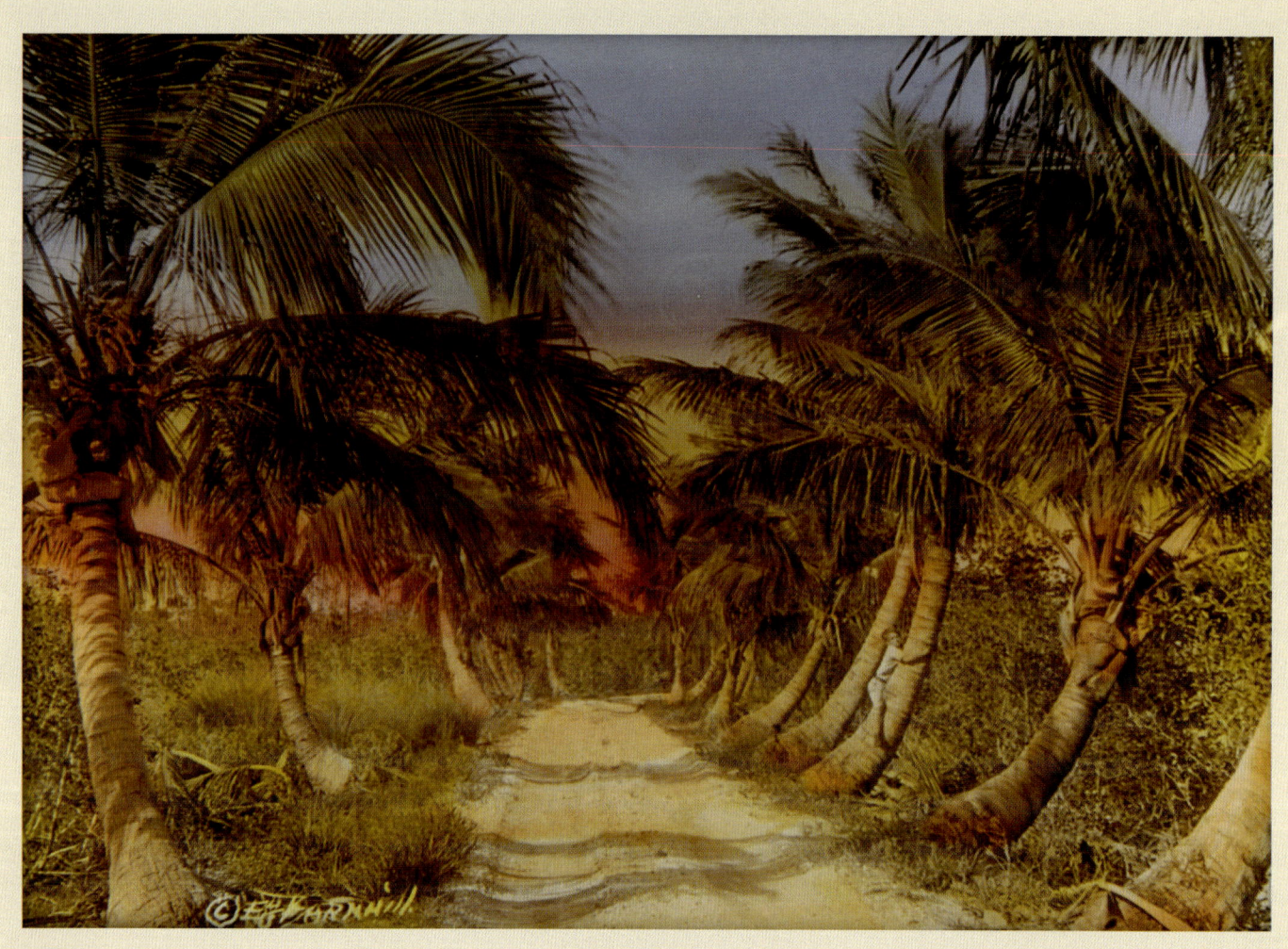

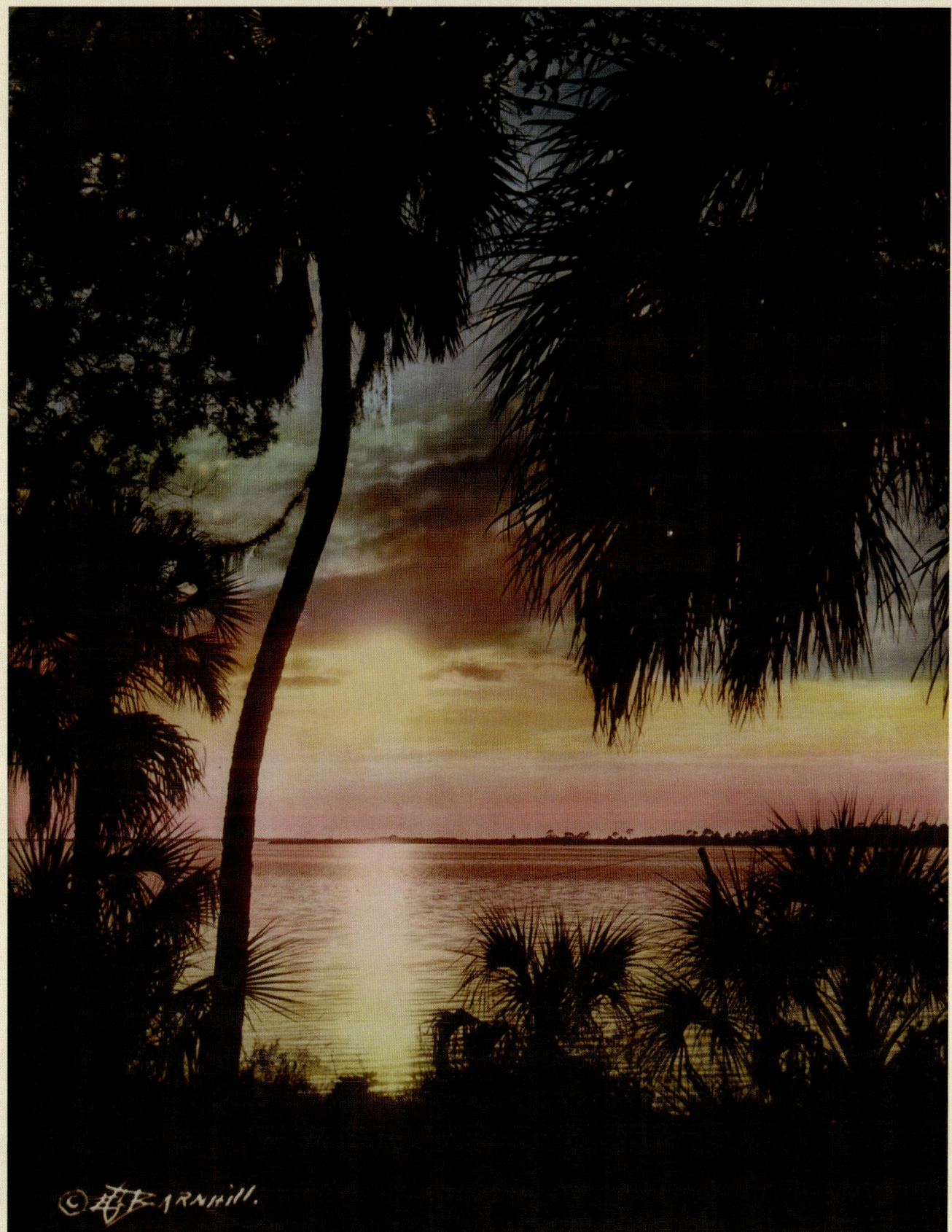

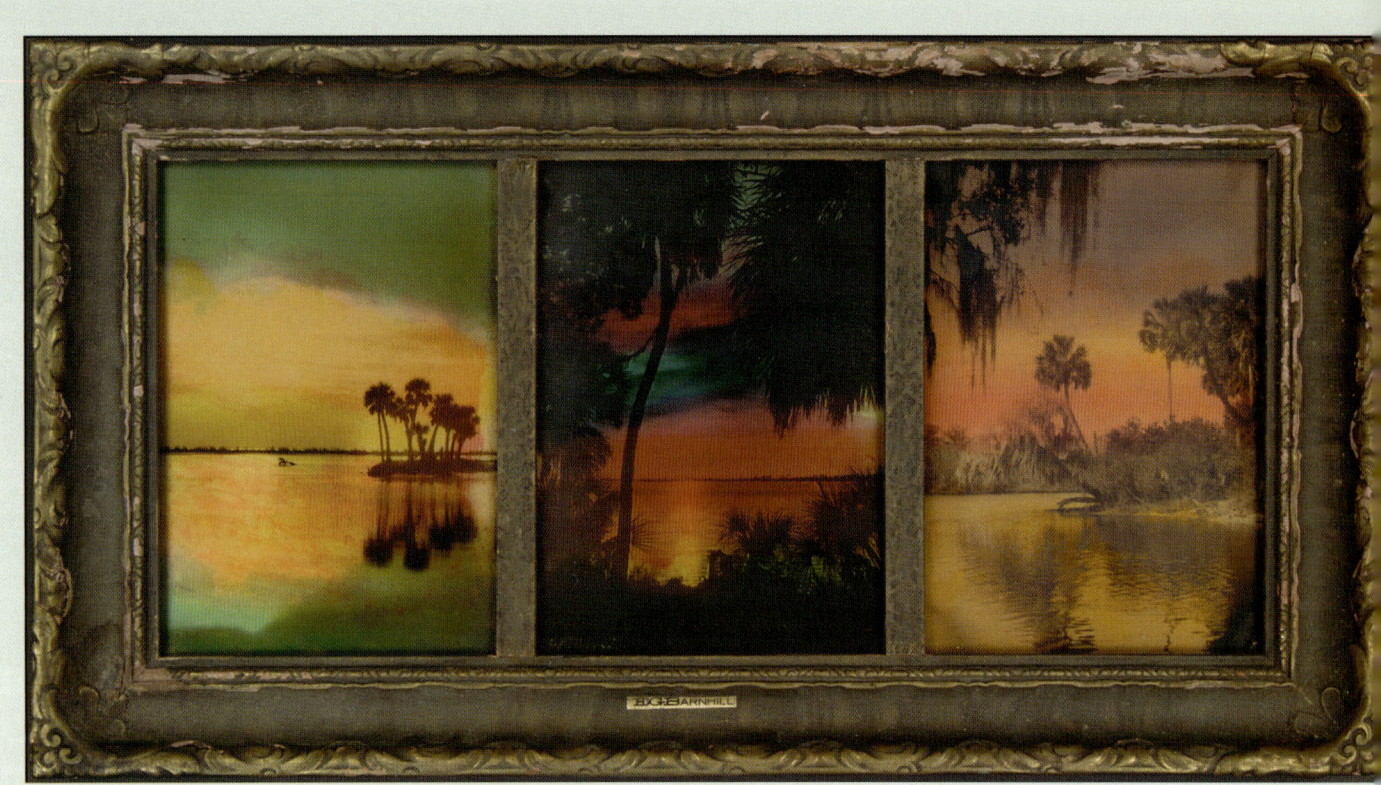

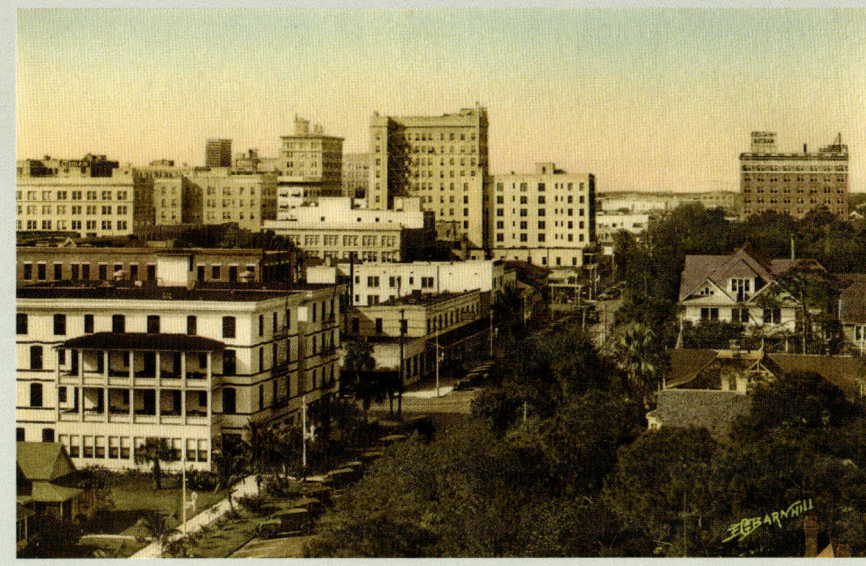

Skyline from Soreno Hotel, St. Petersburg, Florida

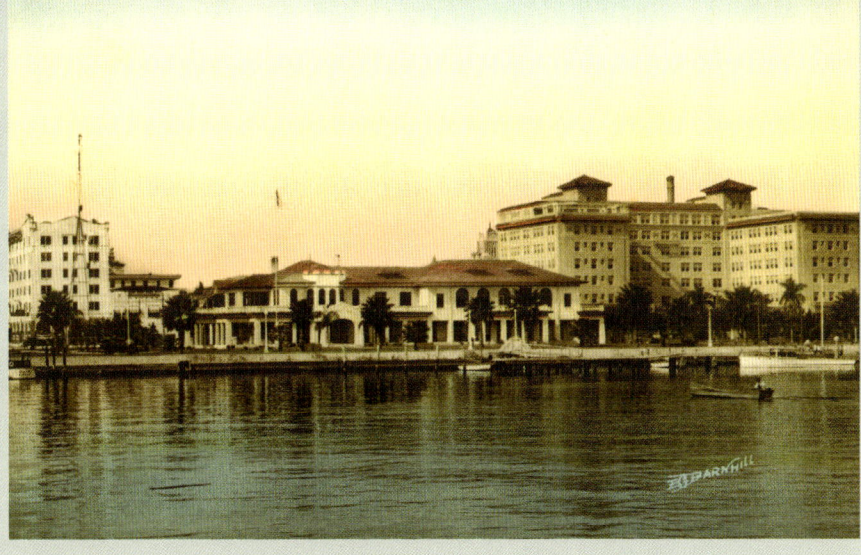

Ponce de Leon Hotel, Yacht Club, and Soreno Hotel, St. Petersburg, Florida

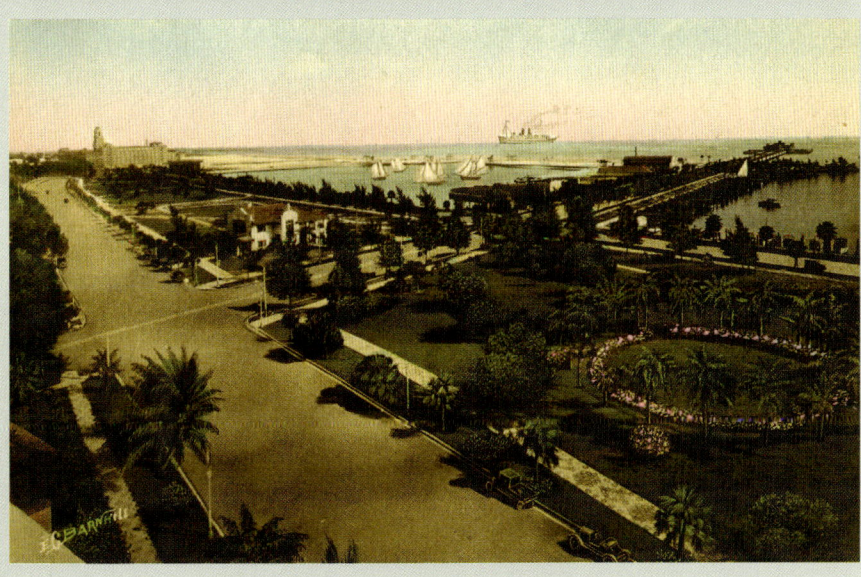

Bay Front Park, Vinoy Park Hotel, and Pier, St. Petersburg, Florida

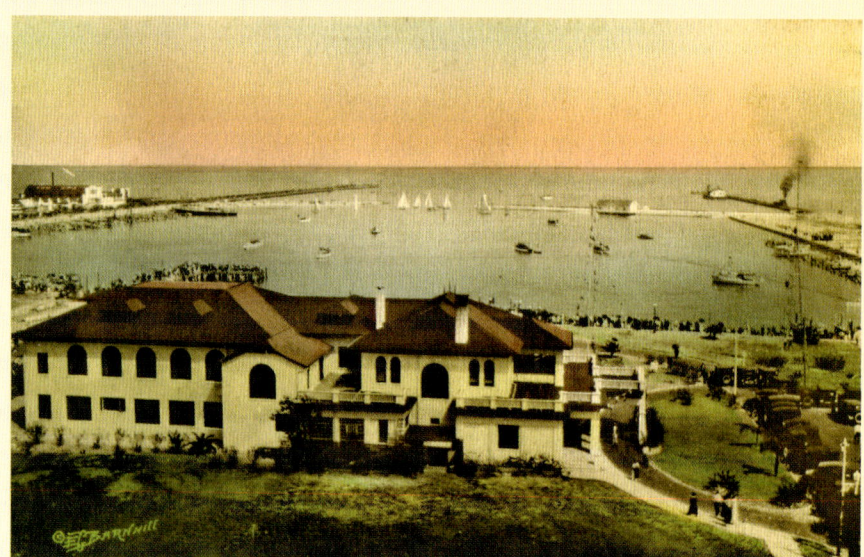

Yacht Club and Basin,
St. Petersburg, Florida

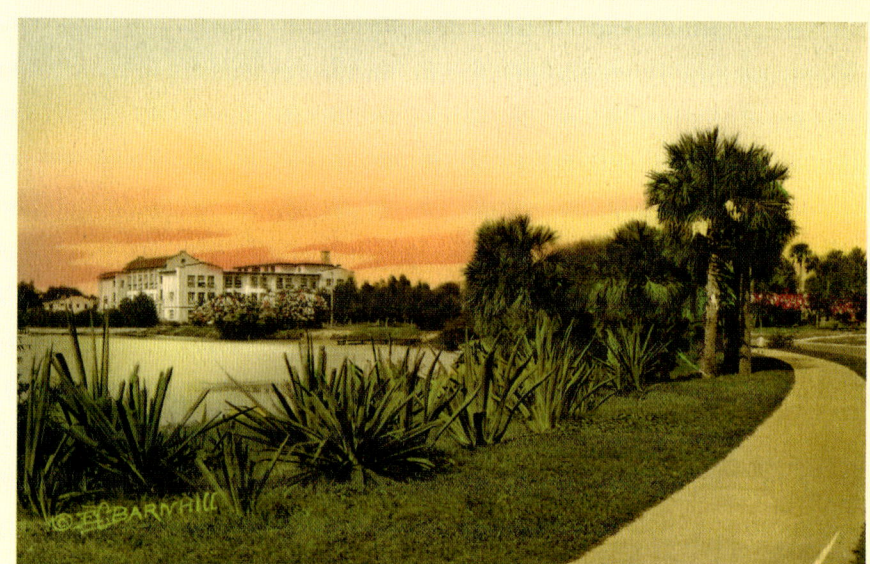

Mirror Lake Walk,
St. Petersburg, Florida

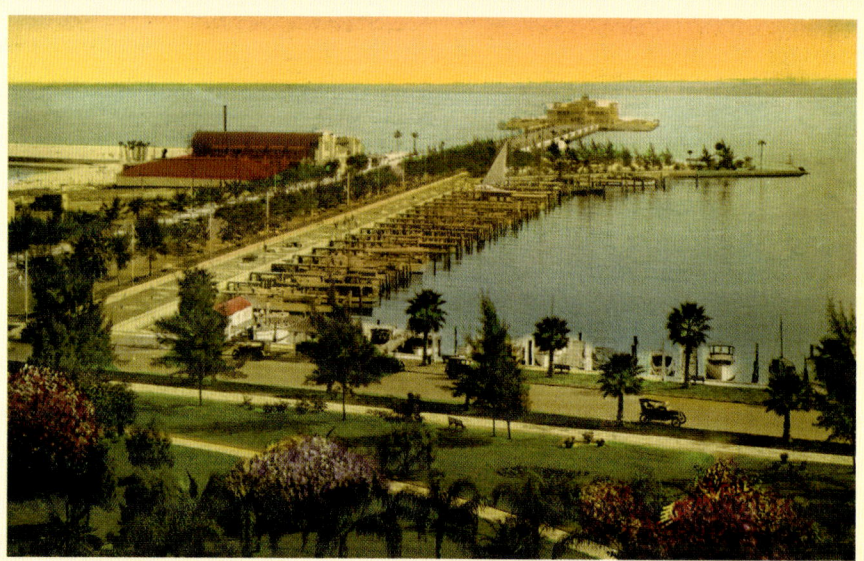

Pier from Soreno Hotel,
St. Petersburg, Florida

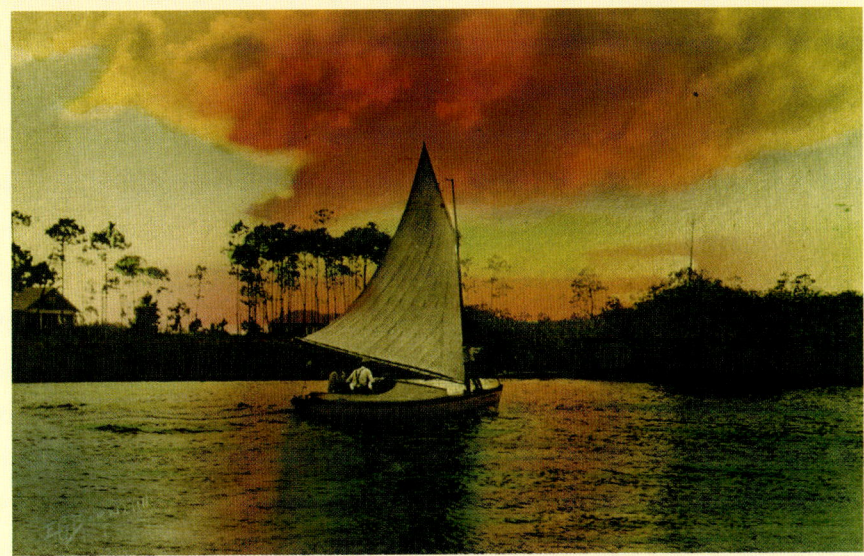

On Picturesque Clearwater
Bay, near St. Petersburg,
Florida

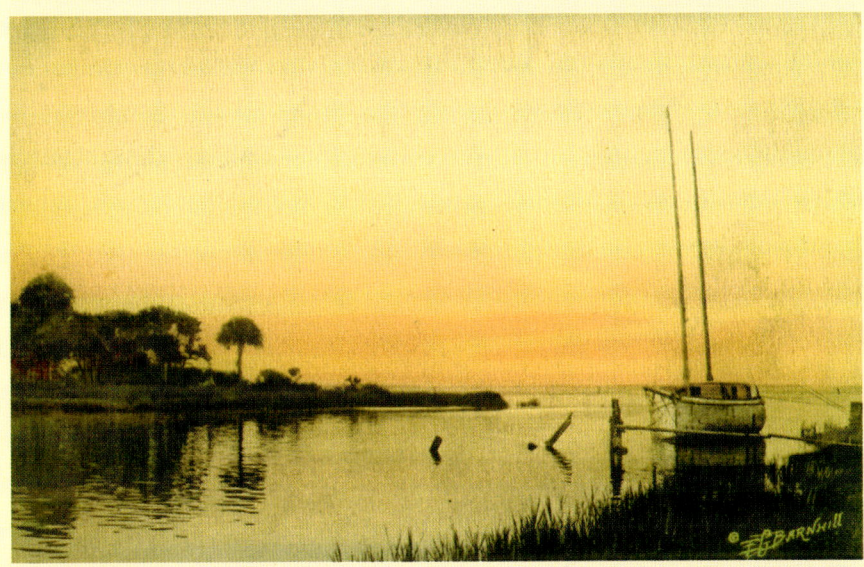

Big Bayou, St. Petersburg,
Florida

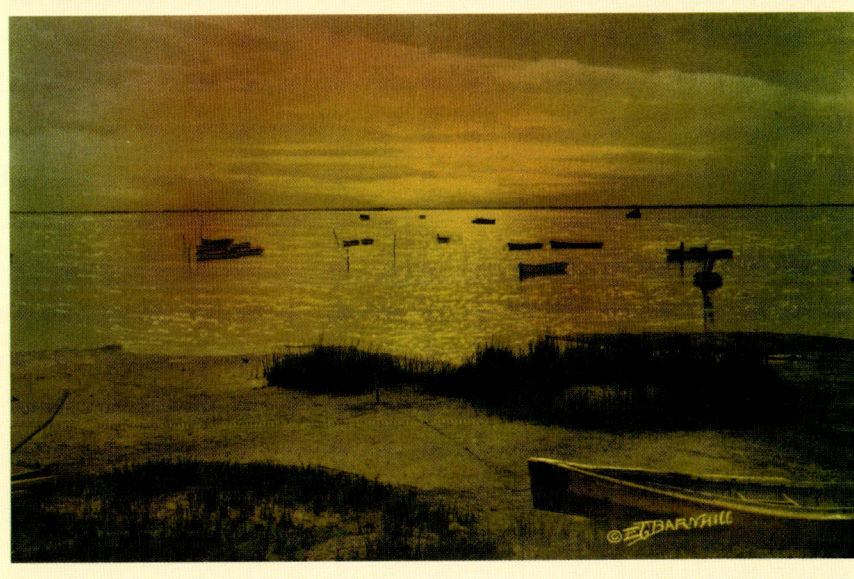

Sunset on Boca Ciega Bay,
St. Petersburg, Florida

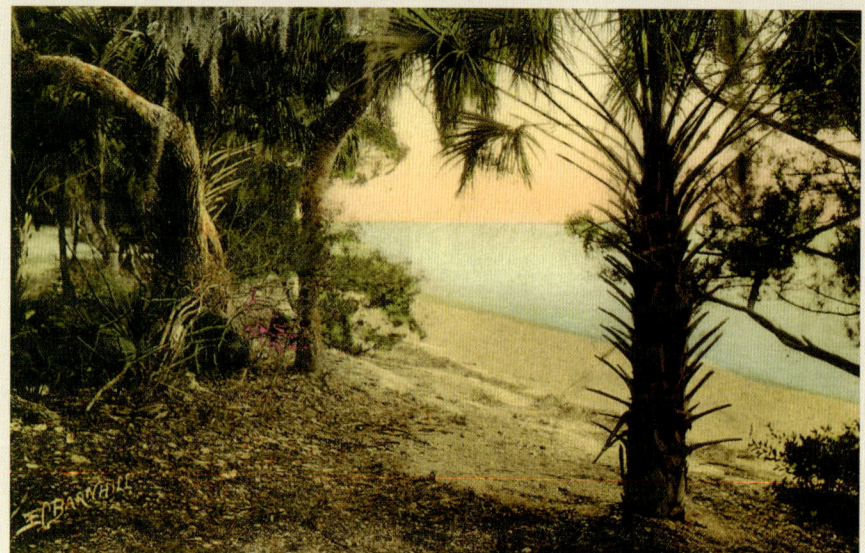

A Bit of Jungle Shore,
St. Petersburg, Florida

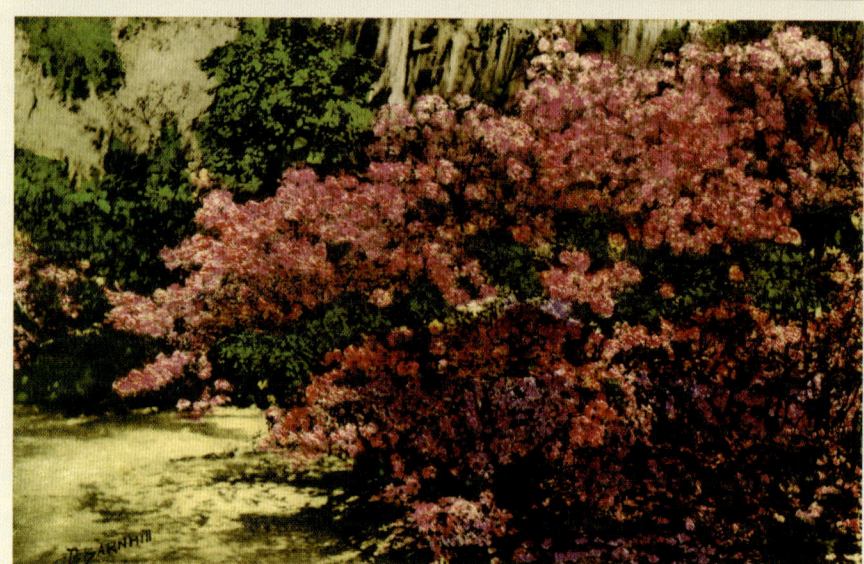

Hibiscus in Bloom,
St. Petersburg, Florida

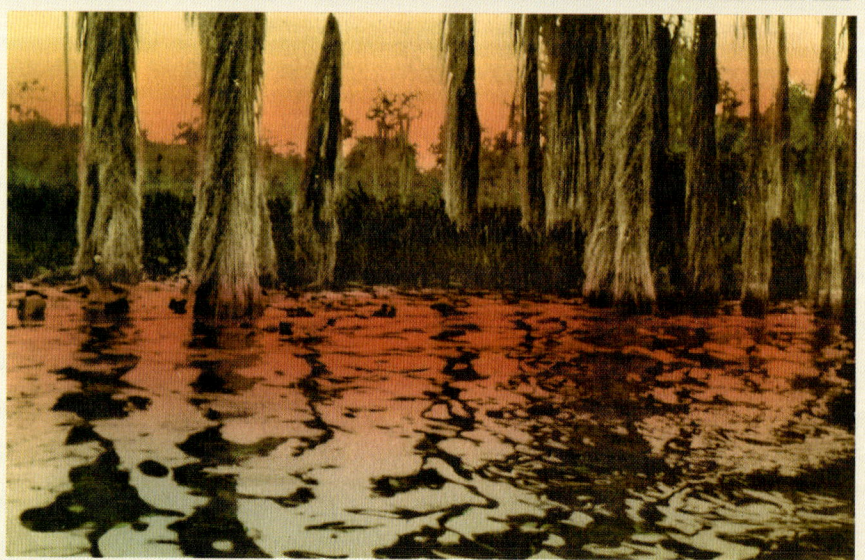

The Ghostly Sentinels,
St. Petersburg, Florida

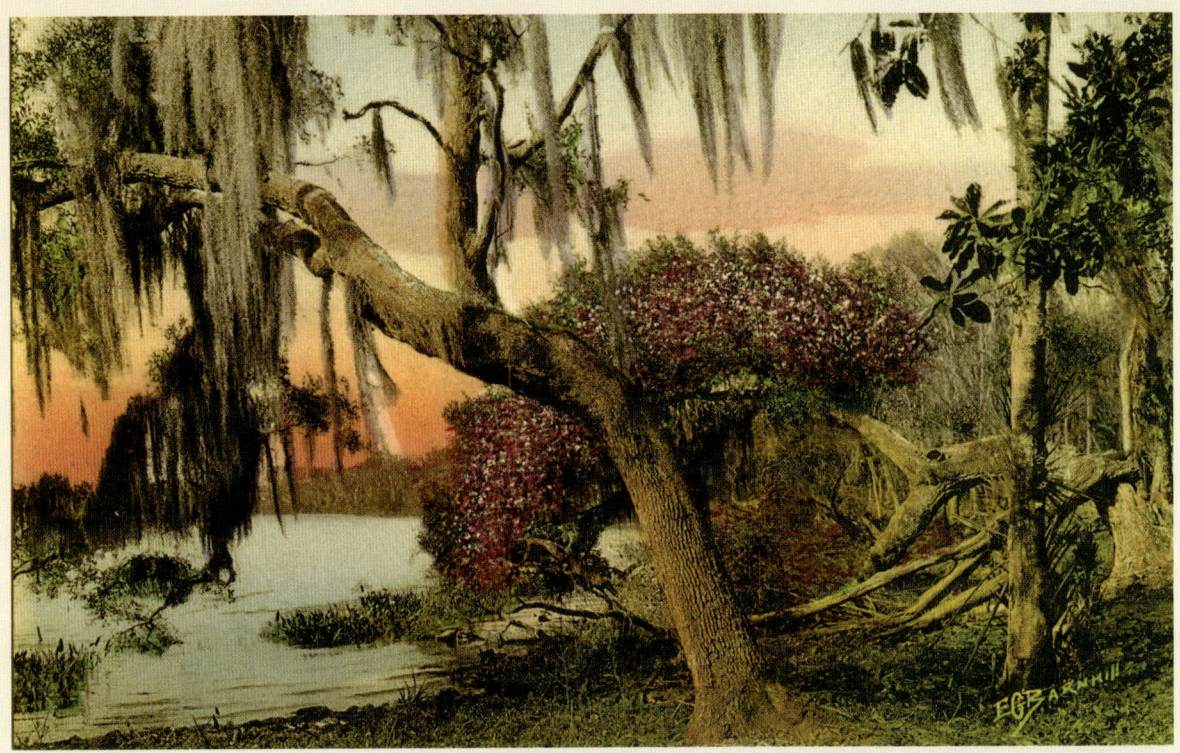

Along the North Shore of Tampa Bay, St. Petersburg, Florida

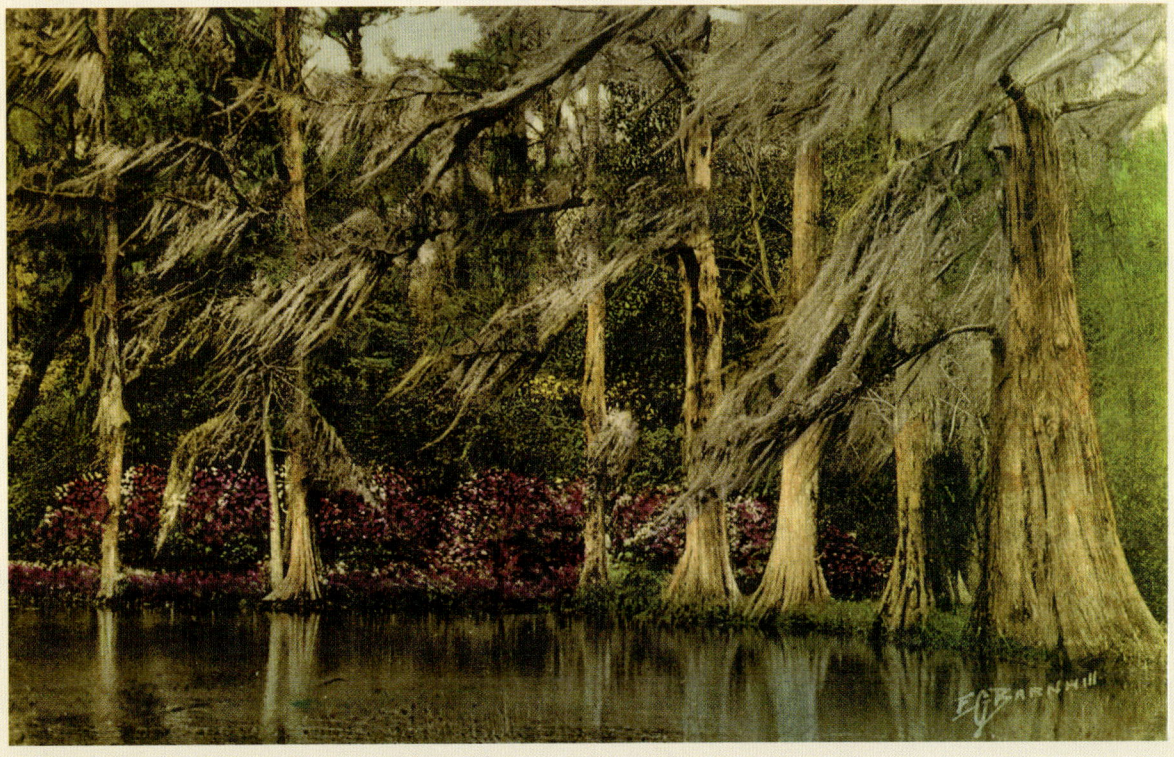

Moss-Laden Cypress Trees, St. Petersburg, Florida

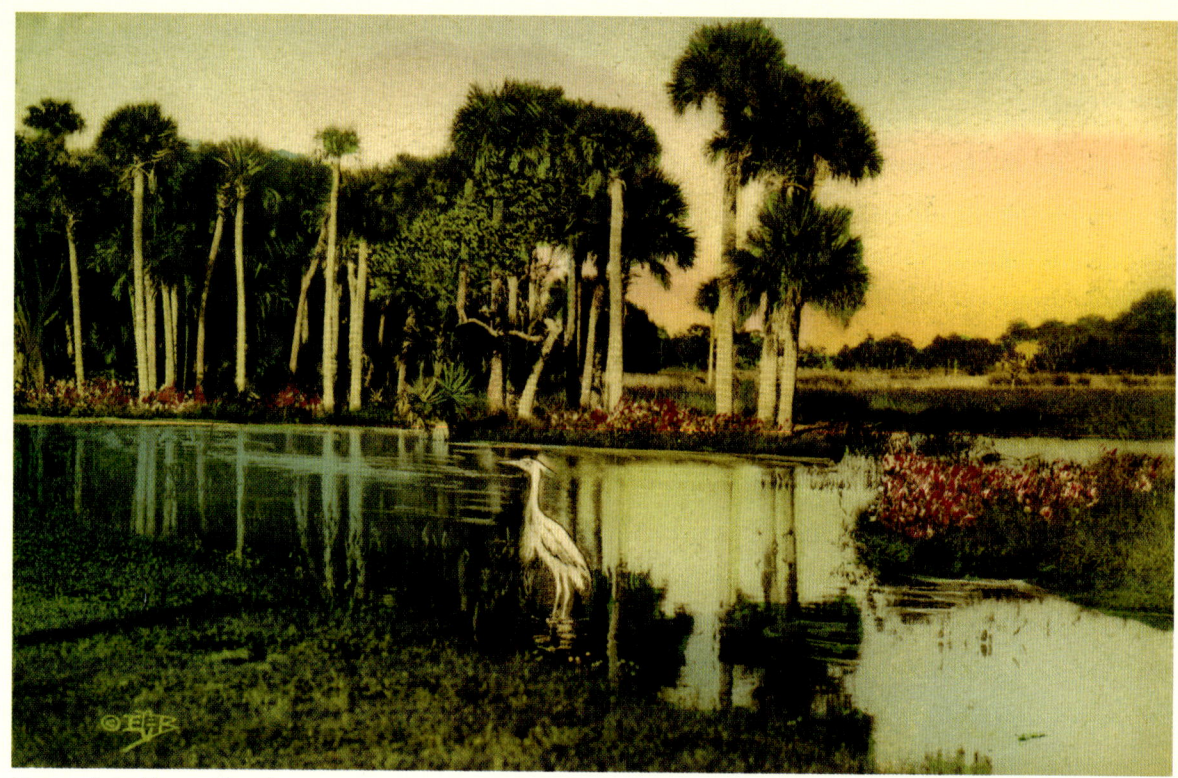

Home of the Heron, Florida

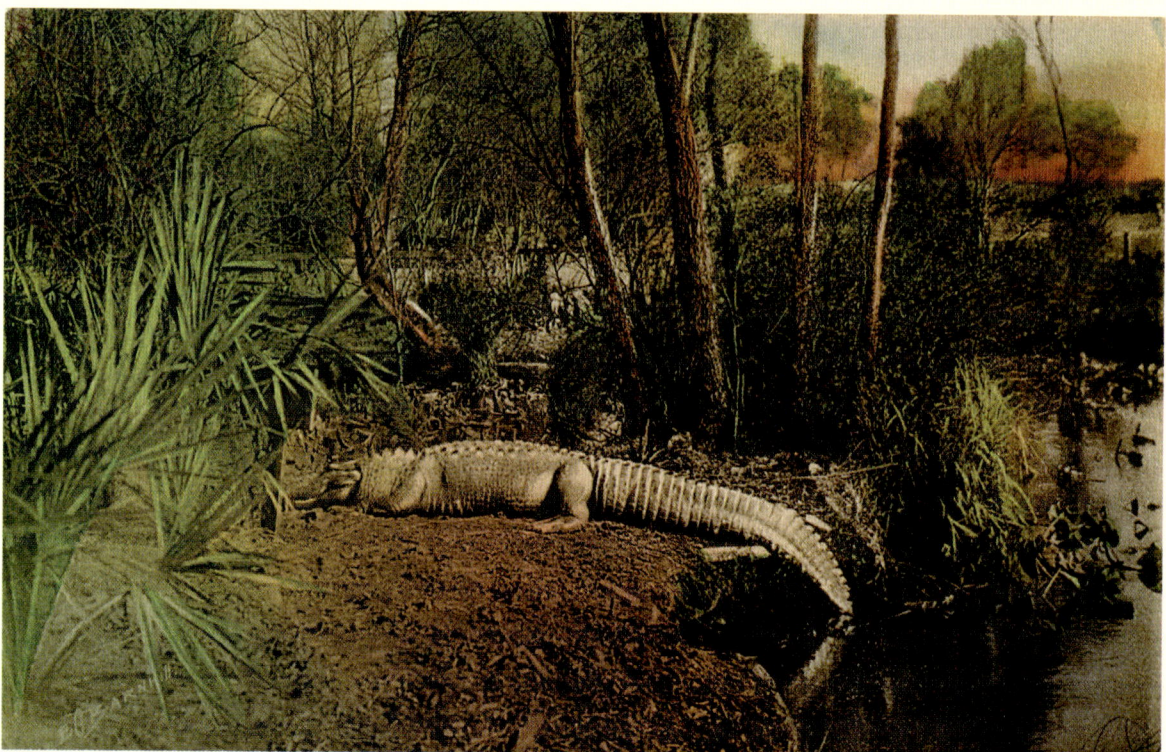

Having a Sun Bath, Florida

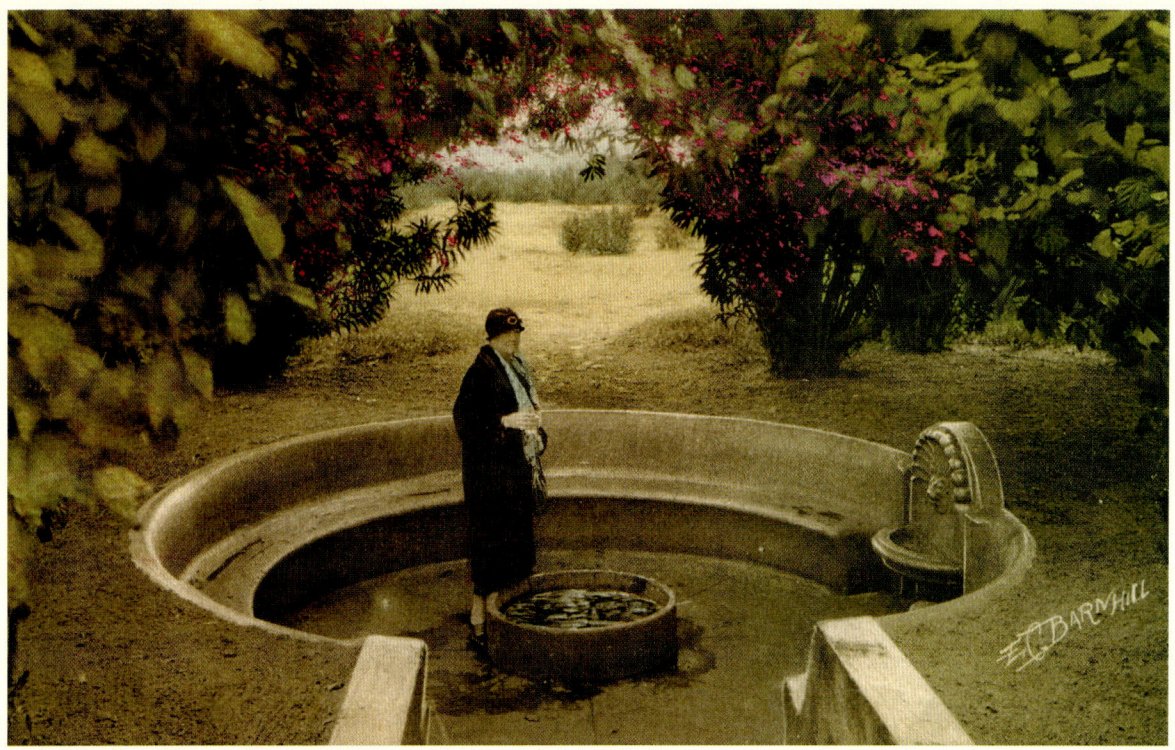

Fountain of Youth, St. Petersburg, Florida

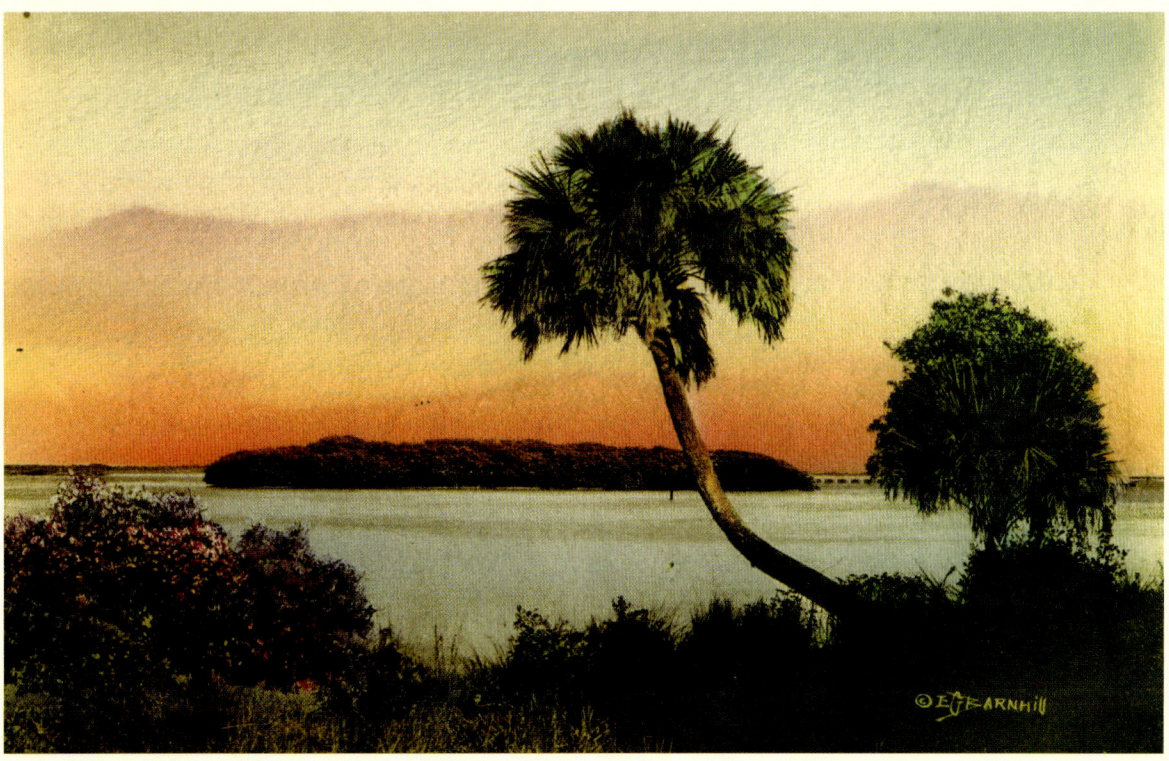

The Island, Boca Ciega Bay, at Pass-a-Grille, Florida

Acknowledgments

The Barnhill families were especially gracious in sharing their histories and remembrances. Early in my interviews, I recognized that they all possess the Barnhill charm—a warm, engaging, and disarming quality. I spent a lot of time with Jack, who was magnanimous during all our conversations. Clayton and Margaret were equally generous and enthusiastic, as was their sister, Betty. Their children, E.G.'s grandchildren Cindy Robb, Peggy Camps, Clay Barnhill, Nancy Hayden, and Linda Scott, greeted me with good cheer and assistance. Linda and her husband, Les, helped in the amassing of Barnhill photographs, and in getting these professionally photographed. E.G.'s late-in-life friend, Virginia Howard, and her assistant, Mary Fisher, at Four Winds Village were helpful as well.

As always, the staff of the University Press of Florida were respectful of Barnhill's lifework; they helped me do it justice. I am grateful to Meredith Morris-Babb, director and my editor; project editor Michele Fiyak-Burkley; copy editor Ann Marlowe; Anja Jimenez and Larry Leshan in design and production; and Romi Gutierrez in marketing. Also, I am indebted to John Knaub, director of photography at the University of Florida, and Jon Nalon, a photographer in Tallahassee, who with skill and pride made the digital files from which the book was printed. They deserve a world of thanks. Barnhill's glass plates posed technical problems that each man solved after great trials and efforts. Watching them grapple with the lighting and processing was inspiring.

I am grateful to many fine and selfless writers, librarians, curators, and dealers, especially those who sympathized with my search to connect Barnhill to Edward Curtis, a generally fruitless, but necessary, task. They helped me ultimately to define Esmond Grenard Barnhill. I thank Mick Gidley, who wrote *Edward S. Curtis and the North American Indian,*

Incorporated, and Barbara A. Davis, author of *Edward S. Curtis: The Life and Times of a Shadow Catcher*. Tracey Schuster of the Getty Research Institute's Research Library, Christine Nelson of Literary and Historical Manuscripts at the Morgan Library & Museum, and James Stack of the University of Washington Libraries' Special Collections Division were equally diligent and kind. Dennis McBride with the Boulder City/Hoover Dam Museum and Jeff Nichols at Westminster College in Salt Lake City helped me to illuminate Barnhill's western influences. Bruce Kapson of Bruce Kapson Gallery in Santa Monica and Lois Flury of Flury & Company in Seattle also offered valuable insights.

Dan McKenna and John McSwain, each a collector and a dedicated historian, helped me sort things out about Barnhill and his times. John and Ellen Leverett helped me better understand their great-uncle, the painter J. R. Wilcox. Archaeologist Bob Carr clarified points about Barnill's Ancient America museum, which he had visited in his youth and which had affected his subsequent interests. Dick and Yvonne Punnett, passionate researchers and archivists of Florida photography, frequently and gladly opened their plentiful files to me, working patiently with me over the long haul.

Kathy Turgeon deserves special recognition. More than a decade before I became interested in Barnhill, she initiated painstaking research into his life. We met after I had completed the draft of my essay. Kathy agreed to share her acquired investigative and authoritative information to ensure that all the factual bases were accurately covered. Together we checked facts and fleshed out certain information about the glimmerman Barnhill. His son Clay once described his dad's life and affairs as "such a mixed-up deal"; Kathy largely straightened them out.

I am inexpressibly thankful to my friend and editor Margie Miller; saying any more would only detract from all she does to help me write and read well. I am grateful also to her husband, Mel, for letting me take up so much of their time.

Of course, I remain humbly and gratefully indebted to my wife, Teresa, and our children, Matt and Jessica, for indulging me in "just one more book."

GARY MONROE is professor of fine arts and photography at Daytona State College. His photographs have been exhibited across the nation and are published in books and exhibition catalogs. He is the author of *Mary Ann Carroll: First Lady of the Highwaymen*, *Silver Springs: The Underwater Photography of Bruce Mozert*, *The Highwaymen Murals: Al Black's Concrete Dreams*, and *The Highwaymen: Florida's African-American Landscape Painters*, and other books and articles on contemporary folk art.